EDMONTON

SECRETS OF THE CITY

EDMONTON

SECRETS OF THE CITY

Charlene Rooke

ARSENAL PULP PRESS

VANCOUVER

EDMONTON: SECRETS OF THE CITY
Copyright © 2001 by Charlene Rooke

ARSENAL PULP PRESS
103-1014 Homer Street
Vancouver, B.C.
Canada V6B 2W9
arsenalpulp.com

The publisher gratefully acknowledges the support of the Government of
Canada through the Book Publishing Industry Development Program for its
publishing activities.

Book design by Lisa Eng-Lodge
Production Assistant Judy Yeung
Photographs, unless otherwise indicated, by Akemi Matsubuchi
Cover photo by Akemi Matsubuchi
Printed and bound in Canada

Efforts have been made to locate copyright holders of source material
wherever possible. The publisher welcomes hearing from any copyright
holders of material used in this book who have not been contacted.

CANADIAN CATALOGUING IN PUBLICATION DATA:
Rooke, Charlene
  Edmonton: secrets of the city

  Includes index.
  ISBN 1-55152-103-2

1. Edmonton (Alta.)—Guidebooks. I. Title.
FC3696.18.R66 2001   917.123'34043   C2001-910891-5
F1079.5.E3R66 2001

c o n t e n t s

acknowledgments

When I first heard the title *Edmonton: Secrets of the City*, I pictured an old-fashioned gumshoe treading unsavoury alleys, nooks, and crannies of the city, digging up dirt, scandals, and sundry tidbits from longtime denizens. That romanticized image was quickly replaced by the reality of cauliflower ear from legion phone calls, sore feet from endless trips to obscure local attractions, and stuffed sinuses from long hours spent in dusty libraries and archives, where the real dirt was gathering on volumes of local history.

Secrets are at their juicy best when they're whispered right in your ear, and among the locals who generously shared lore with me I'd like to single out Marc Halun, Kelly Mekechuk, Eilish Murphy, and Rick and Marion Pilger, who know so much about Edmonton they probably could have written this book themselves. I'm also grateful to the others — among them Michelle Arnot, Danny Baldassarre, Ron and Marnie Beaudoin, Pierre Boileau, Lisa Chambers, Dean Collins, Alan Findlay, Erin Heximer, the McDougall family, Lara Minja, Michele Moon, Dan Sander, Rosann Semchuk, Robyn Stephenson, David Ward, Bruce Weir, and Jennifer Windsor — who dropped me a tidbit or two, along with everyone who sent tips after hearing about the book on TV or in print.

I owe a great debt to the many local historians, writers, and researchers who have trod this path before. Thanks also to the gatekeepers of that knowledge, including employees of the Stanley Milner Library, the City of Edmonton Archives, the Provincial Archives of Alberta, and the Edmonton and Alberta governments.

Two other members of the *Secrets* fraternity, James Martin and Shawn Blore, were generous with their experience and advice. Special kudos to Akemi Matsubuchi for countless hours spent organizing and shooting the fantastic photographs. (Grrrl power note: this is the first book in the *Secrets* series produced by an all-woman team.) And thanks to the whole gang at Arsenal Pulp Press.

Since no tome on Edmonton would be complete without mentioning the weather, I must thank Mother Nature for her kindness over the season I spent researching this book: the warmest and driest winter on record, with a mean temperature of around -3ºC and less than a centimetre of snowfall.

Finally, thanks to my mom and dad, Lori and Phil, and Nicholas for their support during the writing of this book.

introduction

Why is Edmonton is often perceived as the workhorse sibling to its stallion sister city to the south? Yes, this is a city that knows the value of hard labour – and rewards it. Yes, this is a city that believes in slow and steady – in our economy and our everyday lives. Edmonton is a city that doesn't rely on glitz and glamour for its appeal; we're keeping it real. It's a city where you can enjoy both lush green valleys and endless prairie fields. It's the gateway to Canada's burgeoning north. It's a city with a stunningly vibrant arts and cultural scene, and with no attitude, thank you very much.

Most of all, Edmonton is a city with nothing to prove. (After all, we are the provincial capital.) Its residents know how great it is – that's why, smug in their knowledge, they stay. With a healthy streak of reform rebelliousness tempering our conservative nature, Edmontonians are anything but stodgy and reserved: the Festival City celebrates as publicly as it mourns. (Was that an audible collective sob when Gretzky was traded?) We're the first to cut larger-than-life local characters down to size, but also the first to defend our former fortified city to outsiders.

If the world didn't already know all this, it found out when Edmonton hosted the high-profile 2001 IAAF World Championships in Athletics. So bunker down with your green onion cakes, Alley Kat beer, and Java Jive coffee, invest in some local property (preferably located on a former landfill site), and tune your radio to CKUA: we're about to be invaded, after the entire world discovers the well-kept secret of our city.

Should any city loyalists be tempted to fly up in arms about the fact that I was a bona fide resident of Calgary while writing this book, please take comfort in the fact that I spent 25 years of my life in Edmonton, and the last several months there finding out whether the urban legends, local myths, weird facts, and audacious rumours I'd collected over the years were really true. My fleeting absence has only strengthened my belief that Edmonton is one of the quirkiest, most interesting, and eminently liveable cities around.

And a city full of many deep, dark secrets ... although I'm sure I didn't find all of them. Unturned stones and closeted skeletons are welcome at *edmontonsecrets@canada.com* or by mail care of Arsenal Pulp Press – anonymity guaranteed.

There's much more to know about Edmonton than where to find its gigantic shopping mall. Instead, look for missing human remains, a man-made waterfall, or a purple city. Visit the city's strange landmarks, weird museums, hidden tunnels, and famous graves. And if you really want to know secrets like where the mayor gets beaver, where to find a royal biffy, and how to find the magic spot, read on.

As Time Goes By

Old Strathcona's Post Office was once housed in the building at 105 Street and Whyte Avenue that is now home to several restaurants and bars. The clock in the tower of the building was nothing but trouble: when it arrived from Derby, England in 1913 it was too large for the structure, and the tower had to be extended by about two metres to accommodate it. After a mere 40 years it stopped working, and a locksmith and gunsmith had to rebuild the necessary parts to get it running again. By 1976, that post office moved and the building was to sit empty for nearly 10 years. But the clock had become such a fixture of local life that over that time the same locksmith was dispatched, once a week, to wind, clean, and lubricate it.

The clock that currently sits in front of the **Westin Hotel** at 101 Avenue and 100 Street is a close sibling that also went postal at one time. It arrived from Derby in 1909 and its installation delayed the opening of the postal outlet by several months. In 1966 the post office closed, and in 1978 a hotel was proposed for the site. The building was torn down, but the beloved four-faced clock was salvaged, to be rebuilt in the new clock tower that keeps on ticking today.

Biffy in a Jiffy

With Queen Elizabeth II's visit to Edmonton for the opening of the 1978 Commonwealth Games pending, civic officials were anxious to do the right thing by royal etiquette. It seems that, should nature call, the regent cannot possibly make do with facilities shared with commoners – she needs a loo of one's own. In a last-minute decision, city council decided to slap together a $50,000 private biffy, a fully-furnished and carpeted affair, at field level under the stands on the west side of **Commonwealth Stadium** *(11000 Stadium Rd.)*. Sadly, the little loo remained unflushed. Maybe it had something to do with 60,000 spectators knowing *exactly* where Liz was going if she left her seat? Today, it is used as a storage shed, and given its condition – there are holes in the walls and flood damage – it is no longer fit for a queen.

Double Luck

When Edmonton adopted the twin city of Harbin, China in 1985, an elaborate **Chinatown gate** was erected at 102 Avenue at 97 Street, where two blocks of the avenue were renamed Harbin Road. Crafted with traditional tools by Chinese artisans, the 12-by-23-metre gate, covered in thousands of colourful gold and red tiles, supports two lion statues. Following ancient superstition, you can place your hand inside the lion's mouth and rattle its tongue to bring good fortune and luck. (Or, if the lion doesn't like the looks of you, maybe lose your hand.)

If you're wondering what the connection is between Edmonton and its twin city of Harbin ... keep guessing. Edmonton is also "twinned" with Hull, Quebec (a 1960s initiative to twin French- and non-French-speaking communities) and Nashville, Tennessee (reportedly on the whim of a country music-lovin' city councillor). To put a stop to the insanity, in 1999 City Council unanimously voted to curb further twinning arrangements.

Black Gold

Driving in to Edmonton from the south, you might be tempted to think that the oil derrick on the grounds of **Gateway Park** (2404 Calgary Trail, 496-8400) is a mere prop or tourist attraction. In fact, it's the artifact that in 1947 ushered in Alberta's reign as the oil capital of Canada. The Leduc Number 1 was actually located southwest of where it now stands, and the well blew just in time. The Turner Valley oil strike south of Calgary was beginning to run dry, and word was that Toronto-based Imperial Oil – which had drilled 133 dry wells in Alberta and Saskatchewan – was ready to abandon operations on the prairies. It later drilled more than 1,000 wells in the Leduc area, with a tidy haul of 400 million barrels of crude oil.

BALL AND CHAIN

At one time, this law-abiding town couldn't even sustain its own federal prison. Although the **Edmonton Penitentiary**, built in 1906 near where Commonwealth Stadium is today, could accommodate up to 120 prisoners, it was shut down in 1921 because they couldn't keep it full. It's easy to see why: life at the Pen was no free ride, with prisoners being required to grow their own vegetables on the prison's 70-acre farm and mine two nearby shafts for their own coal. After the criminal element vacated, the building's tenant for years was Big 4 Moving and Storage – can you think of a *safer* place to store your stuff?

government secrets

Call a Plumber

Listen up while standing under the "Magic Spot," marked in the marble by a brass dot on the fifth floor of the Legislature. You'd swear you were in the shower … but you won't get wet. The acoustic anomaly was discovered by a maintenance man changing a light bulb after a ground-floor fountain was installed in 1959 to commemorate the first official visit of Queen Elizabeth II. It seems the sound of rushing water in the fountain whooshes up the marble staircase like a sound tunnel and bounces off the ceiling rotunda, which is why the sound of loud, rushing water appears to be coming from overhead.

Speaking of all things plumbing, on the third floor of the Ledge you'll find a glass case containing the province of Alberta's former and current ceremonial maces. The security is hardly necessary for the first, 1906, model: although it looks regal, the mace was hurriedly constructed by CPR patternmaker Rufus E. Butterworth out of a piece of plumbing pipe, a toilet tank float, old shaving mug handles, a bedpost finial, and gold paint; total cost: $150. It was used for 50 years before being replaced by the current (real) gold and silver mace. When *Who Wants to Be a Millionaire?* filmed a Canadian edition in 2000, the mace was the elusive answer to a question about a Legislative artifact that constituted Alberta's first recycling effort.

Down Periscope

Several angled concrete towers built on the Legislature grounds in the 1980s are actually portals that use

mirrors to allow the pedway visitors below to view the grounds, while directing natural light into the underground system.

WILD THING

Royalty may have crowns, the clergy robes, but the mayor of Edmonton has prime beaver. Beaver pelts form the base of the **Mayor's Chain of Office**, a fancy, foot-wide stole edged with white ermineskin and trimmed with a chain and medallions representing various city military and police units. It was presented in 1985 to then-mayor Laurence Decore, who looked like a natty drag queen when he wore it at civic ceremonies. His successor, Jan Reimer, wisely refused to sport it, protesting that she wouldn't wear fur because she objected to inhumane trapping methods. The chain of office is on display on the second floor of City Hall *(100 St. and 102 Ave., 496-8200)* near the mayor's office.

For Your Eyes Only

The eyes have it in the famed portraits by Victor Albert Long, a creator of many official portraits who was renowned for the way he painted eyes that seem to follow the viewer. King George V and the seated Queen Mary hanging on the fourth floor of the Ledge do, indeed, turn an eagle eye on keen observers.

Purple Haze

It's a rite of passage for Edmonton teens, who peer into the huge spotlights pointing up at the Ledge just long enough to temporarily turn the world violet. Our sources say that when you look into the light, it bleaches the rods and cones and fatigues the response of the nerves in the eye. When you look away, the rods and cones signal the brain in a different way, causing you to see things in a contrasting hue — thus purple haze from looking at an orange-hued light. This phenomenon is known locally as Purple City. We in no way endorse such eye-damaging behaviour. You've been warned.

secret tunnels

Courthouse Tunnels

The Edmonton Remand Centre is the local holding facility for those charged with criminal offences while they're awaiting trial. Fortunately, due to a little foresight and planning, the criminal element doesn't have to see the light of day to have its day in court. Underground tunnels connect the **Remand Centre** *(9660 104 Ave.)* with the nearby **courthouse** *(102A Ave. and 99 St.)*, **Brownlee Building** *(10365 97 St.)*, and **Edmonton Police Service** headquarters *(9620 103A Ave.)*.

For security reasons, officials are loathe to say much more about these tunnels. (Although the province is said to be considering opening the Brownlee-courthouse passage to the public, they're mum on the subject.) In May 2000, Steven Gene Anderson (5'10", 160 pounds, black hair, two Pink Panther tattoos) escaped custody while being escorted via underground tunnels to

ZOO TALES

Long before the politically correct days of animal conservation, protecting endangered species, and recognizing zoos as "forced captivity and torture" instead of "good clean family fun," Edmonton had the **Storyland Valley Zoo**. Its props and exhibits were built around storybook and fairy tale themes, like Humpty Dumpty, Mary (of little lamb fame), Noah (of Biblical ark fame), and Old MacDonald's Farm. To use the public pay phone, you had to stand inside a giant bass fiddle — hey diddle diddle. Exactly how it was to teach kids about wildlife and savage exotic beasts remains a mystery — its key message seems to have been that animals are as harmless and amusing as a rhyming couplet.

A highlight of the zoo has always been the cheerful train that chugs around the grounds. On its maiden voyage in 1959, heavily loaded with city bigwigs, the little train just couldn't.... It failed to make it up the first climb and derailed, forcing the big wheels (including then-mayor William Hawrelak) to disembark and shove the locomotive back on its way.

the Remand Centre from the police station, where he had been taken on a breaking and entering charge. While five prisoners and two officers waited to be buzzed through a security door into the Remand Centre, the Houdini-like prisoner escaped his handcuffs and ran for freedom, surfacing in the Brownlee Building and running to freedom down 97 Street. No such dramatic escapes have been reported from the Grierson minimum security facility located in the old **Royal North West Mounted Police Barracks** *(9542 101A Ave.)*, where there were once 12 holding cells for prisoners – although an old tunnel reportedly exists leading from the barracks down to the North Saskatchewan River.

Tunnel of Love

An underground tunnel at the **Faculté Saint-Jean** *(8406 91 St.)*, the University of Alberta's French campus, once connected the residence with a nearby house that in recent years has been used for offices. The three-storey residence, where the brothers of the order of the Oblates of Mary Immaculate lived, began construction in 1910 when the house was built. The two-storey house was a residence for nuns, Les Soeurs de la charité d'Evron. Rumours reportedly circulated about the nuns and priests using the secret underground passageway for illicit rendezvous, which led to the tunnel's eventual closure.

Mine Shafts

Photo: City of Edmonton Archives (EA10-1180)

If you're hiking or biking in the North Saskatchewan river valley and see doors that seem to lead into the river bank, they're not the work of trolls or hobbits. These concrete portals – which you can see from the hiking and biking trails located just west of Ada Boulevard – seal the entrances to several old mine shafts, left over from the days at the early part of the 20th century when close to a dozen coal mines dotted the river valley.

In 1975, the Valley Zoo got serious and began to build an expanded, accredited zoological attraction. It now participates in international preservation and conservation networks. You can even adopt an animal – anything from a Mexican short-tailed fruit bat ($30/year) to a red-footed tortoise ($75/year) – to help the zoo feed and care for its occupants. Humpty Dumpty and pals still remain in the old part of the zoo as a reminder of its storied days of the past. *13315 Buena Vista Rd., 496-6911*

Train Tunnel

Photo: Charlene Rookie

When the High Level Bridge was originally built in 1913, its main purpose was to extend the CNR south from Edmonton proper to the town of Strathcona (now the Old Strathcona area). The train tracks on the top deck of the bridge continued east, parallel with what is today Saskatchewan Drive. In later years, when the south approach to the bridge was rebuilt, the train tracks were housed inside a tunnel that begins at the south end of the bridge and pops up on the east side of the Strathcona House apartments (10883 Saskatchewan Dr.). Once a favourite spot for street people and for drunken university students wandering home at night, the tunnel might have been permanently closed, save for the fact that it contains the fresh-air intake for the apartment tower above. The heavily-graffitied entrance is now fenced off and only open in the summer months, when the High Level Bridge Streetcar traverses the old route.

Pedestrian Tunnel

Photo: courtesy City of Edmonton

At the east end of the James MacDonald Bridge there's a closed-off pedestrian tunnel that once allowed walkers to cross safely underneath the bridge's several lanes of busy traffic. However, it was used less for safe crossing than for other, more nefarious pursuits, and became known as a trouble spot. It's now fenced-off on both sides, so you'll have to take your chances in a real-life game of Frogger if you decide you must cross the bridge at that spot.

GIBSON BLOCK

So-called flatiron buildings became all the rage after the first of the distinctive, triangular-shaped buildings went up in New York in 1902. Edmonton got its own flatiron in 1913, built to capitalize on an awkward-shaped lot at Jasper Avenue and 96 Street. The original owner who became the building's namesake, William Gibson, listed his profession as "Gentleman" on the building's title. He could have used the word "capitalist" — he sold the building just one year later for triple its original value. Until 1978, there were Turkish baths in the basement of the Gibson Block, and when architects and builders examined the derelict building in 1994 they discovered that two of the old bath chambers were still intact, including unblemished tile. They also discovered that the basement actually extends out beyond the rest of the building on the south and east sides, so that the bottom of the sidewalk forms the roof of the basement. Today the Gibson Block is considered the finest example of the flatiron architectural style in Alberta, and the one-time rooming house was restored in 1994 to serve as the Women's Emergency Accommodation Shelter.

Campus Tunnels

While students scurry to and from classes in winter weather that often dips to -30ºC, below campus there are 21 kilometres of brightly lit, marvelously clean tunnels that carry utilities and services to every building. Most of them were built in the 1960s and '70s, although one linking Athabasca and Pembina halls has been around since the '20s. Although they're regularly used by workers in little motorized scooters, the tunnels have always been inaccessible to common folk. That's the official word, although rumours persist that the tunnels were once open to pedestrian traffic, and that a nasty (insert your favourite crime here) caused campus officials to close the gates forever.

Palisades Walkway

Well, it's not exactly a tunnel, it's more of a walkway, and an exclusive one at that. Taking off from 99 Avenue between 104 and 105 Streets (just east of McKay Avenue School), this elevated sidewalk leads directly to the back door of the Palisades Apartments, saving residents the long flight of outdoor stairs down into the river valley to access the building's front door at 8404 118 Street.

Underground Reservoirs

Several huge water tunnels and reservoirs hulk underneath unexpected areas of the city. The Rossdale sewage storage tank, built in 1995, actually extends under the North Saskatchewan River. It can accommodate 50 million litres of storm water or sewage in times of heavy rain or spring runoff, storing it until it can be treated and safely released. There are also massive tanks built to handle storm water runoff from Whitemud Drive and keep the freeway safe. They're located under the freeway at 103 Street, 106 Street (south side), and 111 Street (north side). Several more biggies lurk under Yellowhead Trail, including one where it meets Wayne Gretzky Drive. And those attractive residential man-made lakes? More then 20 of them in the Edmonton area are actually storm water collection reservoirs, and are unsafe for recreational purposes for up to 72 hours after a heavy rainstorm because they collect dirty storm water runoff from area streets.

IT'S A BEAR

Back in the days of the Edmonton Oilers dynasty in the 1980s, hometown boy Mark Messier used to pay homage to his roots by taking the Stanley Cup to St. Albert's rundown **Bruin Inn** for adoration from the masses. That was perhaps the last hurrah for the small white stucco building, which later suffered indignities like being painted purple and having a tacky nightclub called Club Amnesia appended to its back. Back in 1929, the Bruin (named after the Northwest Brewing Company's slogan: "Northwest Beer – it's a bear!") was a classy joint; the "last word in comfort and luxury," said the *Edmonton Bulletin*. It enjoyed a run of popularity through the 1950s, because in Edmonton bars men and women weren't allowed to drink together; whereas just outside the city's north limits in St. Albert (a traditionally Catholic community, no less) mixed drinking received the town's blessing. The grizzled Bruin was recently torn down and replaced by a neo-traditional bright yellow eyesore called **Ric's Bar and Grill**. *24 Perron St., St. Albert, 460-6602*

industrial-size secrets

Bottling Bubbly

An old woolen mill at 97 Street and 103 Avenue fizzed back to life in 1907 when Canada Dry set up shop there, establishing only its second ginger ale plant anywhere (the first was in Toronto). The secret recipe for the delicious elixir was sold to the Yanks in 1923, and the label in those early days featured a drawing of Canada on which Edmonton was prominently marked.

Strange Brews

Photo: City of Edmonton Archives (EA500-136)

The oldest unmodified industrial building in Alberta is the old brick home of **Edmonton Brewing and Malting Co.** in Rossdale (9843 100 St.), which once produced Purple Label beer. A more familiar-looking brew was also produced there: in 1911, the Anheuser-Busch brewery in St. Louis slapped the Edmonton operation with an injunction for using a label that was a little too similar to that found on the famous Budweiser bottle.

Up in Smoke

Which would you rather have, a fragrant cigar rolled on the thigh of a Cuban virgin ... or one rolled by an Edmonton gentleman? The **Edmonton Cigar Factory** was one of the city's biggest employers in the early 1900s, with as many as 90 employees (all men) on the

Photo: City of Edmonton Archives (EA500-243)

payroll at its plant (10046 102 St.). Entrepreneur Harry Shaw imported the raw materials from Cuba and Sumatra, and in his heyday was selling a million of his La Palmas, Major Remos, and La Consequentias a year.

MILITARY SECRETS

Edmonton's **cenotaph**, which now sits in front of City Hall (101 Ave. between 100 and 100 Sts.), has been keeping an old secret since it was built 1936. When it was moved from its old site at 102 Street and 100 Avenue in 1978, a small sealed crate was discovered inside the First World War memorial. A military service association was consulted on the matter, and elected to leave the box and its unknown contents, unopened, in the cenotaph's interior where it remains to this day.

The complex known as the Boardwalk (which encompasses the 1910 Ross Brothers Hardware Building and the 1912 Revillon Building) has housed many tenants over the years, most recently an urban market, shops, and restaurants. It recently got an injection of youth when Edmonton Public Schools established **Centre High** there, a program for repeat Grade 12 students. The school allows flexible, non-traditional study arrangements including part-time studies and summer and weekend classes. An innovative funding formula – including commercial development, business and community, and school board money – funded renovations and equipment for the space, which has 30 classrooms and serves nearly 2,000 students. *100, 10310 102 Ave., 425-6753*

Bum Wrap

Photo: City of Edmonton Archives (EA267-42)

What is today the downtown **Army & Navy** store *(10305 97 St.)* was in 1911 the home of the Great Western Garment Co., better known as GWG. GWG was the Levi's of the north, manufacturing durable work clothes like overalls, twill shirts, and work pants (and later military garments during both World Wars). After the company's heyday with Scrubbies stonewashed jeans in the 1970s, popularity faded and today the label is owned by Levi Strauss. Edmonton's true-blue threads still run deep, as the Levi's plant here *(10660 85 St.)* is one of the largest and most productive in North America.

Watershed Moment

When the City of Edmonton proposed installing a man-made waterfall to cascade off the High Level Bridge, some citizens thought it was a joke. But on civic holidays and special occasions when the water and the spotlights are turned on, it makes for an undeniably pretty sight (if somewhat more of a mist than an actual waterfall). The waterworks is nearly 300 feet wide and 200 feet high – that's higher than Niagara Falls – and spews 11,000 gallons of water a minute. The punchline came when Edmonton cartoonists Delaney and Rasmussen invented a comic strip, *Bub Slug*, in which the eponymous blue-collar hero was Edmonton's waterfall maintenance man. (The two still ink the strip *Betty*, named for Bub's long-suffering wife.)

cheap sleep

Hostelling International

The Edmonton location won the 1998-99 Ivy Devereux Award for the most outstanding urban hostel in Canada. Housed in a former prayer retreat centre in the primo Old Strathcona neighbourhood, the hostel accommodates almost 90 people, boasts a retro games room (complete with orange shag carpet), two big kitchens, laundry facilities, Internet access, a barbecue deck, and costs 15 bucks a night. When can we move in? *10647 81 Ave., 988-6836*

not-so-cheap sleeps

Fantasyland Hotel

Rent a Polynesian, Victorian, Arabian, Hollywood, African, Roman, Western, Igloo, or Truck theme room (many with features like hot tubs and round beds) and marvel that a place like this exists outside Las Vegas. *17700 87 Ave., 444-3000*

Glenora Bed & Breakfast Inn

Run by the Freeland family in the 1912 Buena Vista building, this B&B has 21 cozy rooms, some with kitchenettes. Rates include breakfast at Nina's restaurant downstairs, and the High Street area has good restaurants and shopping. *12327 102 Ave., 488-6766 or 1-877-453-6672*

Neighbourhood Tours

During Historic Edmonton Week (late July-early August) the Historical Society of Alberta and its local chapter, the Edmonton and District Historical Society, offers tours touching upon various aspects of Edmonton history, including a walking tour of the Old Glenora neighbourhood and a bus tour of post-War modern architecture sites downtown and in the Oliver neighbourhood. *429-2797 or visit www.albertahistory.org*

For hours of self-guided fun, pick up the booklet **Historical Walking Tours of Downtown Edmonton** (available at City Hall, the Gateway Information, and the City of Edmonton Archives, among other locations), which contains the following four routes that can easily be linked together or completed separately. The booklet has lots of pictures for easy identification, and even has a handy architectural glossary so you can toss around terms like "jerkinhead roof." Allow time along the way for coffee, lunch, or window shopping. Call Alberta Community Development *(431-2339)* for information on other walking tour booklets.

La Bohème

Host Ernst Eder has made this restaurant and B&B a local mecca for French and Moroccan cuisine, Argentine tango, and European hospitality. Legend has it that the Austrian immigrant opened it with $40 and a second-hand stove in 1979. The six suites have claw-footed tubs and rates include continental breakfast. Located in the 1912 Gibbard Block in the Highlands district, close to jogging and cycling trails.
6427 112 Ave., 474-5693

Macdonald Hotel

A 1991 renovation restored this former jewel in the Canadian Pacific Hotels crown to its 1916 lustre. Now under the Fairmont Hotels umbrella, the Mac has hosted many celebrity guests, including British royalty from the Queen Mother to Mick Jagger. Mick reportedly eschewed the hotel's fine cuisine and cooked his own pasta meals on a little hot plate in his room.
10065 100 St., 429-6424

Union Bank Inn

A $5 million renovation of the Northwest Trust building (built as the Union Bank in 1911) resulted in the creation of this tasteful boutique hotel, which has 34 rooms with unique designs and contains the acclaimed **Madison's** restaurant.
10053 Jasper Ave., 423-3600

The Heritage Trail

Beginning at the Macdonald Hotel and ending at the Legislature, this red-brick trail passes plaques and interpretive signs commemorating events, people, and places in Edmonton's history.
Approximately 1.5 kilometres, or 1.5 hours

Jasper West and Warehouse District

Visit all the major commercial buildings of the early 20th century in the blocks between 100 and 104 Avenue and 107 and 104 Street.
Approximately 1.75 kilometres, or 1.5 hours

Downtown and Rice Howard Way

Walk through the heart of the city, once and again a thriving commercial district.
Approximately one kilometre, or one hour

Jasper East Village

The old part of downtown, west of 97 Street, is the site of a contemporary revitalization of many of its fine historic buildings. Stroll this one in broad daylight.
Less than one kilometre, or about 45 minutes

If someone tries to sell you a house with a stunning river valley view, be wary, be very wary. Like an anorexic supermodel, these properties are beautiful but unstable, and have a propensity for slipping over the edge. That's exactly what happened in the autumn of 1999, when the home at 4112 Whitemud Road tumbled 30 metres to its death (nobody was hurt). Two neighbouring homes later had to be pulled down because they posed safety hazards. Erosion is the historical culprit, helped over the years by extensive coal-mining along the river's banks (as early as 1911, College Avenue School, which was located on the current day Macdonald Drive, sank into a mine shaft) and by homeowners who flouted building codes.

In fact, the city faced so many complaints from hillside homeowners over the years, it has recently resorted to caveats, engineering reports, and development agreements to protect itself from a landslide of lawsuits. That's the case with a palatial house fronting Blackmud Creek ravine, which city building codes recommended should be set back about 13 metres from the property's edge. Not only did the owners build closer, they installed an elaborate underground sprinkler system that weakened the riverbank even further. In 1992 the front yard slid into the ravine; the rest of the house, shored up by concrete pillars, is still holding.

BIG-TICKET PROPERTIES

In the market for some property? A nearly 300,000-square-foot former hospital, perhaps, on a 10-acre lot? (A mere $6 million.) Or how about a 90-acre parcel of land on Edmonton's southeast outskirts? (A steal at $7.5 million.) These and other mega-bargains can be found on the Alberta government Web site (www.gov.ab.ca/realty) which tends to be Edmonton-heavy in its listings (unsurprisingly, given that we're the provincial capital). So far, it's not an e-commerce site, so you'll have to put away that platinum card and actually call a realtor to seize any of these deals.

BIG-TICKET CONDOS

According to the realtors in the know, Edmonton's most prestigious high-rise towers are these three.

The Arcadia
10019 119 St.

Le Marchand
11503 100 Ave.

9929 Saskatchewan Dr.
The name says it all

Crumbling Hotel

Photo: City of Edmonton Archives (EA500-121)

The distinctive, cupola-crowned brick and sandstone facade of the **Alberta Hotel** was a hallmark of 98 Street and Jasper Avenue from 1903. In its early years, it was the finest hotel in town: Prime Minister Wilfred Laurier stayed there in 1905 when Alberta entered Confederation. It had Edmonton's first front-desk bell system, first passenger elevator, and first running showers. With a new Federal Building slated for the site in 1984, the historical building was carefully dissembled and preserved, in the hopes that it could later be reconstructed on another site. So far, it hasn't. Today, the carefully numbered and recorded pieces of the hotel are scattered at half a dozen storage sites around Edmonton awaiting resurrection. Five years ago, the reconstruction of the Alberta Hotel was one cornerstone of the proposed 30,000-square-foot Old Towne Market development between 96 and 97 Streets. But the plan floundered, and nobody else has offered to pick up the pieces.

PEELING ORANGE

The old clapboard **Orange Hall** in Old Strathcona *(10335 84 Ave., 432-7077)* is the original home of the Loyal Orange Order, Chapter 1164. Today it's used for various community functions and performances, but legend has it that the basement still holds the secrets of the past: dusty locked cupboards are said to hold a 1915 black leather Bible and minute books dating back to the Orangemen's first local meetings in 1895.

Secret Vistas

The best panoramic view of Edmonton used to be from the Vista 33 observation deck high up in the old AGT building (now called **Telus Plaza South**, *10020 100 St.*); it was closed in 1993. Other pleasing vistas of the city are available from these spots:

Strathearn Drive
Gallagher Hill
Saskatchewan Drive
La Ronde (the revolving restaurant on top of the Chateau Lacombe)

famous and infamous houses

Not an Igloo

When Edmontonians talk about the Eskimo house, they're talking about Dave McGregor's place at 9259 92 Street. When Edmonton hosted the Grey Cup in 1997, he painted his house in bold green and gold stripes and added the team's EE logo on the front. As if the neighbours weren't happy enough about the paint job, it has had the unintended effect of making the house a hot drive-by destination for hooting, horn-honking fans after victorious home games.

His Home Is His Castle

Photo: Charlene Rooke

What kind of a man would give his garage a Middle Ages facelift, complete with turrets and knights in armour? Well, the torturous-looking sculpture on the lawn of 5524 111a Street will give you a hint to its occupants' occupation: it's fashioned from old pieces of dental equipment. And you thought only lances and pots of boiling oil were used for medieval torture....

NO BONES ABOUT IT

Rowand House — better known as Rowand's Folly, for its elaborate three-storey construction, including real glass windows which were imported from England in barrels of molasses — has been re-created in Fort Edmonton Park as a monument to the fort's longtime chief factor, John Rowand. But there's no trace of Rowand or his remains on site. The man himself died unexpectedly on an 1854 trip to Fort Pitt (in modern-day Manitoba) and was buried there. However, his friend George Simpson later insisted on honouring Rowand's lifelong wish to be buried in his hometown of Montreal. The remains were exhumed, and Rowand's bones inexplicably put on a slow boat to England. Four years later they found their way back to the port of Montreal, where Rowand was finally buried in Mount Royal Cemetery in 1858.

Art For Folks

GOING DOWN IN HISTORY

Edmonton's last remaining wooden grain elevator came down in a heap in 1999, making room for a new traffic interchange. Located at the junction of Ellerslie Road and Gateway Boulevard, the 30-metre-high landmark was torn down at a cost of about $20,000 – $70,000 less than it would have cost to preserve it and move it elsewhere, which, despite all the kerfuffle about demolishing the heritage structure, nobody anted up to do. In their heyday in the 1950s, there were more than 1,500 wooden grain elevators in Alberta; today it's estimated that there are less than 200. The classic, twin-peaked silhouette of the old-fashioned structures still decorates the St. Albert skyline, as it has two original Alberta Wheat Pool grain elevators (from 1906 and 1929), which are both registered provincial historical resources. *Grain Elevator Park, Meadowview Dr., and Mission Ave.*

You might call Dave Fillion's Bonnie Doon-area garage *(9002 92 St.)* a work of folk art ... then again, you might call it a pile of junk. The exterior walls are plastered with objects ranging from coffee cups and trophies to an old fireplace and bathroom fixtures. The theme carries into the junkyard, which contains treasures as diverse as a small lighthouse, a fence plastered with vinyl LPs, and two sets of wind chimes made from Fillion's old false teeth.

This Little Piggy

Construction methods have advanced since the days of the fabled three pigs – straw is now a viable building option. There is a straw-bale construction house in Stony Plain (just west of Edmonton) and another in Sherwood Park (just east of the city). The buildings are typically reinforced with fencing wire and finished with cement stucco.

Double Barons

The house built by William Magrath *(6240 Ada Blvd.)* in 1912 sits on the Highlands area street, Ada Boulevard, that he named for his wife. The elaborate 14-room mansion had an indoor pool, a billiards room, and a ballroom. Right next door lived his business partner, Bidwell Holgate, who employed the same architect, Ernest William Morehouse, to design another grand 20-room mansion (6210 Ada Blvd.). The real estate barons, who snapped up 23 lots in the Highlands area for a mere $35,000 in 1912, personally paid to have the city's streetcar line, sidewalks, street lighting, and sewer and water lines extended to the neighbourhood. However, after the real estate market went bust the next year, Magrath and Holgate both eventually lost their houses to the city for back taxes. In recent years, the Magrath house was known as the Bishop's Mansion as it housed the bishop of the Ukrainian Catholic Diocese; Holgate House has been operated as a bed and breakfast.

Pocklington House

Peter Pocklington couldn't leave town fast enough for most Edmontonians, and indeed the gavel had barely banged down on the last auction item before Puck's house went on the block, too. The Tudor-style, Old Glenora home was priced at $2.9 million and nearly sold at the end of 2000 for a bargain $1.8 million to an oral surgeon and his wife. But the province of Alberta – one of Pocklington's many money-hungry creditors – made a court challenge that forced the couple to bump their offer to $2.3 million.

That's $300,000 more than the ransom a masked gunman demanded when he took Pocklington hostage at the house in 1982. (He also wanted to escape via the Pocklington private jet.) The 11-hour standoff at the house ended when a police officer fired a single shot from his M-16, hitting both Pocklington and his captor in the arm. The kidnapper, recent Yugoslavian immigrant Merko Petrovic, had actually planned to kidnap Pocklington's wife Eva, but apparently bonded with Peter: he even wrote him a couple of letters from prison.

Cat House

This 1914 house, nestled in the old-money enclave of St. George's Crescent, is a traditional Tudor-style home with one unique feature: a porcelain cat that has been perched on the roof since 1928, when the feline was purchased in Normandy by George and Margaret O'Connor. The couple, a former Alberta chief justice and newspaper theatre critic, respectively, named the house The Graenon, Irish for "sunny place." That must have been before the hedge and poplar trees got so big … now it's more of a shady place.

Time in a Capsule

Fuelled by millennium fever, around 10,000 time capsules were buried in North America in the last century. Edmonton is no exception, leaving no cornerstone unturned without a time capsule underneath. Herewith, a look at some hidden and exposed treasures in the Edmonton area.

Location: **Former Immaculata Hospital in Westlock**
Contents: A candy tin filled with pins, coins, comics, letters, and a copy of the local newspaper, the *Westlock Witness*.
Expiry date: Buried in 1949 and unearthed July 1997. With the hospital slated for demolition, a 90-year-old retired doctor remembered the capsule, sealed in the building's cornerstone, and saved it from certain destruction.
Posterity: Site is now an IGA grocery store; time capsule is now in the Westlock Museum.

Cat House II

When the SPCA called in June 1999, the house at 6234 112 A Street contained 83 sick, starving cats, truckloads of cat feces, and two women (sisters Anne and Lucy Abolins) who were apparently oblivious to the situation. Don't forget the 116 other cats (and one dog) found dead in plastic bags in the garage, which the sisters claimed had died of "natural causes." All the animals in the house had to be euthanized, but so complete was the damage to the rental property that it later had to be razed to the ground, with the demolition site posing a biohazard for days. Charged under the Animal Protection Act, the sisters were fined $2,500 each.

Rutherford House

Alberta's first premier built this brick mansion on what is now the U of A campus. Today, as a Provincial Historic Site, Rutherford House (*11153 Saskatchewan Dr., 427-3995*) is home to guided tours, costumed historical interpreters, a ubiquitous gift shop, and the Arbour Restaurant.

Artistic Statement

A local landlord made an eye-popping statement when he painted three apartment towers known as the **Picasso Buildings** in stripes of sherbet and shamrock green. Their motto (painted on the top of one of the towers): "Don't judge a book by its cover" – indeed, the buildings are attractive on the inside. Word has it that the properties have changed hands and may soon be repainted.

The location of **Fort Edmonton Park** *(Whitemud Dr. and Fox Dr., 496-8787)* does not mark the spot of the original Fort. It was first built in 1795 by the Hudson's Bay Company north across the river from the current town of Fort Saskatchewan. It was moved to what is now downtown Edmonton in 1802, relocated briefly between 1810 and 1813, then returned to that site, near what is now the Rossdale power plant. It moved for the final time in 1830, to a site on the present-day Legislature grounds.

When the West was won and Fort Edmonton dismantled in 1915, the timbers and some artifacts were salvaged and stored on a farm outside Edmonton. Although the 100-year-old wood may have been in no shape to build with, in the late 1960s the city went back to retrieve the material to build Fort Edmonton Park. But it was all gone. Some say the farmer burned it as firewood; others say errant Boy Scouts on a camping trip were the culprits. The only original artifact in Fort Edmonton today is the old safe, which was recovered from another nearby farm and is now installed in Rowand House. When a locksmith finally got it open, the safe contained documents verifying its authenticity, and a tin of very stale cookies.

architect magnets

Life at the HUB

When it was built by the Students' Union in 1972, the **Housing Units Building** on the U of A campus was hailed as an innovative application of the "covered street" design. The building consists of a long galleria lined with retail shops, a huge 292-metre skylight on top, and student housing on either side with windows opening right onto the mall. *Canadian Interiors* called HUB "bold, imaginative and yet practical." For years the campus considered it a big white elephant: construction

Location: **City Hall**

Contents: Silver coins, a one-dollar bill (what's that, you ask?), a copy of the *Edmonton Journal*, and rolls of enthralling microfilm detailing city council planning and building minutiae.

Expiry date: Laid beneath the cornerstone of the new City Hall in 1954; exhumed in 1989 when the building was torn down.

Posterity: The cornerstone and capsule were placed by popular mayor William Hawrelak. He scored Canada's biggest mayoral victory in 1951 but resigned in 1959 amidst conflict of interest allegations. He was re-elected in 1963 and again resigned under a cloud; re-elected once more in 1974 but died in office of a heart attack in 1975, proving that in time, a metal capsule will outlast a Teflon mayor.

costs went $1 million over budget, and the housing and retail spaces were chronically vacant. In April 1976 the university made the deal of a century, buying the beleaguered building for a token buck. Today it is home to several food outlets, booming businesses, and some guy with a huge collection of Coke cans stacked in his window.

Cardinal Virtues

Mercurial Metis architect Douglas Cardinal is currently embroiled in a dispute over his over-budget, internationally-acclaimed design for the National Museum of the American Indian in Washington, D.C. Those familiar with his curvilinear Canadian Museum of Civilization in Hull will recognize several lesser-known examples of the Calgary-born architect's work found in Alberta: St. Mary's Church in Red Deer, **St. Albert Place** (photo above) northwest of Edmonton, and the Edmonton Space and Science Centre.

Like an Egyptian

Architect Peter Hemingway always insisted that the inspiration for his four glass pyramids that form the **Muttart Conservatory** had less to do with any New Agey properties generated by the shape than with practicality: high ceilings and lots of light for the thousands of varieties of plants that grow there. Gene Dub continued to riff on the pyramid theme with his design for the new **City Hall**, which is capped off with yet another glass pyramid.
9626 96A St., 496-8735; 100 St. and 102 Ave., 496-8200

campus curiosities

Founded in 1908 on River Lot Five, a picturesque swath on the south bank of the river, the University of Alberta takes its green and gold colours from the autumn colours of the river valley. You can count on anything that old to have plenty of eccentricities, and the campus is no exception. These secrets are courtesy of *New Trail*, the University of Alberta alumni magazine.

Forgotten Learning

The **Arts Building**, completed in 1915, was supposed to have two major stone carvings representing ancient and modern learning. Due to a shortage of qualified stonemasons (and, truth be told, funds), plain stone blocks mark the building's entrance where the carvings should have been. The distinctive stone sundial, which blithely reads, "I count only the sunny hours," was a gift from the class of 1930.

Well-aged Whiskey

In the oldest building on campus, **Athabasca Hall**, eight pristine whiskey bottles, complete with original corks, were found concealed in the ceiling plaster when the former residence and teaching building was renovated into offices in 1978.

Biological Hazard

Campus legend has it that the parts of the **Biological Sciences Building** construction were jobbed out to several contractors – who didn't exactly see eye to eye. Tales of doors that opened to brick walls, a classroom entrance hidden in a closet, and showers containing electrical outlets are legion. Reportedly, a four-metre python was once lost in the labyrinthine building for several days. Another construction debacle appeared in the **Civil Engineering Building**, which was built without women's

CEMETERY TOURS

Many of Edmonton's founding fathers (and a few pioneering sisters) found their final resting places at city-owned public cemeteries. Among the headstones at **Mount Pleasant Cemetery** are many names familiar from Edmonton streets and landmarks: Hugh Calder, John Gainer, Frederick Keillor, Robert McKernan, Robert Ritchie, Alexander Rutherford, and John Walter. Three of the Famous Five women's rights advocates – Henrietta Mills, Nellie McClung, and Emily Murphy – are also buried in Edmonton cemeteries.

washrooms. Hey, in 1960 who would've thought you'd need them? Half the men's washrooms have since been converted, and there have been lineups ever since.

Persons House

Just east of the campus is the humble **Emily Murphy House** *(11011 88 Ave.)* where Emily Murphy lived from 1919 until her death in 1933. She was the first woman magistrate in the British Empire and one of the Famous Five who contested the Persons Case that gave women the right to vote in Canada, but better known under her best-selling fiction pen name, Janey Canuck. Fittingly, the Faculty of Law's Student Legal Services is the current tenant.

Written in Stone

Just in case you didn't get enough trig homework, Pythagoras' theorem is etched in the cement in front of the **Mechanical Engineering Building**. The concrete block was salvaged from the sidewalk of a math professor's house when the home was demolished.

Keeping the Flame Alive

The stylized metal sculpture of a dove outside the **Students' Union Building** once lit up the field at Commonwealth Stadium as the official flame tower of the 1983 World University Games in Edmonton. The piece was built by architectural technology students at NAIT, with production costs donated by the Sawridge Indian Band.

Shot in the Arm

In 1923, Banting and MacLeod got the Nobel Prize for developing insulin as a treatment for diabetes – and James Bertum Collip got the shaft. The University of Alberta professor had made the trip east to help the University of Toronto researchers make the breakthrough that would lead to their lauded discovery. A plaque on the third floor of the old Medical Building (the current **Dentistry/Pharmacy Centre**) marks Collip's former stomping grounds.

A favourite local underground tale involves undertaker Sam McCopland, who circa 1900 was known for his aggressive marketing techniques, like distributing fans with his number on them at hospitals during summer heat waves. His phone number included the digits 6666, which McCopland was wont to pronounce, "sick, sick, sick, sick." Tours given by the Edmonton Municipal Cemeteries in association with the Edmonton and District Historical Society (from the May long weekend through September of each year) cover the Edmonton *(11820 107 Ave.)* and Mount Pleasant *(5420 106 St.)* cemeteries and some of their famous inhabitants. *434-1817 or 439-2797*

weird museums and collections

Secret Labs

City of Edmonton Artifacts Centre

Photo: Charlene Rooke

Find anything from an old bottle to an old carousel horse at the Artifacts Centre. Tucked into the hillside, this little-known warehouse is located in the Deco-styled storage building of the old O'Keefe's Brewery, now part of a Parks and Recreation storage yard. Occasionally open for tours (typically during Historic Edmonton Week every summer) by curators Bruce MacDonald and Sherry Haley, it houses Emily Murphy's magistrate's chair, 7,000 old bottles salvaged from the Rat Creek Dump when it was bulldozed during construction of Commonwealth Stadium, and the old neon sign from Mike's News, along with bolts of vintage fabric, baby carriages, an old traffic light, and items too numerous and sundry to catalogue here. The period artifacts for city-run historical attractions (Fort Edmonton, John Walter Museum) come from here.
10542 Fort Hill, 496-1490

Photo: Charlene Rooke

As the northernmost research-intensive university in the world and one of the largest universities in Canada, the U of A has a whole whack of weird facilities.

Catch the Fever

A **Biocontainment Level III laboratory** is designed to handle lethal bugs like Venezuelan equine encephalomyelitis (who knows what that is, but it sounds nasty) and yellow fever. That means double doors, separate air intakes, and full protective gear for researchers. The U of A has one of only a handful of these labs in Canada, located in the Heritage Medical Research Centre.

Feeling Hot

Harry Burns has been set on fire nearly 2,000 times, but always emerges unscathed. Burns is the morbid nickname given to a fibreglass mannequin at the U of A's **MEANU** (Mechanical Engineering Acoustics and Noise Unit) in east Edmonton, which researchers use to test protective clothing. He's the only dummy of his kind in Canada.

Kennedy Collection

Rob Fakeley digs wax – in his house, he has a lifesize figure of former U.S. president John F. Kennedy, which he bought through the *Bargain Finder* several years ago from a defunct wax museum for $900. It's part of his massive collection of Kennedy memorabilia that includes audio recordings, magazines, and documents like tickets and invitations with presidential cachet.
465-2826

Dental Museum

Many curators would give their eye teeth for the U of A Faculty of Dentistry's collection of old dental implements and natural history specimens related to the jaws and teeth. The collection, which can only be viewed by appointment, is unique in Canada.
U of A, 4065 Dentistry/Pharmacy Building, 492-5194

E.H. Strickland Entomological Museum

From giant silk moths to Mexican ground beetles, this collection of buggy specimens is among the best in Canada. Caddisflies, butterflies, and other creepy crawlies are here in abundance, but mostly hidden away in storage cabinets, so appointments are necessary.
U of A, 2-18 Earth Sciences Building, 492-3991

Provincial Museum of Alberta

Several warehouses full of wacky stuff that, at any given time, isn't on display at the museum is carefully catalogued and stored. Among the riches are a 30,000-year-old fossilized lion's jawbone salvaged from a local gravel pit, a piece of the Red Baron's plane, and the canary cage from an old coal mine.
12845 102 Ave., 453-9100

Pressure's On

Two large concrete planters outside the **Chemistry Building** are more than meets the eye: they're actually big safety valves that would contain the damage in the unlikely event that the underground chemical storeroom had an, uh, mishap. Over in the basement of the **Earth Sciences Building**, researchers have the country's only geological press that can create artificial diamonds in just a couple of weeks. The **Power Plant**, now a popular student bar, has always been host to chemical experimentation. Back in 1923, professor Karl Clark invented a process to extract oil from the sticky tar sands – a process that's still in use (in modified form) in massive plants in Alberta's north.

McKay Avenue School Museum

The province's oldest school was actually named for Dr. William MacKay, but the name was incorrectly carved in sandstone. Inside the charming red-brick building built in 1904, you'll see authentically restored classrooms from various eras. The top floor has also been restored to its former use: in 1906-7 it was Alberta's first legislature. An older wooden schoolhouse (complete with outdoor biffy) on the grounds has an interesting history: during the construction of the brick school, its 1881 wooden predecessor was sold to the contractor as a storage shack. Later, it was hauled down into the river valley and used as a residence in Rossdale. (It would have floated away during the 1915 flood had its owner, David Mawhinney, not secured it with cables.)
10425 99 Ave., 422-1970

Textile Collection

The U of A's Faculty of Human Ecology has more than 16,000 textile pieces in its collection, the most famous being the frilly pink Klondike-style dress Princess Di wore during her 1983 visit. Originally designed as a costume for a BBC television production, the dress was later bought at auction by Calgarian Michael Smith, who donated it to the collection. Local theatre groups often peruse the collection to get inspiration for period costumes.
U of A, 1-15 Human Ecology Building, 492-1502

Telephone Historical Centre

Don't be shocked when Xeldon the talking robot pops out of the wall during the multi-media presentation included with your admission — it *will* be the highlight of your visit. Unless, of course, you have a jones for old phones (including a few brave but warped survivors of house fires) and the wonders of fax and Internet service. Did you know that push-button phones were originally

Two Joes

St. Joseph's Basilica *(10044 113 St., 488-7295)* was in the spotlight in 1988 when hockey star Wayne Gretzky and actress Janet Jones were married there with an entourage of 22 attendants and a crowd of 5,000 gathered outside. Across town, the grand **St. Josaphat's Cathedral** *(10825 97 St., 422-3181)* is renowned for its seven copper cupolas and its elaborate frescoes. Using hand-tinted egg tempera, Ukrainian artist Julian Bucmaniuk modelled the faces of saints and prophets after local parishioners, and used the ugly mugs of Hitler, Lenin, Stalin, and Khruschev for figures he painted in Hell.

Big Stuff Country

Our horizons are bigger and so, it seems, are our public monuments (witness the monstrous mall — nearly five million square feet — in the city's west end). Citizens of Edmonton and northern Alberta believe bigger is better, as evidenced by this bizarre big stuff located in Edmonton and around central and northern Alberta.

Photo: Charlene Rooke

Got Milk?
A giant milk bottle bearing the ECD logo, which used to perch on the roof of the Edmonton City Dairy building, now sits in the Bonanza Park area of Northlands. Built in New York in 1928, the bottle is more than seven metres tall and weighs eight tons. There's also a big, four-storey high boot in front of the west end Western Boot Factory.
10007 167 St.

installed in Edmonton phone booths to overcome the problem of dials freezing in winter? Or that the city had Canada's first 911 phone service? Now you know.
10437 83 Ave., 433-4068

Girl Guides of Canada (Alberta Council) Archives and Museum

If you like the naughty schoolgirl look that comes from Girl Guide uniforms, badges, pins, and souvenirs, this one's for you. They also have a library of material about the Guiding movement around the world and a collection of slides and tapes.
11055 107 St., 424-5510

Alberta Association of Registered Nurses Museum and Archives

The main claim to fame of this collection is one of only three "Florence Nightingale" lamps known to exist today. Other artifacts include uniforms, military decorations, and photographs from the province's nursing history.
11620 168 St., 451-0043

Bible Wax Museum

Back in the 1980s, curious visitors who made the cut (past the curator's pet squirrel monkey, Enrico) could visit the homemade wax museum in Larry Q. Lawson's basement. Among the handcrafted treasures were Moses, Judas, the Virgin Mary, and a life-size Jesus sitting on a patch of artificial turf. Sadly, the museum seems to have melted into obscurity.

Cult Library

Somewhere in the city, behind locked doors, is an unusual library that contains everything from anti-Semitic tracts to files on various quasi-religious sects. Items from the collection have been used to help prosecute cases of hate-mongering, and because of the sensitive nature of much of the material its keeper has received threats … so we can't say any more about its location.

secrets of the orders

Saint Anthony of Edmonton

At the southwest corner of the University of Alberta's French campus, **Faculté Saint-Jean** *(8406 91 St.)*, is a small stone grotto, a shrine to the Virgin Mary. It was built by the Faculté's former caretaker, Oblate brother Anthony Kowalczyk, with rocks he gathered by hand from Mill Creek ravine (he had lost one arm in a sawmill accident, so that was no small feat). Kowalczyk arrived at the college around 1911 and stayed until his death in 1947.

In 1952, local Catholic leaders began the long process of seeking canonization of Brother Anthony as a saint for the many miracles he is said to have performed. Reportedly, he would often say a small prayer to get a piece of broken machinery working. And a woman who prayed to Brother Anthony when she was hospitalized with a life-threatening heart virus in 1990 believes she was cured through his intervention. Before the Residence Saint-Jean was recently renovated, one room there was believed to be so vividly inhabited by a spirit that students wouldn't stay there – Brother Anthony, perhaps?

Secrets of the Mall

Love it or hate it — and most Edmontonians lean toward the latter — **West Edmonton Mall** is Alberta's number one tourist attraction. When the mall was built in 1981 it was all about shopping, but today it's increasingly becoming a "family entertainment complex." (That doesn't mean it's not still a nightmare destination for last-minute Christmas sprees.) Here are some of the famous and infamous features of West Ed (as the locals call it).

Guinness World Records are held by the mall for the biggest shopping centre (1999) and biggest parking lot (1998). It also claims the world's largest indoor wave pool, amusement park, lake, and rollercoaster.

Facilities include a casino, bingo, comedy club, day spa, nightclub, hotel, chapel, skating rink, bowling alley, submarine ride, driving range and mini golf, arcades, movie theatres, and more than 800 stores and 100 places to eat and drink.

He Left His Heart in Calgary

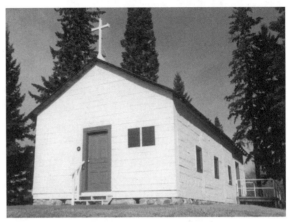

Father Albert Lacombe was revered in the Metis community he founded in St. Albert, just north of Edmonton. **Father Lacombe Chapel** *(Mission Hill, St. Albert, 459-7663)*, Alberta's oldest log structure, reportedly sits on the exact spot where he and Bishop Grandin stood when they envisioned the mission there. Founding Catholic Fathers Lacombe, Grandin, and Leduc are all buried in the crypt of the St. Albert parish church — Father Lacombe without the generous organ he was so famous for (his heart, you pervert). After he died in 1916 at the Lacombe Centre he had founded in Calgary, it was placed in a jar and kept for years by the nuns there. It was eventually buried behind the Lacombe Centre's main building *(146 Ave. and Bannister Rd. S.E., Calgary)* where it reportedly remains to this day, despite a major fire that occurred in 1999.

Give Jesus a Hand

Motorists travelling north on St. Albert Trail used to face the sight of a large statue of a seated Jesus, beckoning to his flock, in front of **St. Joseph's Seminary and Newman Theological College** *(15611 St. Albert Tr., 447-2993)*. The thing is, at first glance he seemed to be not so much beckoning as, well, flipping the bird. In the 1980s, the statue was not only moved significantly back from the road, but also appeared to have been modified to relieve Jesus of the ambiguous digit.

Hidden Chapels

If you've *way* overextended your credit cards, you may want to pray at the **Marketplace Chapel** on the second level of Phase III at West Edmonton Mall (near Fantasyland Hotel). It is so-named because the marketplace is where Jesus reputedly did much of his early preaching. If it's the study gods you'd rather invoke, there is not only the tiny gem of a chapel in **Old St. Stephen's College** on campus, but the gorgeous stained-glass dappled chapel at **St. Joseph's College**, and a small multi-denominational chapel tucked into **HUB Mall**.

Columbus' Santa Maria – an exact replica, that is – was constructed in Vancouver and trucked to the mall, where it is a popular location for wedding ceremonies.

Area covered by the mall is the equivalent of 48 city blocks.

Mall rats aren't rodents, they're the homeless teens who loiter in the mall by day and reportedly live, eat, and sleep in its warren of back corridors by night.

Fantasyland got a reality-check when Walt's people took exception to WEM's use of the Disneyland trademark and took legal action to protect the name. The amusement park is now called Galaxyland.

The Mindbender triple-loop rollercoaster is rated number one in the world for G-force.

Theme areas of the mall include Europa Boulevard (with a rare collection of Ming Dynasty vases and replicas of the crown jewels of England) and Bourbon Street (a taste of old New Orleans, complete with lifelike statues of Storyville hookers).

Deaths at West Ed over the years have included three people killed in a June 1986 rollercoaster accident, a diver killed while servicing the submarine ride in 1987, and in 2000 a young man who drowned after apparently jumping into the mall's man-made lake on a drunken prank, and a worker painting a mall pet store who fell on his head. A man was fatally stabbed on Boxing Day in 1996 in an incident reportedly related to gang violence – not in a dispute over heavily-discounted sale goods.

Church Firsts

The first permanent building outside the walls of Fort Edmonton is the 1887 wooden **McDougall United Church**, which stood where the 1909 brick version is today *(10086 101 St.)*. The original structure was restored and is now displayed at Fort Edmonton. Just down the road on 1920 Street at the Fort, you'll also see North America's first formal place of worship for Muslims, the **Al Rashid Mosque**. Edmonton's first synagogue is no more – in 1958, the former Beth Israel Synagogue became **St. Boniface Roman Catholic Church** *(9510 101 Ave.)*. Local legend has it that the synagogue entrance originally faced east, but that after a car crashed through the front doors the entryway was moved to the back of the building. And from Whitemud Drive in the city's southwest, it's impossible not to spot the golden statue of the angel Moroni topping the **Mormon Temple** *(Whitemud Dr. and 53 Ave.)*, the first one in Edmonton. Nearly half of all local Mormons can't even attend – they aren't spiritually qualified to enter this sanctum. Before it was dedicated by the Mormon leader in 1999, it was open to the public for tours, and thousands of the curious streamed through. Local builders say the place indeed seems built to withstand The End: like all Mormon temples, it is designed to last 1,000 years.

Building a Following

The construction of **Holy Trinity Anglican Church** *(10037 84 Ave.)* was enough of an ordeal to try even the strongest faith. A basement foundation was dug in 1906, but without the necessary funds for construction a temporary structure, which became known as the "basement church," was erected. When construction resumed in 1912, it was with Clinker brick (a low-cost building material often used for fill or even paving) from the local Pollard Brothers brickyard – a savvy decision that saved the congregation a bundle. Although the distinctive naturally coloured, burnt looking finish of the brick was once considered undesirable, the attractive Holy Trinity church started a neighbourhood renaissance for building with Clinker brick that's still evident today. And it wasn't a long winded sermon that blew the chimney off of **Knox Presbyterian Church** *(8403 104 St.)* in 1910, it was a tornado-force wind – much to the surprise of the nearly 600 worshippers gathered there for a Sunday School rally.

Edmonton's first recorded traffic accident happened on April 27, 1893 when Finch's cart collided with Osborne's buggy at 101 Street and Jasper Avenue. Since then, our transportation methods have become more sophisticated, from low-flying planes to traffic rotaries, rat holes, and Big Brother-style traffic monitoring. Also look out for bodies hidden in bridges, missing gold bricks, and fragments from the Red Baron's plane.

Deep Pockets

Imagine stealing about four dollars from each of the 600,000 people living in Edmonton, and you'll have some idea of the magnitude of the theft of former Edmonton Transit LRT repairman Salim Kara, who was convicted in 1996 of stealing $2.3 million from 1981 to 1994. The trial, at which Kara was sentenced to four years in jail, revealed that while frequently alone on night shifts and ostensibly fixing the fare boxes, Kara would use a telescoping antenna attached to a magnet to extract coins (mainly loonies, after their introduction in 1987) from transit coffers. On the bright side: if the two-dollar coin had been around at the time, he probably would have stolen twice as much.

At the time of his arrest, the $38,000-a-year repairman had a $1 million term deposit in his name and had built a Riverbend home (with a heated, four-lane driveway) worth nearly $1 million. Most of his ill-gained assets were turned over to the insurance company that covered the city's losses over the period of his thefts.

Wondering how this volume of theft – about $900 a day for 13 years – went undetected left Edmontonians scratching their heads. Security cameras taped Kara with his hand deep in the cookie jar on at least one occasion before his arrest, but a colleague taped over the incident because it looked "incriminating." The trial also revealed that employees collecting coins from the fare boxes didn't bother to check whether amounts agreed with totals the boxes automatically calculated, or chalked discrepancies up to mechanical errors. The bank where Kara deposited massive quantities of rolled coin never questioned his explanation: that he was a video arcade owner. The nimble-fingered thief eventually served only 11 months of his sentence before being released on day parole.

Driving in Circles

Edmontonians have been chasing their tail lights for 50 years, thanks to an early city planner with a penchant for throwing crescents, circles, and curves at local drivers. Noel Dant, a planner trained in England and hired in Edmonton in 1947, brought the idea of "rotaries" (better known today as traffic circles) to the Prairies. Originally, the circles were one canny way for the city to hold large tracts of land from development until a proper intersection was built. However, in theory the circles are an excellent way to handle volumes of traffic coming from four different directions. As they rely on natural gaps in traffic to allow even flow, traffic circles cease to work efficiently if traffic dominates from any one direction (or if some idiot decides to suddenly exit from the inside lane of the circle).

Over the years, several of the original circles (such as the one at Groat Road and 107 Avenue) have since been removed when traffic flow became too heavy. There remains a pseudo-circle at Saskatchewan Drive and 87 Avenue that's more of a three-sided operation, similar to the accident-prone arrangement that was recently removed in front of the Bul Go Gi House restaurant at 87 Avenue and 92 Street. There's also a "half-and-halfer," as transportation planners are wont to call it, at St. Albert Trail and 118 Avenue — a traffic circle that's signal-operated, instead of free-flowing. Oddly, although traffic statistics show that there have been approximately half as many accidents at that circle since the lights were installed, the average cost per accident has more than doubled. Planners speculate that the signals allow drivers to move at faster speeds than a free-flowing circle does, meaning that collisions are more serious when they occur. Or maybe people are just more confused by the lights.

Today, traffic circles are as scarce as hen's teeth in Canada, with only five traditional traffic circles left on major arterial roads in Edmonton:

142 St. and 87 Ave.
142 St. and 107 Ave.
83 St. and 90 Ave.
101 St. and 118 Ave.
85 St. and 98 Ave.

GRID LOCK

Much as we have Noel Dant to thank for traffic circles, one C. Gordon Mundy is the man behind our mercifully logical street numbering system. As anyone who grew up in the 'burbs can tell you (St. Albert, for instance, is all named streets), Edmonton's street grid — which has as its centre 101 Street and 101 Avenue — allows intuitive logic to prevail when looking for an address. Mundy was a map-maker who, in 1914, took the city's grid of existing numbered streets and named avenues (of which only Jasper Avenue remains) and rationally numbered them. Streets get larger as you move east to west, and avenues get larger as you move south to north; odd-numbered addresses are on the south side of the avenue, or the east side of the street. The main impetus for the change came from the Fire Department, which got hopelessly confused on calls because different stretches of the same avenue were renamed as they were enveloped by new subdivisions.

Red-Light Districts

In the mid-1980s, Edmonton installed a system of video cameras on major routes to keep an eye on traffic trouble spots like McDougall Hill, 98 Avenue, and the Quesnell, Capilano, and High Level Bridges. Every 20 seconds or so, black and white photos of the area were broadcast back to monitors in two control rooms, so the city could alert the media, post warnings or special speed limits, or dispatch road-maintenance equipment or tow trucks to the trouble spots.

Sounds ingenious, right? Perhaps it was, while it lasted. The cameras (described as "extremely outdated technology") haven't worked for a couple of years, and replacing them with expensive new cameras and fibre-optic cable isn't in the budget. The cameras are still there for the eagle-eyed to spot, but they no longer see anything.

Running red lights has always been a serious problem in Edmonton, as evidenced by these slightly tongue-in-cheek traffic etiquette guidelines from a 1975 city guidebook: "Green: the light is about to turn amber, go fast. Amber: the light is about to turn red, go fast. Red: if you are stopped, stay stopped; if you are stopped in the intersection or are not yet stopped, go very fast."

By 1998, running red lights was causing up to 1,500 collisions a year and $8 million in damages, prompting local police services to install red light cameras. The Sherwood Park RCMP installed the first in North America, at Wye Road and Ordze Road, in April 1998 – sending out warning tickets to errant motorists even before Bill 215 made the cameras' evidence admissible in court. Soon after, Edmonton launched a pilot project at a single intersection, where traffic accidents declined by almost half over the next year.

Although relatively new to Canada, red-light camera systems have been used since 1968 in Western Europe, Australia, and the U.S. The cameras work on a similar principle to photo radar: the camera is connected to the traffic signal and to sensors buried in the pavement, just in front of the stop line or crosswalk. It is triggered by any vehicle passing over the sensors after the signal has turned red. To reduce ticketing errors, it takes a second photograph that shows the violating vehicle in the intersection (which allows police to avoid ticketing drivers making a legal right-hand turn on the red light). Tickets (for a hefty $57) are automatically sent to the vehicles' registered owners. Should you decide to protest your innocence, "There's not much of a defense," says a Police Service spokesperson, since the date, time of day, time elapsed since the beginning of the red light, and speed are all recorded with the image.

Between 1999 and 2000, although the number of vehicles monitored by red-light cameras doubled, the number of tickets issued dropped by 53 percent. That could have something to do with the deterrent effect of the signs announcing the cameras' presence that are posted at every monitored intersection ...

or Edmontonians could actually be learning safer driving habits. Currently, six red-light cameras rotate through the following 12 locations:

  Whitemud Dr. (westbound) and
    Gateway Blvd. (northbound)
  23 Ave. and Gateway Blvd.
  97 Ave. and 105 St.
  118 Ave. and 73 St.
  127 Ave. and 97 St.
  Jasper Ave. and 116 St.
  137 Ave. and St. Albert Tr.
  137 Ave. and Manning Dr. (southbound)
  Yellowhead Tr. and 156 St.
  101 Ave. and 50 St.
  Argyll Rd. and 75 St.
  100 Ave. and 170 St.

secret roads

Keillor Road

For years it was the city's most beloved shortcut, and its closure was mourned by many. This circuitous, winding route connecting Saskatchewan Drive to Belgravia Road became solely a pedestrian and cycle path in 1996 after years of complaints from area residents about increasing traffic volumes.

Fort Hill

If you're in the Old Strathcona area and need a quick shortcut down into the river valley, get yourself onto 87 Avenue approaching 106A Street. You'll see one sign pointing down Fort Hill, and another warning you that it's a one-way passage – except for city maintenance vehicles. We're not advising that you flout this traffic convention, of course, but if you happen to be on a bicycle or on foot you'll find that the road leads past a Parks and Recreation storage facility on the right, and shoots you under the Saskatchewan Drive overpass, which frames a very pretty view of downtown like a big proscenium arch. You'll pop out on Walterdale Hill, about halfway down the hill to the Kinsmen Sports Centre.

**SHARE A CAR,
SAVE THE EARTH**

Does $500 for a 1999 Toyota Tercel sound like a good deal to you? It does to members of the **Carsharing Co-operative of Edmonton**, which allows members access to a communal car for a one-time membership fee ($400 of which is refundable), a small monthly administration fee, and low usage rates of two dollars an hour and 35 cents a kilometre. Members can reserve the car up to a year in advance. When it's not being used, the car sits in a central location (*10511 Saskatchewan Dr., 432-5098*), behind the Environmental Resource Centre. The car-sharing movement first started in Germany and Switzerland in the 1980s and has been gathering speed in Canadian cities like Vancouver, Victoria, Toronto, Montreal, and Quebec.

Lavigne Road

NO DOUGHNUTS HERE

So you're driving along 50 Street with jaggy, low-caffeine nerves and riding a sugar low when you spot a Tim Horton sign in the distance and race in the direction of its siren call. Alas, the sign on 93 Avenue doesn't loom large as you approach — it's kiddie-size. The miniature Tim Horton Doughnuts is part of the **Kiwanis Safety City** *(4831 93 Ave., 1-800-301-6407)*, a fenced-in block that resembles a mini-golf course but is actually used to teach children's road safety programs. There are also mini McDonald's, Canadian Tire, and Crystal Glass stores, kid-size pedestrian and railroad crossings, and traffic lights. Kids get to tool around Safety City on neat motorized scooters, making it a popular destination for birthday parties that are both fun *and* educational. There's also a bicycle safety program available.

Chances are you've seen this small pocket of houses as you cross the James MacDonald Bridge, but the residential area of Lavigne Road is somewhat tucked away in the city's grid (as in, not even on some maps). This cluster of a dozen-plus houses is accessed with a quick right off Saskatchewan Drive at 91 Avenue. Follow the hill down Lavigne, then around the curve to the left, and you'll find yourself driving through a small park and popping out on Queen Elizabeth Park Road, right across from the entrance to Queen E Pool. It makes a handy shortcut if road conditions are good on the steep, top part of Lavigne (watch that speed limit in the park, though). The area that is now Lavigne Road was once known as Skunk Hollow ... hmmm, maybe that's why they keep to themselves.

Hillside Crescent

Tucked into the north bank of the river just below Ada Boulevard, this quiet little crescent supports only a few houses, including one so grand it has its own private gate and drive. To find it, take the downhill turn from Ada Boulevard at 44 Street.

road hazards

Plugging the Holes

Our unpredictable, freeze-and-thaw winter weather is hell on wheels – that is, the damage gaping potholes can do to vehicles. In an average year, more than 400,000 potholes form, most in the winter and spring when water seeps into cracks in the road, then freezes and expands, breaking up the pavement. Repairs cost the city hundreds of thousands of dollars a year. To report a particularly jarring one, call the tips line. *496-1700*

One Big Sandbox

Due to perennially icy driving conditions, a lot of sand is dropped on Edmonton streets every winter – approximately 150,000 tonnes. Ever wonder what happens to it all when the sweepers come by in the spring to clean it up? In eco-friendly Edmonton, about 40 percent of it is recycled for future use. The reclaimed material is enough to fill 625 railway cars.

Paint It White

What would be the worst possible colour to paint a snowplow? If you said white, you may be able to land a job with the City of Edmonton. Civic snowplows used to be painted a colour called "grabber blue," a tint that had some problems (it was discontinued by the paint manufacturer, and there was that little problem of lead pigment). These days they're plain white, and carry a City of Edmonton decal identifying them. Watch out for that white blur whizzing by you in a cloud of flying snow on the highway.

More Old Trains

If steamy, chugging journeys are your thing, don't miss these.

Fort Edmonton Park

You can eat, meet, or ride in old-time comfort. There's an old-fashioned steam engine that does a circuit of the park, and a streetcar that swings down 1905 Street. If you're looking for an out-of-the-ordinary meeting or event location, try the Fort's A-1 Business Car. It's a restored first-class coach, originally called the Prince Rupert, that was built in 1912 for the Grant Trunk Railway and once used for meetings by travelling big-wigs. These days you can rent it for groups of up to 20 people, and the park can even arrange catering. *496-8774*

A Trolley Good Time

Alberta Prairie Steam Tours
Departing from Stettler (186 kilometres southeast of Edmonton), they offer scheduled trips, special events (like murder mysteries, staged train robberies, and dinners), and charter booking for old-train fanciers. Two trains, a 1920 steam engine and a vintage 1958 diesel, lead almost daily summer excursions to Big Valley to the south, where you'll find a 1912 Canadian Northern Railway station and museum.
P.O. Box 1600, Stettler;
403/742-2811

Edmonton is the only Canadian city besides Vancouver that still operates trolleys, or bus-like vehicles that operate using overhead power lines and regular rubber tires. (They're distinct from streetcars like Toronto's, which operate on overhead power sources but use metal rails, like train cars.) Old-timers sometimes refer to them as "trackless trolleys," to distinguish them from Edmonton's earlier, now defunct, streetcar system. The first trolleys arrived on a shipment all the way from England in 1939 – months late, because the original ship they were transported on was sunk by a German submarine en route to the port of Montreal.

Circa 1913, an early, streetcar-style line was established that became known as the Toonerville Trolley (after a popular comic strip of the day). The route ran on 104 Street south from Whyte Avenue to 76 Avenue, and west to the McKernan Lake recreational area around 111 Street, where it came to an abrupt end. The conductor would stop, rearrange the trolley apparatus from the end car to the car that was now facing forward, reverse the direction of all the seats to face back to where they'd come from, re-install his controls on the front car, and head back to the city. At least once, when darkness prevented the driver from spotting the end of the track, the streetcar shot off the end and deep into the bush. The drivers were known for performing little errands and favours for their regular passengers on the route, and once for even delivering a family of lost ducklings back to McKernan Lake.

A streetcar was commandeered in the early 1940s to create a travelling streetcar library – the first of its kind in North America. The service was wildly popular, attracting hundreds of borrowers a day when it parked in various Edmonton neighbourhoods. The library streetcar operated for a decade, until 1951.

Photo: City of Edmonton Archives (EA160-794)

The *Edmonton Queen*, the 400-passenger, Mississippi-style paddlewheeler that was launched in 1995, is the grandest – if not the first – riverboat to ply the waters of the Fort Saskatchewan. Two early riverboats, the *Northwest* and the *City of Edmonton*, transported cargo during the week and passengers on the weekend, often on picnic excursions to Big Island. Much humbler was the first cable ferry, built in the pre-bridge days of 1882. It was a bona fide floating platform attached to an overhead cable with pulleys, so that the force of the current would gently nudge it across the river. It could hold six animal-driven carts and several passengers, and was a transportation boon – the equivalent of a modern superhighway – for early settlers. The early schedule of tolls was 25 cents per vehicle, 10 cents per foot passenger, and a bargain rate of a nickel for every additional sheep, hog, calf, or colt – and the canny operator, John Walter (whose early homestead is the John Walter museum today) charged double the toll before sunrise or after sunset. Today, excursions on the *Edmonton Queen (Rafter's Landing, 424-2628)* include short cruises between the Walterdale and Capilano Bridges, some with dinner or live entertainment.

HIGH LEVEL BRIDGE STREETCAR

The High Level Bridge hadn't been used by streetcars since 1951, but an old-fashioned traincar once again trundles across the top of the bridge today. The Edmonton Radial Railway Society (the folks who run the old steam train at Fort Edmonton Park) run a regular route between Old Strathcona *(103 St. at 84 Ave.)* and a downtown stop near the Grandin LRT station *(109 St. and 98 Ave.)*, from the Victoria Day long weekend in May until Thanksgiving. It makes intermediate stops at the Granite Curling Club *(8620 107 St.)* and at the hiking path at the south side of the bridge *(90 Ave. just west of 109 St.)*, and sightseers can board or get off at any stop. The streetcar leaves the south side on the hour and half-hour, and the north side at 15 and 45 minutes past the hour, every day between 11 a.m. and 4 p.m., with extended hours in August during the Fringe Theatre Festival. If your streetcar is named desire, they also take bookings for group or special occasion charter trips *(437-7721)*. Don't be surprised by the Japanese-language ads lining the car's interior: the well-used vehicle was purchased from Osaka, Japan.

Plane in Vain

A jilted lover, a pilot's license, and the open skies combined to produce an impromptu daredevil air show in the early morning hours of September 23, 1992, when Randy Mock set out to show his seven-months-pregnant former girlfriend "something spectacular." Mock called Dawna Lorenz at her parents' north-end Edmonton home at 12:30 a.m. and implored her – with his vague but dire warning – to watch the skies. In the wee hours of the morning, he repeatedly buzzed the home and surrounding neighbourhood, alarming residents and police. His 1969 Cessna came within 50 feet of tree and housetops and occasionally sputtered and stalled as if running out of gas, necessitating the evacuation of many nearby homes. Despite Mock's repeated radio pleas to the airport tower to have Lorenz come out of the house and talk to him, she and her family managed to slip out of the house and drive to safety. Good thing, too – at about 3:15 a.m. Mock crashed his plane squarely into the home's front door, showing his top-notch flying skills by gliding neatly between two large trees to do so. Mock was critically injured in the accident and died one month later; miraculously, nobody else was hurt. But he *did* get her attention.

FLIGHTS OF FANCY

Known as the "Gateway to the North," Edmonton became a popular aerial shortcut and pit stop for aviators setting world speed and distance records in the 1920s. Parker Cramer, the first man to fly from Siberia to New York, stopped here in 1929. Wiley Post landed in Edmonton during his around-the-world flight in 1931, but ended up taking off from the paved road known as Kingsway Avenue today (formerly Portage Avenue) because the airport's field was too muddy to use.

Heavy as Bricks

Edmonton-born bush pilot Max Ward earned his wings in the RCAF before turning entrepreneur, eventually helping develop Canada's north by flying supplies to miners and prospectors in remote locations. (This incarnation of Wardair bore little resemblance to the luxury passenger airline he later founded, which was named the best airline in the world in the 1980s.) On one of those northern flights, Ward unwittingly participated in a gold theft. Gold bricks being transported from northern mines into Yellowknife were frequently among his cargo, and on one flight a light-fingered passenger managed to substitute two lead bricks for gold ones during a stopover. Even when Ward handed the man his extraordinarily heavy suitcase at the end of the trip, he didn't catch on to the scam. The theft was finally discovered, but not before the thief made it all the way to Cuba.

Pedestrian Right of Way

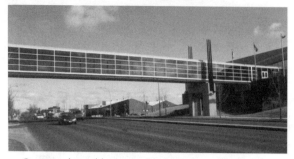

Our weird neighbours to the south (in Calgary) call them +15s (huh?), but in Edmonton the covered walkways that protect scurrying downtown workers and shoppers from winter's icy chill are known as pedways (shorthand for pedestrian walkways). Should you find yourself in a *Way Downtown*-style bet to stay indoors, here's the quick way to negotiate Edmonton's downtown walkways: buildings that are part of the system display green pedway signs, marked with a cute little pair of oxford-shod black feet indicating the level where you'll find the walkway. Feet at the top of the sign indicate an above-ground pedway, feet in the middle indicate street-level indoor passage, and on the bottom mean an underground walkway. If all else fails, there's always the sidewalk.

Off the Radar Screens

Most motorists probably think the dip in Yellowhead Trail where it passes north of the Edmonton Municipal Airport (now called City Centre Aiport) is just a topographical feature. Not so, says a city streets engineer. The dip was deliberately built into the road so the big rigs that frequent the Yellowhead won't be inadvertently picked up by the airport's radar. The slower speed of the trucks — not to mention their distinct lack of wings — are other features airport staff have used to distinguish the road warriors from the flyboys.

WING IT

Some unusual art decorates the new south terminal at the Edmonton International Airport. Its not the landscape that's unfamiliar — patchwork prairie fields, puffy clouds, endless horizon — it's the medium: airplane wings. The old mahogany and spruce airplane wings that now rise vertically out of the floor were sourced from a salvage yard near Villeneuve. The aerial views on *Wings* were painted by David Janzen, who has interesting origins, too. He is the son of John Janzen, former Edmonton superintendent of parks, for whom the John Janzen Nature Centre is named.

Photo: City of Edmonton Archives (EA289-148)

Ironic, for a province that's rat-free, that Edmonton's most distinctive traffic feature was once nicknamed the Rat Hole. The dark, foreboding tunnel was built in 1928 to guide two-way traffic on busy 109 Street under the CNR tracks. No matter how many overhead lights were installed, a trip down into the Rat Hole was always as dark (and approximately as safe) as a descent into the deepest reaches of the earth. Drivers entering the hole would turn on their left turn signals to make sure oncoming drivers could see the corner of their car. Despite signs clearly marking the tunnel's clearance height, many a traffic jam was caused by an over-ambitious trucker getting his rig stuck in the entrance. The Rat Hole was removed in 2000, and now a big, ugly intersection marks the spot at 104 Avenue and 109 Street.

Hub of Activity

Despite the snazzy new $130-million terminal at the International Airport, Edmonton isn't exactly one of the world's major air hubs – anymore. For a period during the Second World War, Edmonton's was the busiest airport in North America, with a record-setting 865 arrivals and departures on one day in September 1943. (Just think of the lineups at check-in.) Military intelligence had pinpointed Edmonton as the shortest air route to Alaska, and after Japan attacked the Aleutian Islands in June 1942, Edmonton became an aviation hotspot for American aircraft en route to Russia. The British Commonwealth Air Training Plan's #2 Air Observer School also trained pilots, navigators, and observers out of Edmonton during the war.

troubled bridges

Weekend warriors who just can't wait for that next trip to Jasper or Banff have been spotted climbing city bridges, including Groat, Quesnell, and Beverly. Not only are the climbers a potential liability nightmare for the city, their anchors can create openings for water to seep into the bridge, where it could freeze and crack the concrete. The River Valley Rangers have been slapping red-handed climbers with $110 tickets, and warning signs have recently put the writing on the wall.

Low Level Bridge

Photo: City of Edmonton Archives (EA25-19)

It doesn't get the attention of its taller, younger sibling the High Level Bridge, but the workhorse Low Level has a storied history of its own. None other than Donald Ross – one of Edmonton's early city builders and the name behind the Rossdale district – shucked his coat to drive in the last red-hot rivet that finished the bridge on April 2, 1900. As it was being constructed in 1899 the river flowed high, and another few metres were fortuitously added to the concrete piers. Good thing – during the flood of 1915, that extra height might have been the difference between the bridge standing strong or being swept away. Or, could it have been the steam locomotive the made the difference? Our sharp-thinking founding fathers, wary that the bridge might be washed out not only by floodwater but by debris that the river would lodge against it, bolstered the bridge by driving a steam engine onto it for stability. The extra weight helped the Low Level hold its course, and it survived the flood.

Initially built as a northbound railway bridge, by the 1940s vehicle traffic was so heavy that the bridge was twinned to span both directions. In more recent years, the Low Level has been a popular destination for Engineering Week pranks by high-spirited University students: at various times, both a motorcycle and a mannequin (a gorilla mannequin, to be precise) have been suspended from the bridge.

Kings of the Road

Anthony Henday Drive
Named for the Hudson's Bay explorer who, in 1754, became the first recorded white man to enter what is now Alberta.

Groat Road
Marks the east boundary of what was once River Lot 2, purchased by the ambitious settler Malcolm Groat in 1870.

James MacDonald Bridge
Takes its name from the late former city engineer who worked on five of the bridges that span the North Saskatchewan River.

Manning Drive
Honours Ernest Charles Manning (father of Preston), Alberta's longest-serving premier (from 1943-68).

Mayfield Road
Pays homage to the renowned Edmontonian fighter pilot Wop May, who used the Sproule farm, located around the modern-day intersection of St. Albert and Yellowhead Trails, as his landing strip.

High Level Bridge

It's hard to believe that this decidedly old-fashioned-looking trestle bridge was once the fourth-largest in Canada, but that was indeed the case in 1913. The High Level Bridge took $2 million, three years, 500 men, 1.4 million rivets, and 8,000 tonnes of steel to build – and several human lives. Some accounts say three men died during construction, some say four. (Perhaps the difference can be accounted for in the persistent but unprovable local rumour that one body lies encased in the bridge's cement pillars.) A young bridge worker from Lacombe, Alberta was the first casualty, crushed to death on his sixth day of work by a pile driver in 1910, the early days of construction. Later, a worker fell from the concrete piers to his death and another was buried in a cave-in of the riverbank.

After the bridge opened, trains and streetcars rumbled across its top deck, and pedestrians and vehicles on its bottom deck – usually. On June 30, 1932, some rambunctious University of Alberta students decided to drive a car across the train deck in the wee hours of the morning, with tire tracks revealing that the car came within several perilous centimetres of the edge. Just a few years later in 1935, traffic on the bridge was so heavy that a baby was born in a car on its deck, her mother stuck in a traffic jam en route to the hospital. A birth of another kind nearly threatened the bridge on the centennial of Confederation in 1967, Canada's birth as a nation: starry-eyed civic officials proposed painting the High Level gold to commemorate the occasion (a proposal that was wisely voted down). One thing that never changes: drivers just don't believe that beam dangling at the bridge's north end, warning of a low clearance on the south side. Stories of oversize transport trucks being trapped at the south portal, plugging up traffic on the bridge for hours, are common.

Tommy Banks Way

Named for the jazz legend in 1999 (before he became a Canadian senator) and runs past the Yardbird Suite at 103 Street and 86 Avenue.

Walterdale Bridge

Named for John Walter, an early Edmonton homesteader who operated a sawmill, lumber yard, and ferry service in the river valley.

Wayne Gretzky Drive

Capilano was named for Edmonton's most famous sporting son at the same time his 99 jersey was retired in October 1999.

Whyte Avenue

Carries the name of Sir William Whyte, the onetime second-vice-president of the Canadian Pacific Railway.

Quesnell Bridge

Not only is the Quesnell Bridge a great place to get into an accident in the winter or into a traffic jam at any time of year, but in 1995 a murderer proved it was a good place to stash unwanted human remains. Quesnell, like the Beverly Bridge to the east, is supported by hollow concrete pillars. For the purposes of a University of Alberta research study, a tube leading into one of the Quesnell Bridge pillars was installed. Donald Smart must have been intimately familiar with the bridge's structure when he was seeking to get rid of the head, arms, and legs of victim Jo-Anne Dickson. (He had already, using a copy of *Gray's Anatomy* found in his apartment, carefully severed them from her torso, which he stuffed in a suitcase and threw into the river.) He stuffed some of the remains down the tube and into one of the bridge's hollow pillars, where they were found several months later by an unlucky bridge maintenance worker. In 1997, Smart was convicted of second-degree murder.

Edmonton Incline Railway

Photo: City of Edmonton Archives (EA462-34)

Think of it as a big, primitive escalator. Or maybe as the shortest rail line ever in Edmonton. The Edmonton Incline Railway was the solution to early commuters' problems: once travellers crossed the Low Level Bridge from Strathcona on the south bank, they still had to get up the steep north bank of the river to reach downtown Edmonton. Often they carried large, heavy loads of building materials, and in bad weather horse teams and wagons struggled to make it up McDougall Hill. An early entrepreneur created a hoist, with one platform going up and one going down, and charged a nickel a person or 15 cents for horses and a wagon, round trip. Once the High Level Bridge opened in 1913, the lift became obsolete. One local historian surmises that the engine is still buried in the riverbank, somewhere in the vicinity of the Chateau Lacombe Crowne Plaza (*10111 Bellamy Hill*).

LOCK, STOCK, AND BARREL

In the gold rush years of the late 19th century, Edmonton became known as the last outpost on an alternate, inland route to the Klondike. One prospector who stopped here to stock up didn't even make it out of town, thanks to his ramshackle vehicle. Instead of loading up a traditional cart, C.L. Smith of Houston, Texas took three big empty whiskey barrels, filled them with all his supplies, and mounted them on axles. (Think of them as early prototypes of monster truck tires.) Pulled by a team of two horses, Smith's bizarre vehicle almost made it to the town of St. Albert on Edmonton's northern outskirts before falling apart. Chalk the ill-conceived contraption up to faulty construction, or maybe to all that whiskey he had to drink to empty the barrels.

FOUNTAIN OF (ROAD SAFETY) KNOWLEDGE

Wilbert McIntyre was a beloved physician from Edmonton's early days who died in 1909, prompting the construction of the McIntyre Fountain at the intersection of 83 Avenue and 104 Street. The fountain became an unwitting target for careless Edmonton drivers, including one city planner who, during the holiday season in 1952, inadvertently took the final run at the landmark during a late-night drive home. (Can you say "impaired," everyone?) The fountain was dismantled and the pieces promptly lost; it took until 1991 for the Old Strathcona Foundation to rebuild the McIntyre Fountain, which now sits near the Strathcona Library.

Lead-footed Edmonton drivers have put millions of dollars into city coffers since 1993, the year photo radar was first used in the city. Statistics from that year showed that Edmonton drivers were seven times more likely to be ticketed than their speedy counterparts in Vancouver. Although photo radar has had trouble shaking its cash-cow image in Edmonton and elsewhere, local statistics seem to support its record at improving safety: before photo radar introduction (1987-92), Edmonton averaged 40 traffic fatalities and more than 32,000 collisions per year. That number dropped to 30 fatalities and approximately 26,000 collisions per year after photo radar was first used (1993-95), a change attributed at least in part to photo radar enforcement. Tickets run a mere $65 for going 15 kilometres over to a hefty $100 for driving 25 kilometres over the speed limit. Staving off accusations of sneakiness, police use signage to inform motorists of many standing photo radar locations. And during any given week, you can find a complete list of photo radar sites on the Edmonton Police Service Web (www.police.edmonton.ab.ca, follow the link for "news wire").

Signs of the Times

Edmonton motorists got a shock in 1990 when signs boldly marked "Fatality" began cropping up on city streets. The cross-shaped markers, installed at sites where fatality accidents had recently occurred, were intended to increase awareness of traffic safety. Soon after their inception, non-Christians objected to the signs' shape, which was changed, in a connect-the-dots fashion, to an eight-sided box shape that in a macabre way resembles a coffin. The signs go up the second working day after a fatal accident, and remain up for six months. They are not installed in residential areas (out of courtesy to the family of the deceased, who may live in the area), and not against the family's wishes. Since Edmonton introduced the signs, other North American cities have been interested in the unique and cost-effective program: following a sharp rise in traffic fatalities from 1983-89, the fatality numbers dropped and plateaued after introduction of the signs. One unexpected effect: the signs sometimes become magnets for mini-shrines to the deceased, surrounded by photographs and floral tributes after high-profile accidents.

More recently, the city has begun replacing the traditional schoolhouse-shaped, blue signs with two child figures that mark school crossings with bright (nine times brighter, to be exact) fluorescent yellow ones. Apparently, they're hoping that, "I didn't see the sign officer, honest," will become an excuse of the past.

Accident Hotspots

According to the Edmonton Police Service, you're most likely to crash your car at these 10 city intersections, which had the most accidents in 2000:

23 Ave. and Gateway Blvd.
137 Ave. and 97 St.
87 Ave. and 170 St.
Yellowhead Tr. and 127 St.
95 Ave. and 170 St.
Wayne Gretzky Dr. and Fort Rd. at Yellowhead Tr.
Yellowhead Tr. and 149 St.
Groat Rd. and 118 Ave.
118 Ave. and 97 St.
107 Ave. and 142 St.

Penny-Pinching Parking

Membership Has Its Privileges

If you happen to be meeting a tweed-and-corduroy, elbow-patched colleague at the University of Alberta's Faculty Club for lunch, don't forget to mention that to the attendant at the parking lot in the campus' far northwest corner to get the special club rate of two dollars (a far cry from the seven-dollar deposit usually required) between noon and 2 p.m. One could, theoretically, cash in on the cheap rate to go do business elsewhere on campus, but that would be dishonest, right?
116 St. south of Saskatchewan Dr.

Park in the Heart

Look for the logo – a square green sign with a big white P and a small red heart – for sweet parking deals. At locations sporting the signs, a loonie will get you three hours of parking during the daytime on weekends, and a toonie will cover you from 6 p.m. to 1 a.m. any night of the week.
Downtown Business Association, 424-4085

Downtown Dollar

Loonier than a loonie and funnier than any normal money, Edmonton's own urban buck is this custom-minted currency, a little gift-with-purchase you can often scam from participating downtown stores, banks, and services. The coin can be used at certain downtown parking meters, parking lots and parkades, and on Edmonton Transit. Makes a cool souvenir, too.
Downtown Business Association,
424-4085

A looming figure in Edmonton's storied aviation history is famed First World War fighter pilot Wilfred "Wop" May. On his first combat mission overseas, he did battle with Baron Von Richtofen – alias the Red Baron – and won. Richtofen was shot down and killed during the chase, but May survived and went on to start Edmonton's first commercial airline and was instrumental in establishing Blatchford Field (later known as the Edmonton Municipal Airport, now called City Centre Aiport), Canada's first municipal airport, in 1926. It became particularly well-known three years later when May and fellow pilot Vic Horner made a heroic flight north to Fort Vermilion – in an open-cockpit plane, in -30ºC weather – to deliver much-needed diphtheria vaccine. He was also the pilot who helped catch the Mad Trapper of Rat River (a.k.a. Albert Johnson) in 1932, the first time a plane was used to track a fugitive in Canada. One of his early planes, the *City of Edmonton*, now graces the entrance to the Reynolds Museum in Wetaskiwin.

Unquestionably, the Edmonton Transit Service's Route 8 is the busiest in the city. with 19,712 boardings per day. The Number Eight is a longish route that runs from the Mill Woods neighbourhood in the city's deep southeast to Abbottsfield in the northeast, travelling through the Bonnie Doon, NAIT, and downtown areas along the way. During the morning rush hour, the portion of the route taking commuters from Millwoods into downtown is the busiest, and as you'd expect the pattern reverses in the late afternoon. To ensure a comfy, uncrowded transit trip, at peak hours avoid these other busy routes, ranked here by total number of boardings per day:

Route 9 (Southgate to Northgate, Rossdale to NAIT)
   13,628

Route 6 (Mill Woods to downtown, Millgate to downtown and university)
   11,611

Route 1 (West Edmonton Mall to Capilano Mall)
   8,736

Route 5 (Westmount to Coliseum)
   8,437

Route 4 (West Edmonton Mall to Capilano Mall)
   7,738

Route 2 (Lessard to Clareview and Highlands)
   7,385

Route 10 (Coliseum to Clareview)
   6,517

Route 106 (Lessard to Capilano and West Edmonton Mall)
   5,671

Route 3 (Jasper Place to Cromdale)
   5,109

Fun Transit Facts

Well, maybe they're not that fun but they're interesting. Well, maybe they're not that scintillating … but we bet you didn't know them before.

Routes (including LRT, trolley, bus, and Service Plus van):
144

Bus stops:
5,133

Transit shelters:
1,141

Transit benches:
2,000

Vehicles in fleet:
863

Total employees:
1,704

easy riding

An excellent cycling map of the city is available from the Citizen Action Centre in city hall and from bike-friendly spots around the city. It shows paved and unpaved trails, service roads, bus routes, and bicycle racks, trails, lanes, paths, and routes. Included are basic bicycle traffic safety and laws, a signage guide, and transit information (like the fact that riders can take bikes on the LRT, except during rush hours). Here are some other useful bicycle resources to keep your wheels turning:

Population served:
658,000

Service area:
700 square km

Annual ridership:
43,041,689

Total kilometres:
32,587,746

Operating expenses:
$105,072,842

Revenues:
$54,220,703

Power consumption:
17,950,122 KWH

Diesel fuel consumption:
16,050,785 litres

* All figures for 2000.

River Valley Trail Report Hotline
496-2959

Edmonton Bicycle Commuters Society
433-2453

Edmonton Bicycle and Touring Club
424-2453

Alberta Bicycle Association
453-8518

Bicycling Education Society of Edmonton
421-0241

You've never seen Edmonton's outdoors in quite this way, including all manner of bugs and vermin, panning for gold, and a big stinky lake. On the sporting front, find out how Edmonton plays home to a runner's paradise, when Rocket Richard made his return here, why Edmonton caused a Stanley Cup scandal, and where to find the mascot capital of the world.

Photo: City of Edmonton Archives (EA423-59)

Gold in Them Thar Waters

The words Edmonton and gold usually prompt associations with the Klondike gold rush of the 1890s, but gold can also be found closer to home. Way back in 1860, a lucky young man named Tom Clover struck it big sluicing for gold in the North Saskatchewan River, giving the area of Clover Bar its name. Records show that in 1896, $50,000 in gold was removed from the river. To declare the grand new Legislative Building open in 1912, the Duke of Connaught unlocked the doors with a key made of locally panned gold.

Even today, you still see the odd prospector panning in the river. Gold panning involves scooping some river gravel, mud, and water into a shallow pan, and swirling it around to remove the coarse grains and leave the fine ones, including the relatively heavy gold particles, behind. The best places to look for this fine, or so-called flour gold, are the river's grassy banks or gravel bars, especially along the inside bank of a turn in the river, which tends to trap the heavier gold particles. Favourite spots include Groat Bridge and, just outside of town, the Devon Bridge.

Photo: Rob Galbraith/Edmonton Journal

Although many Edmontonians find the circumstances too painful to recount, the date of August 9, 1988 is burned into the city's collective memory: the day Wayne Gretzky was traded from the Edmonton Oilers to the Los Angeles Kings, and the day Peter Pocklington indisputably became the most-hated man in Edmonton's history (although a long, nasty strike at the Pocklington-owned Gainers meat-packing plant may have also had something to do with it). The trade happened a mere three weeks after Gretzky married Hollywood starlet Janet Jones in the most star-studded wedding Edmonton had ever hosted. (There was some speculation – not borne out by the last decade of entertainment history – that Jones' career was the impetus for the trade.) The Oilers had just won their fourth Stanley Cup, Gretzky was at the height of his fame and popularity as the greatest player in hockey history … and Pocklington traded him away for two players, three first-round draft picks, and $18 million. (Repeat: *$18 million*.)

Perhaps a little history is in order, to prove how Gretzky's presence in Edmonton literally changed the face of hockey in the city. Peter Puck bought the World Hockey Association Oilers team in 1977, and within two years wrangled the team into the National

Hockey League. He made a bold prediction: that within five years, the unproven young team would win a Stanley Cup. His ace in the hole was the skinny 17-year-old from Brantford, Ontario named Wayne Gretzky. The kid was signed to a long, 20-year contract (symbolized by his jersey number, 99 – the year it would expire).

John Ducey

One of the first six people to be inducted into the Canadian Baseball Hall of Fame. Well-known as a player and umpire, Ducey's name previously graced Edmonton's Triple A ballpark (now rebuilt as Telus Field, one of the best parks in its league in North America).

Clarence Campbell

You know he was the former president of the National Hockey League and the namesake of the league's Campbell Conference, but less well-known is the fact that the Edmontonian was also a Rhodes Scholar and a semi-pro baseball player.

In 1982 and 1983 the Oilers reached the Stanley Cup finals, and in 1984 they won — just in time to make Pocklington's audacious prediction come true. Four cups later, Pocklington exercised the terms of Gretzky's contract to trade him.

Gretzky's legacy to the city of Edmonton is marked with a heroic statue outside the Skyreach Centre where he played for nine years, and the renaming of Capilano Drive as Wayne Gretzky Drive in 2000, the same year that he received an honourary doctorate from the University of Alberta.

Alex Decoteau

Canada's first Native police officer (he was hired in 1909), he was a talented runner and the only Alberta competitor in the 1912 Olympics in Stockholm, Sweden. Decoteau died at age 30 in the First World War.

John Hougan

The original ski-jumping eagle: he broke the national record at Connors Hill in Edmonton in February 1913 with a 109-foot jump (and bested his own record by three feet the following year).

X Marks the Spot

When the Edmonton Oilers won their first Stanley Cup in 1984, the thrill of victory went straight to the big head of team owner Peter Pocklington. Perhaps out of a sense of filial loyalty, Pocklington snuck the name of his father, Basil Pocklington, onto the team roster to be engraved on the Stanley Cup — although Puck senior had never played for the Oilers. (At age 69 at the time, he was a little long in the tooth to be drafted). The name was dutifully engraved with the rest of the list on to Lord Stanley's impressive silver vessel, but when the National Hockey League discovered Pocklington's transgression it ordered the "extra" name removed. Hockey Hall of Fame curator Philip Pritchard confirms that several unsightly Xs are now scratched over the offending name on the cup.

Hockey Pool

In 1988, with the Edmonton Oilers still enjoying the post-season glow of sporting victory with the Stanley Cup, fleet-footed Oiler Glenn Anderson suffered a personal tragedy. During a house party at his Edmonton home, his friend George Varvis died as a result of an apparent drowning incident in Anderson's pool. Varvis had spent some time in the hot tub before going in the pool to cool off, where he apparently fell asleep. Varvis was pulled from the pool and Anderson performed CPR on him, but although Varvis revived and even walked into the hospital emergency room himself, he slipped into a coma and died a few days later. All kinds of lurid rumours circulated — including one that drugs were involved in the incident — all of which Anderson denied. No charges were laid in the apparent accidental death.

river trivia

As outdoorsy Edmontonians will not hesitate to tell you, they love their North Saskatchewan River Valley. In a rare incident of civic vision, the development of a river valley parks area began way back in 1915 on the recommendation of landscape architect Frederick Todd. It is the largest and most continuous sprawl of urban parkland in North America, nearly 22 times the size of New York's Central Park. A space that big holds a lot of secrets. Here are a few.

Impressive Measurements

The river valley encompasses nearly 75 square kilometres and has more than 100 kilometres of ravines.

Green Space

Edmonton has the second-most parkland per capita of any Canadian city, out-greened only by Victoria.

Lava Lab

When the Dudley Menzies LRT Bridge was being built, a cut into the riverbank revealed a layer of ash from the eruption of Oregon's Mount Mazama nearly 7,000 years ago.

Hotbed of Industry

Several businesses – including John Pollard's brickyard, Fermin Bedard's Strathcona Tannery, John Walter's mill, and several coal mines – once thrived in the river valley, and vestiges of them can still sometimes be seen (look for remains of bricks in the south bank just west of the LRT bridge).

GO ESQUIMAUX

The Canadian Football League Edmonton Eskimos team traces its lineage to a rugby club called the Esquimaux that played a unique version of traditional English rugby (and apparently took some liberties with traditional English spelling). After a few early runs at the Grey Cup in the 1920s, the team folded and re-emerged after the Second World War. At that time, they acquired the distinctive green and gold colours they still sport today, more by accident than by design. The University of Alberta Golden Bears football team had folded, and the Eskimos bought two boxes of used football equipment, including the university's green and gold jerseys, for the new team's use. Used jerseys? Apparently the CFL didn't pay any better then than it does now.

secrets of the flora and fauna

Lily of the Valley

In the 1890s, noted California horticulturalist Luther Burbank arranged with Donald Ross, owner of Edmonton's first hotel (and namesake of the Rossdale area), to supply and ship to him 1,000 tiger lilies. Ross sent his children out scrambling in the river valley for the plants, which Burbank later bred into the domestic tiger lilies that now grow all over the world.

Dutch Treat

Tree fanciers know about the massive oaks of the antebellum American South and the giant redwoods of the Pacific Northwest, but how many know about Edmonton's 60,000 elm trees? That population of trees is the largest disease-free group of American elms in the world — so far. The threat of Dutch Elm Disease and other tree-eating pests, like a black fungus called *dothiorella*, is an annual concern. Some of the earliest (some date back as far as 1911) and most spectacular elms are along the boulevards of Whyte Avenue and have been registered as local historic resources. A particularly stocky one at 89 Avenue and 100 Street has even been named the girthiest in the city, with a diameter of 118 centimetres. The collective value of the elms is estimated at $420 million.

TEA IN JAPAN

In the midst of the Devonian Botanic Garden sits a little slice of Japan, the **Kurimoto Japanese Garden**, one of only a handful of Japanese gardens in northern latitudes. (Winter is hell on bonsais.) The garden, named for Yuichi Kurimoto, the first Japanese graduate from the University of Alberta (which runs the Devonian), includes an elaborate entrance gate, bridge, bell tower, and an *azumaya*, or shelter, for tea ceremonies. Built in 1990, the garden is *kaiyou*, or strolling, style, and in typical symbolic fashion its features interpret the broader Alberta topography of lakes, mountains, forests, and hills. At the top of the bell tower is a black ornament, called a *giboshi*, that represents Buddha's head. Go ahead, just try to give the bell a ring: it weighs 1,500 pounds. *Five km north of Devon on Hwy. 60, 987-3054*

Healthy as a Horse

A giant horse chestnut tree downtown has survived the climactic odds and thrived in Edmonton for the last 70 years. Located in the parking lot behind the HSBC bank on Jasper (10561 Jasper Ave.), the tree was planted by an immigrant from Prague who used "conkers" or shoots from his native land. (It's sometimes referred to as the Holowich tree after him.)

Vermin

The Alberta Department of Agriculture started its war on rats in the 1950s, making ours the first and only officially rat-free province in Canada. It's a zero-tolerance effort: a 500-strong rat colony found on a farm in southern Alberta was quickly

Photo: Provincial Archives of Alberta (A17202b)

eradicated in the summer of 1991, as were a few unlucky rats that hitched a ride on a truck from Saskatchewan into Edmonton recently. There's actually an eight-member rat-control team, based out of Vermilion, that patrols Alberta's eastern border for the intrusive pests. Alberta is still officially rat-free, although employees of certain Edmonton restaurants might beg to differ.

Buggy Facts

Lady and the Bug
Edmonton's **Muttart Conservatory** uses – annually – nearly 300,000 ladybugs to control insect pests on its many species of rare and native plants.
9626 96A St., 496-8735

Beautiful Butterflies
The tropical butterfly house at the **Devonian Botanic Garden** contains more than 30 species of the exotic winged creatures. The Devonian is also home to the second-largest collection of microfungus in Canada, and its other wonders include a rhubarb collection (50 species), orchid greenhouse, and lily, peony, iris, herb, alpine, and desert gardens.
Five km north of Devon on Hwy. 60, 987-3054

Peticide

Edmonton has the unfortunate distinction of being the dog and cat-killing capital of Western Canada. Around 8,000 pets are put to sleep here each year, far more than in Vancouver or Calgary. That statistic was part of the impetus for the city's controversial cat bylaw, which requires owners to register their felines for as little as $10, if the animal is neutered and carries microchip or tattoo identification. The city pound *(Yellowhead Tr. and 128 St., 496-8860)* can house up to 100 dogs and 120 cats. If your Fifi or Fido goes missing, check *www.gov.edmonton.ab.ca/animalcontrol* for pictures of animals that have recently been picked up.

Birds of Prey

In the 1970s, as few as one breeding pair of peregrine falcons were left in Alberta. Today, a few peregrine pairs make Edmonton their annual breeding ground: one fierce mama annually nests on or around the 13th storey of the Clinical Sciences building on the university campus, and another nested high up on the Telus tower for several years. Lately, one pair seems to have decamped at the **Canada Trust Building** *(10104 103 Ave.)* and another has been spotted nesting on the side of an **Inland Cement** *(12640 156 St.)* silo. Spring is the best time to spot them wooing and cooing, but beware: peregrines tend to be defensive of their territory, and the small but mighty predators can be aggressive against humans.

Groundhog Day

Every day is groundhog day for workers at **CBC Radio** *(7909 51 Ave.)*. For the last decade, a posse of Richardson ground squirrels (the proper name for the reclusive little rodents) have made Swiss cheese of the CBC building lawn, which is riddled with hundreds of holes made by an estimated 500 animals. A few years ago, when the critters started making their way into the building and chewing electric cables, a mass "control" effort was attempted, but they're b-a-a-a-c-k.

Bloodsuckers

Edmonton's unique combination of typically heavy summer rainfall, hilly topography, and poor-draining clay soil creates perfect conditions for the breeding of mosquitoes. The mosquito season stretches from mid-May to mid-July, but anti-mosquito spraying targets the larvae in the spring. Heavy rainfall and melting snow can create puddles where masses of *Aedes vexan* (the most common of six species found locally) can breed in as little as five days. The city controls a 1,700-square-kilometre larval zone, largely with helicopter spraying, with about a 90 percent success rate at killing the little bloodsuckers. The sensitive can call the Spray Line (496-TREE, then press 2) to find out times and locations (and take comfort in the fact that they stopped using DDT in 1972). If you're planning a picnic check weekly summer updates of mosquito activity on the Web: *www.gov.edmonton.ab.ca/comm_services/* (follow the link for "parkland services")

Mean and Green

The Edmonton Eskimos enjoy the only major natural turf playing field in Canada at Commonwealth Stadium. The hardy grass is planted in half a foot of a sand and peat moss mix, with another foot and a half each of washed sand and washed rock below, resting on a weeping tile and clay base for drainage. It's high-maintenance, because it not only needs frequent fertilizing, but the lines have to be repainted every time the grass is cut. When Edmonton hosted the 1984 Grey Cup it got an uninvited blizzard, leaving groundskeeping staff scrambling to clear the field before game time. Only in Edmonton would you see people shovelling and sweeping the grass....

Punchy Pugilists

In the scrappy, Western tradition, Edmonton has produced a legacy of fine boxers over the years. (An apocryphal tale has it that former Selkirk Hotel bartender Jack Kearns went on to manage the American slugger Jack Dempsey, but that's another story.) The first was Louis "Kid" Scaler, a national lightweight champion circa 1910. Heavyweight Vern Escoe was already the Canadian champion when he moved to Edmonton in 1953 to continue his career. In the early 1960s, Doug Harper won the Canadian light-heavyweight title and Wilf Greaves won the Commonwealth and Canadian middleweight titles. The winning streak continued when local boxer Bill McGrandle won the featherweight title in 1966, and 18-year-old Allan Ford became the youngest boxer ever to capture a Canadian title, leading the lightweight class from 1968 to 1972. Scotty "Bulldog" Olson held the Canadian amateur championship and USBA and IBO flyweight belts in the 1980s, and Edmonton's Ken Lakusta and Willie deWit were both Canadian heavyweight champions in the early 1990s.

Things Built on Garbage

Before the city went recycling-mad, it seemed to go through landfill sites faster than a baby goes through disposable diapers. But we know how to make use of them: the old **Clarke Stadium** was the legacy of garbage and of colourful local politician "Fighting Joe" Clarke — not the morose, jowly, current-day Joe Clark, but an eight-time alderman and five-time mayor from 1912-37. In 1929, he obtained a 99-year lease on federal government land for just a dollar. The land was home to not only the Rat Creek Dump, but a sports stadium that bore Clarke's name and later the nearby Commonwealth Stadium. Other scenic sites built on old city dumps include:

Jackie Parker Park
Whitemud Dr. and 50 St.

Rundle Park
29 St. between 113 and 118 Aves.

The Ultimate What?

It's the sport in which you score points by advancing a disk into an endzone. If you haven't heard of it, well, get with the program, because the 2001 Canadian Ultimate Championships were held in Edmonton, bringing 70 teams and nearly 2,000 players to the city. Invented by some New Jersey kids in the late 1960s, the sport – which is the "ultimate" combination of elements from soccer, rugby, basketball, and volleyball – still has a gonzo, underground appeal. It also has a unique feel-good ethic: the sportsman-like players themselves, not referees, make the calls under a rule system known as the Spirit of the Game. Edmontonian Kiersten Stead, who is active in the Edmonton Ultimate Organization (www.edmontonultimate.org), is considered one of the world's best Ultimate players.

FIRE IN THE SKY

Who needs fireworks when you've got a spectacular annual meteor shower? The Perseids is a natural show that plays in repertory across the sky for a few days every August. The name comes from the visual impression that these pretty "shooting stars" (actually burning chunks of galactic debris) appear to be coming from the constellation Perseus. Evenings in mid-August, away from the city lights, you can spot up to 50 in an hour. Try viewing this phenomena from the **University Observatory**, on the roof of the Avadh Bhatia Physics Laboratory (492-3439), open to the public most Thursday evenings from September to April.

The Rocket Rides Again

At age 67, well past his prime but well before his death and virtual canonization in 2000, Maurice "Rocket" Richard laced on the blades to skate on the outdoor ice in -30ºC weather at Riverdale Rink. A famous hockey-player muse (Guy Lafleur, in the original script) plays a pivotal role in the stage and later screenplay Life After Hockey by Edmonton's Ken Brown. When it was filmed as a movie in 1989, The Rocket was paid a modest fee to appear as himself in a few scenes. He chose his own costume, the Canadiens jersey he wore when he played his last Stanley Cup game in 1960. The acting gig must have beat those embarrassing Grecian Formula commercials he'd been doing to pay the bills.

Wetland Wonders

Saving the wetlands might not sound as exciting, say, as saving the rainforest, but the **Big Lake** area just northwest of Edmonton is one of the most important wetland areas in Alberta. Almost 200 species of birds have been observed by naturalists at the site, which forms a major staging area for many migrating birds. If American avocets, tundra swans, Franklin's gulls, and Canada geese are your thing, you'll want to spend some quality time on the observation platform. There are also pike, walleye, and perch in the lake and river, but no fishing allowed – they're for the birds. Warning: wetland is just a really nice word for large quantities of algae and decaying vegetation, so be prepared for the fact that Big Lake gives off a very *distinctive* odour. *Access from Riel Dr. or Red Willow Park in St. Albert*

Ride 'Em, Cowboy

Our neighbours to the south like to brag about that little rodeo they call the Stampede, but it's Edmonton that hosts the biggest indoor sporting event in Western Canada. The **Canadian Finals Rodeo** came out buckin' in 1974 and draws the elite cowboys from nearly 100 summer rodeos across Canada for an indoor championship at Northlands. A three-quarters of a million dollar purse is at stake as around 90,000 spectators look on every year, watching cowboys compete in bareback, saddle bronc, and bull riding, not to mention calf roping, steer wrestling, and barrel racing (for the ladies). Miss Rodeo Canada is crowned, there's a Black Tie bingo fundraiser, a chili cook-off, and plenty more action packed into five days in November. *7300 116 Ave., 471-7210*

Secret Society of the Elk

Elk Island National Park

Canada's oldest national wildlife sanctuary is the only park in the world with free-roaming herds of bison. Two species – plains and wood bison – live in the park, and the herds' territory is split down the middle by the Yellowhead Highway for good reason: the herd of plains bison here is the largest and purest in the world, no animals having been added since the herd was moved to Elk Island in 1909, three years after the park was created. So thriving are the bison herds, that around 150 excess animals are sold each year to populate other areas. In addition to over 1,000 bison, there are also nearly 2,000 elk, 500 beavers, 350 moose, 165 deer, and 100 coyotes in the massive park, which contains a 3,043-yard, nine-hole public golf course.
45 km east of Edmonton on Yellowhead Hwy.

Nature Calls

A former Edmonton Parks and Recreation superintendent with vision created the first nature and observation centre of its kind of Canada. Founded in 1976, the **John Janzen Nature Centre** *(Whitemud Dr. and Fox Dr., 496-2910)* offers activities like nature walks, workshops, and talks in the heart of the river valley (just southwest of Fort Edmonton Park). In addition to its ever-popular programs for school groups, the centre offers family activities like sleigh rides and bonfires in the winter and birdwatching in the summer. At 75 cents admission per child (adults are $1.25, or $3.75 for the whole family) there is no better way to entertain a pack of kiddies on one of those "I'm bored" afternoons.

Ukrainian Cultural Heritage Village

A re-created historical village of more than 30 buildings and staff in period costumes interpret the history of Alberta's Ukrainian settlers from 1892 to the 1930s. Activities like horse-drawn wagon rides and tours of the typical homesteads and farmsteads are supplemented with special events during the summer months. *45 km east of Edmonton on Yellowhead Hwy.*

Lost Guides

A gourmet meal at the end of the day more than compensates for the fact that you're a saddle-sore greenhorn. Edmonton's **Lost Guide Adventure Tours** *(8715 68A St., 469-9602)* offers guided horseback tours of the eastern slopes of the Rocky Mountains (west of Rocky Mountain House) and meals like cornmeal blueberry pancakes with maple syrup and bratwurst, or filet of salmon with herb cream vermouth sauce (complete with wine and dessert). Run by Marc Halun, Bill Wesson (both local schoolteachers), and Wesson's chef wife Sherry, the company's six-day, $600 U.S. trips have been wildly popular with international tourists since a glowing review of one of the trips ran in *American Way*, the American Airlines in-flight magazine, in 1999. An added bonus: Wesson and Halun (a.k.a. the Ranger Creek Wranglers) are known to bring out their guitars and croon a few tunes around the campfire.

Photo: City of Edmonton Archives (EA189-2)

MARGARET KINNEY   CAPT. ELSIE BENNIE   J. PERCY PAGE   GLADYS FRY   MILDRED McCORMACK
GUARD   GUARD   COACH   CENTRE   FORWARD
DORIS NEALE   MAE BROWN   MARGARET MacBURNEY   BABE BELANGER
GUARD   GUARD   FORWARD   FORWARD

The most winning team ever in the history of basketball has nothing to do with Michael Jordan or Wilt Chamberlain. It was a group of women who were "ladies first and athletes second," who played in demure bloomers and tunics (until they scandalized the world by wearing T-shirts and shorts when they played in Rome in 1930), and who hailed from Edmonton. The Edmonton Commercial Grads won an amazing 502 of 522 games from 1915 to 1940, regularly scoring 70 or 80 points a game in an era where 30 points a side was considered high-scoring. Ontario-born James Naismith, who had invented basketball in 1891, remarked in 1925, "In my opinion the Grads have the finest basketball team that ever stepped out on a floor."

In 1914, Edmonton high school teacher J. Percy Page began coaching the girls' team at McDougall Commercial High. The next year, when some of the graduating girls wanted to stay on to play, the Grads were born. So dedicated were team members that in 25 years only 38 women hit the boards for the Grads. They crossed many barriers in sport at a time when women were only beginning to be accepted in aggressive team competition: long before women's basketball became an Olympic sport (in 1976), they won the unofficial world championships at the Paris Olympics in 1924, and at

Cross-Country Skiing

Edmonton grooms up to 200 kilometres of local cross-country ski trails every winter in local ravines and parks, an intensive effort that requires about an hour of work for each kilometre of ski trail. Many parks have washrooms and warm-up shelters that are open all winter. Ski equipment can be rented from many local sporting goods stores or from U of A's Campus Outdoor Centre. P-153 Van Vliet Centre, 492-2767

Local skiers show up in droves at these popular local sites:

Capilano Park and Gold Bar Park
109 Ave. and 50 St.

Kinsmen Park
91 Ave. and 108 St.

Mill Creek
95A St. and 82 Ave.

Riverside Golf Course
Rowland Rd. and 84 St.

Terwillegar Park
Rabbit Hill Rd. West

Victoria Park
116 St. and River Valley Rd.

Whitemud Park
Keillor Rd. and Fox Dr.

William Hawrelak Park
9330 Groat Rd.

Wm. Hawrelak Park

Mini Golf

For the thrill of the artificial turf and the agony of defeat by a nine-year-old kid, nothing beats mini golf. Humiliation awaits you at these courses, especially Planet Golf at West Edmonton Mall, where there are always plenty of spectators.

Golfdome
10104 32 Ave., 430-3663

Fun House
9103 31 Ave., 450-2695

Planet Golf
Entrance 8, West Edmonton Mall,
483-7888

St. Albert Trail Go-Karts
13633 St. Albert Tr., 452-1625

Schanks
9927 178 St., 444-2125

Whitemud Amusement Park
7411 51 Ave., 465-1190

subsequent Games in Amsterdam, Los Angeles, and Berlin. No shrinking violets, the ferociously competitive Grads once popped a teammate's dislocated knee back into place right on the court (a few minutes later, she limped back into the game).

By 1940, the Second World War restricted international travel and hometown fans tired of the Grads' continual landslide victories. The team faded into obscurity, but not without leaving a bizarre rumour of its legacy. Perhaps as a backlash to seeing women in competitive sport, some whispered that three-quarters of former team members had developed cancer or given birth to stillborn children. No proof was ever provided, although Coach Page offered a standing $1,000 reward for it. A handful of former team members are still alive today.

Hooped

NBA stars Charles Barkley and Karl Malone suffered a defeat in Edmonton in 1983 as part of the U.S. team competing in the World University Games. The two were among hundreds of world-class university athletes who slept in Lister Hall and schlepped around HUB while the Games were hosted on the U of A campus. While the Canadian basketball teams brought home the gold, the American team, including the two future superstars, had to be content with a bronze medal.

The Baby and the Birkies

Imagine yourself cross-country skiing 55 kilometres with a 5.5-kilogram pack strapped to your back, followed by a giant Viking feast. You'd think the Birkebeiner Ski Festival would make sense only to Norwegians, but 2,500 skiers from Edmonton and around the world race the course every year at the Blackfoot Recreation Area, located about 35 kilometres east of Edmonton on Highway 16. The Birkie celebrates a Norse legend about two Birkebeiner warriors who rescued the infant crown prince of Norway during a civil war in 1206. The pack represents the weight of the infant; the distance re-creates the warriors' journey over two mountain ranges. Birkebeiner races are held every year in Norway and the U.S., but the Edmonton race (on the second Saturday in February) is the only one in Canada and the biggest classic-style cross-country ski festival in North America.
102, 9920 63 Ave., 430-7153

Little Houses on the Prairie

The current site of the **John Walter Museum** *(9100 Walterdale Hill, 496-4852)* has the three homes Walter built for his family over the years (all refurbished and reconstructed after arsonists hit the site in 1998 and 1999). However, there used to be another house on the premises – a tiny log cabin, with furnishings scaled down to size. The house belonged to the Walter family's handyman, a four-foot dwarf named Henry Collins – better known to history by his Cree name, Muchias ("the worthless one"). The son of a Hudson's Bay employee father and a Native mother, he began working for John Walter in 1870 and remained with the family well after Walter's own death and almost until his own death in 1939. Although a rumour persists that a small log storage shed on the site today is indeed Muchias' old house, in fact his original log cabin was torn down in the late 1940s.

Toboggan Hills

Seven Hills in St. Albert used to be the undisputed king of toboggan hills, until its hazardous bumps were flattened out. Find your thrills on these local hills:

Argyll Park
83 St. and 63 Ave.

Emily Murphy Park
Groat Rd. and Emily Murphy Park Rd.

Gallagher Hill
95 Ave. and 97 St.

Government House Park
Groat Rd. and River Valley Rd.

Jackie Parker Recreation Area
50 St. and 45 Ave.

Laurier Heights
139 St. and 78 Ave.

Mill Woods Park
23 Ave. and 66 St.

**Rundle Park
(Walton's Mountain)**
113 Ave. and 29 St.

Whitemud Park
Keillor Rd. and Fox Dr.

Bunny Hills

Although Jasper is only a few hours away, Edmontonians hit the slopes on a smaller scale at several local ski hills. A bonus is that several of the hills make their own snow, so even if conditions in the mountains are sub-standard a pleasant day of skiing can be had within a few minutes' drive. All offer ski and snowboard lessons and rentals.

Edmonton Ski Club
9613 96 Ave., 465-0852

Rabbit Hill
Nisku, 9 km south of Edmonton on Highway 2, 6 km west on Highway 19, 955-2440

Snow Valley
Whitemud Park, access on 119 St. south of Whitemud Dr., 434-3991

Sunridge
10980 17 St., 449-6555

Built to Last

Photo: Charlene Rooke

For years, vestiges of a gold-rush era community could still be found on Edmonton's riverbanks, in the form of stone chimneys that once heated cabins on Miner's Flats (the current-day Laurier Heights). Stones held together with a mortar of mud and straw proved remarkably resilient, and some stood well into the 1950s. Today, you can still see a sturdy stone chimney in Terwillegar Park, in a clearing built into the hillside just off one of the recreational trails, about a kilometre east of the open off-leash area. Opinion is divided as to what the structure originally was: Doug Frost of the River Valley Rangers patrol and maintenance crew speculates that it may be the remains of a farmhouse from a cattle ranch once situated in the area, while others think it is an old miner's or trapper's cabin. Whatever its origins, the site now predominantly serves as a popular bush-bash site for local teens on weekends.

Big and Yellow

It has nothing to do with food, but the **Universiade Pavilion** (built for the 1983 World University Games) is universally known today as the Butterdome. From a distance the canary yellow-clad structure does look like a big slab of the fatty stuff, and it even has melting problems: it becomes somewhat of a mini-avalanche zone every spring, as drops of melting snow cascade down its curved surface. Come to think of it, maybe there is a tangible food link here: within the Van Vliet Physical Education and Recreation Centre you'll find an indoor track, a pool, and facilities for volleyball, basketball, tennis, badminton, gymnastics, soccer, and European handball to help you work off those extra-buttery calories.

Hazardous Greens

The **Kinsmen Pitch and Putt** nine-hole golf course is constructed on land that was once the Strathcona coal mine. From 1905 to 1911 nearly 80,000 tonnes of coal were mined from three major seams in the area, and the old shafts likely still snake under the turf. The site was the location of one of the worst mining disasters in the history of Alberta in 1907, when on June 8 a fire broke out in the engine house and spread to the mine shaft. The fire claimed the lives of five miners, and one man who went down to try to save them. Besides the human toll it was also a financial disaster for its three prominent owners (a who's who of Edmonton list including a Walter, Ross, and Rutherford); they didn't have insurance, and losses were estimated at $10,000, a massive sum at the time.

Gone Fishin'

Anglers come home with burbot, walleye, goldeye, sturgeon, whitefish, sauger, and pike after fishing the waters of the North Saskatchewan river. Exercise caution, though: fish caught in the North Saskatchewan River may contain amounts of mercury above safe levels (0.5 parts per million) for eating, as a result of natural mercury in the soil. Women of childbearing age and children under 15 shouldn't eat locally caught fish at all, and others should stick to one meal a week or until they start to glow, whichever comes first. Here are a few popular local fishing spots (although any self-respecting angler doesn't share his favourite fishing holes):

Beverly Bridge

Dawson Bridge

Goldbar Park

Hermitage Park

Quesnell Bridge

River Valley Road

Whitemud Park

Rumpus Rooms

When regular, stay-at-home-watch-TV kind of fun just won't do, amusements like go-carts, batting cages, bowling, billiards, laser tag, and arcade games await at these local emporiums:

Laser Quest
10829 105 St., 424-2111

Playdium
West Edmonton Mall, 444-7529

Red's
West Edmonton Mall, 481-6420

Schanks
9927 178 St., 444-2125

Whitemud Amusement Park
7411 51 Ave., 465-1190

What do the Kelloggs Tony the Tiger mascot, the Toys 'R' Us Geoffrey the Giraffe, the A&W Root Bear, and the Mars M&M all have in common? These famous mascot suits have all been built by **International Mascot Corporation** *(9350 49 St., 465-7906)*, the Edmonton-based world leader in mascot costumes with offices in New York, Atlanta, and Madrid. From humble materials like foam, fake fur, and fleece the company crafts unique team and corporate beasts, including waterproof (for ever-popular aquatic tricks) and inflatable mascot costumes. They also store, clean, and maintain mascot costumes at their Edmonton warehouse.

parks for paws

With more than 40 off-leash areas, Edmonton is a great place to be a dog. If you are one, or know one, check out these popular river valley dog parks, especially on a busy Saturday when sniffing possibilities are endless. Be warned: bring your pooper-scooper, because failing to pick up after Fido can earn you a $70 fine.

Buena Vista Great Meadow

North of Laurier Park and Buena Vista Dr.

Mill Creek Ravine

Access from 68 Ave. and 93 St.

Terwillegar Park

Access via Rabbit Hill Rd.

"Edmonton's not really a skating centre. Very few good skaters have come from Edmonton," Toller Cranston remarked in the 1970s. That lovable little gnome should be forced to eat those words several times over. A whole generation of championship Canadian skaters hails from Edmonton's **Royal Glenora Club**, including four-time Canadian champion Kurt Browning. Two-time American national and 1992 Olympic champion Kristi Yamaguchi trained there for two years, and at various times skaters Michael Slipchuk, Kristy and Lisa Sargeant, Susan Humphreys, and Jamie Salé have also used Edmonton as their training ice. Toller, eat your heart out.
11160 River Valley Rd., 482-2371

Skating Rinks

Skating on outdoor ice is the quintessential Canadian winter experience. (Or, if indoor skating is more your temperature, 20 rinks around the city offer free public skating; call 496-4999 for times.) On Sundays in the winter, the John Walter Museum has old-fashioned skating and dogsled races, too.

City Hall
1 Sir Winston Churchill Squ.

Jackie Parker Recreation Area
50 St. and 45 Ave.

Legislature Grounds
97 Ave. and 109 St.

Mill Woods Park
23 Ave. and 66 St.

Rundle Park
113 Ave. and 29 St.

Victoria Park Oval (speed skating)
116 St. and River Valley Rd.

William Hawrelak Park
9330 Groat Rd.

The Coasters

Photo: City of Edmonton Archives (EA16749)

DOWN ON THE FARM

And you thought fraternity brothers were the only animals on campus....

Nestled in the crook between Fox Drive and 61 Avenue about two kilometres south of the main campus is the University of Alberta's **Edmonton Research Station**. Commonly known as the University Farm, it is a rural oasis in the middle of a dense residential neighbourhood of the city. This high-tech, modern site for dairy, poultry, and swine research includes such facilities as two barns accommodating 165 cows and an eight-unit milking parlour — much more sophisticated than the agriculture faculty's first digs, a small barn near Athabasca Hall that housed the animal science labs.

Long, long before the Mindbender roller coaster was even a gleam in the Ghermezian brothers' eyes, there was a smaller, humbler roller coaster in Edmonton, at East End Park (the modern day Borden Park). Built in 1915 in the rickety wooden style of the day, it was one of the hit attractions of the annual Edmonton Exhibition for many years, and along with an outdoor pool, a zoo, a band shell, and a picnic area, helped make Borden Park the place to be on a sunny summer afternoon.

River Valley Crickets

You might think that a city like Victoria, given its impeccable British pedigree, would have been the first Canadian city to establish a cricket club. Sorry, old chap, but in fact the oldest cricket club in Western Canada was established in Edmonton in 1882. The Edmonton Cricket Club played early games against the Fort Saskatchewan team from upstream and a Strathcona team from across the river. By 1912, the sport had enough of a following that the Edmonton and District Cricket League was formed. Today the league has 10 active teams, many of which practice at a pitch located within the Victoria Park golf course.

The Edmonton Cricket Club itself is one of the few Canadian clubs to have its own private practice ground, located in St. Albert.

It's no secret to Edmontonians that the river valley is a mecca for runners, but it has been officially sanctified by the running bible *Runner's World*. The August 2000 issue of the magazine lauds Edmonton for having a "gigantic running community and more kilometres of accessible forest-in-the-city than any urban area in the world." The article recommended several running routes in the river valley, including one toughie it called the "Rambo loop" (we're tired just thinking about it).

The other phenomenon to put Edmonton on the North American running map has been the **Running Room** *(8533 109 St., 433-6062 and three other Edmonton-area locations)*, the chain of specialty stores founded in 1984 in Edmonton by John Stanton out of the living room of his house. Today, the company has 40 stores and annual sales of more than $20 million, and is reportedly eyeing the U.S. market for expansion.

Take a Dip

Edmonton has more than a dozen public swimming pools, some of them (including Eastglen and Confederation) treated with saline, not chlorine — good news for those with skin problems, allergies, or bright-coloured bathing suits. You'll also find a wave pool and giant slide at the Mill Woods Recreation Centre, and extras like saunas, whirlpools, weight rooms, and kiddie pools at many city leisure centres. The real standouts, though, are the seasonal outdoor pools. Enjoy them — but discreetly covered, please. In the summer of 2000, police reported a spate of incidents involving voyeurs and flashers hiding in bushes around the pool and, uh, *enjoying* the view.

Borden Park Pool
11200 74 St., 944-7511

Fred Broadstock Pool
10515 158 St., 496-1486

Mill Creek Pool
8200 95A St., 944-7415

Oliver Pool
10315 119 St., 944-7416

Queen Elizabeth Pool
8900 106 St., 944-7480

Paddles Up

One of the nicest ways to see the city is from the river, which is a popular canoeing destination. Several tour groups will provide your group with canoes, lifejackets, and even a shuttle to return you to your launch point. Some of them also do trips outside the Edmonton area, including central Alberta and the Rocky Mountain region to the west.

Alberta Canoe Holidays
970-3015

Dream Seeker Adventures
Red Deer, 403/886-2960

Moon Shadow Adventures
905-0110

Strathcona Wilderness Centre
Hwy. 16, 20 minutes east of Edmonton, 922-3939

fore

Edmontonians have been chasing that silly little white ball with a stick since 1896, when the Edmonton Golf and Country Club was founded in 1896 on what is now the Legislative Grounds. Edmonton opened Canada's first municipal golf course in 1907, and Victoria Golf Course is still one of the busiest public courses in the country.

The Edmonton area has more golf courses per capita than anywhere else in Canada, including the new, eagerly anticipated, Jack Nicklaus-designed Northern Bear Club, a high-end public course 35 kilometres southeast of the city. The following local courses have made the *Score* magazine ranking of the top 100 courses in Canada in recent years:

Belvedere Golf and Country Club
Sherwood Park, 467-2000

Edmonton Country Club
62 Ave. and Country Club Rd., 487-1150

Edmonton Petroleum Golf and Country Club
215 St. and 9 Ave., 470-0701

Glendale Golf and Country Club
12420 199 St., 447-3529

Mayfair Golf and Country Club
9450 Groat Rd., 432-0066

The Ranch
West on Stony Plain Rd., 470-4700

Windermere Golf and Country Club
19110 Ellerslie Rd., 988-5501

Wolf Creek Golf Resort
Ponoka, 403/783-6050

A dog's gotta eat. And if that dog lives in Edmonton, he'll eat well.
This city has a unique melange of culinary influences, ranging from
French Canadian to Eastern European, including both fast food and
S-l-o-w F-o-o-d (no kidding … their logo is a snail). Our local delicacies
include foodstuffs like kubassa burgers, pocket dogs, and chunks of fried
dough, but at the same time we consistently claim Culinary Olympic
Gold. The best part is, you can dine out in Edmonton regally for prices
that represent shockingly good value when compared to other North
American cities. Start your culinary tour here.

Slow Food

Their logo is a snail, and their motto is, "for the defence of and the right to pleasure."
The Italian-based international **Slow Food** movement has an Edmonton convivia (fancy
word for chapter) *(431-1802)* that gathers 8-10 times a year for activities like foraging
for urban weeds and other wild edibles, a foodie tour of Chinatown, or the annual Earth
to Table event in Calgary. The mandate of Slow Food International includes enjoying
local, artisan-made and prepared food and wine – for example, at the international level
they have written a formal manifesto in defence of raw-milk cheese – and even extends as
far as a Slow Cities movement, an international consortium of towns striving to improve
quality of life for their citizens.

Steak a Claim

Hy's Steak Loft *(10013 101A Ave.,
424-4444)* is an Edmonton institution, a
steak house in the traditional vein. Under
the gorgeous Tiffany glass skylight, enjoy
specially cured, juicy beef (and a
selection of seafood, chicken, and lamb
dishes). Bonus: when you ask for it rare
here, they really know what you mean.
The new kid on the chopping block is
the **River City Chophouse**. Located in what has been a doomed location for restaurateurs
(11811 Jasper Ave., 482-11400) – once upon a time a Maxwell Taylor's, Senor Frog's,
and Lone Star outlet – it's operated by the team behind Overtime and Iron Bridge. A
sleek, modern makeover is the setting for steaks, chops, and prime rib. Then there's the
celebrity quotient: former Edmonton Oiler Kevin Lowe is an investor.

Perogies, those humble dumplings of eastern European origin, have recently been spotted on trendy restaurant menus from New York to Vancouver stuffed with everything from squash to quail. You'll also see their manufacturers names splashed across sponsor banners at many running races and triathlons, and these starchy little bundles are many a carbo-loading athletes' dream food.

Authentic Ukrainian cuisine has long been a staple in Edmonton, an area that traces many of its descendants back to the old country. One huge success story has been the Mackowecki family's Edmonton-based Heritage Frozen Foods, whose Cheemo brand has sealed up the perogy market from the prairie provinces to the Pacific northwestern states. (They make enough perogies annually to circle the globe.) The traditional filling is potato spiked with onion and cottage cheese, and cheddar cheese and pizza fillings are unorthodox but delicious. Boiled then briefly fried in butter with some onions, served with a dollop of sour cream, this is comfort food Edmonton-style. Heritage also makes traditional Ukrainian cabbage rolls stuffed with a hearty meat and rice mixture.

To dish up Ukrainian specialties outside your own kitchen, head east to the **Mundare Sausage House** and

Uncle Ed's Place *(11401 50 St., 471-1010)*, where you can find the most famous Ukrainian-style sausage in Alberta, made by the Stawnichy family since 1959. Although the smokehouses and plant are still located in Mundare, this Highlands-area retail outlet has a spotless meat case packed with pepperoni, ham, bacon, wieners, and sausages along with what must be an Edmonton original, kubbie (short for kubassa) burgers, that are fantastic when grilled on a barbecue. Adjacent to the meat shop is Uncle Ed's, a humble eatery where

Private Rooms

Organizing an intimate wine dinner, a Super Bowl party, or something in between? One of these venues is sure to be ideal; book 'em in advance.

Boston Pizza Party room

It has a big-screen TV, a pool table, a staffed bar, and best of all you don't have to clean up after your moronic, cheese-eating friends. The old lounge below the Whyte Avenue BP is yours for the renting ($125) and holds up to 80 people.
10854 82 Ave., 433-3151

Characters

A long, narrow private room is separated from the restaurant by French doors for privacy. For a mere 50 bucks you can have it all to yourself for groups of up to 20.
10257 105 St., 421-4100

Fort Edmonton

The park offers a number of dining spots and can also arrange catering when you book one of its many rental facilities, including the railway salon car, Blatchford Field Air Hangar, Jasper House Hotel, Kelly's Saloon, or Reed's Tea Room.
Whitemud Dr. and Fox Dr., 496-8787

the perogies, cabbage rolls, sauerkraut, and of course, sausage, are as homemade and authentic as you'll find anywhere. The venerable **Russian Tea Room** *(10312 Jasper Ave., 426-0000)* is another good bet for comforting borscht, perogies, and other eastern European specialties.

The Hardware Grill

Not only can this capacious dining room be partitioned to accommodate private parties, they've recently added an intimate wine cellar dining room (for 10-12, with a "chef's choice" $75/person menu) and a conference room (holding up to 45) downstairs.
9698 Jasper Ave., 423-0969

Hy's Steak Loft

With a capacity of 110, Hy's can accommodate anything from a private business meeting to a wedding in its banquet room — and no extra rental or service charges.
10013 101 A Ave., 424-4444

Il Portico

The basement wine cellar makes a cozy room for up to 40 people, with the room charge of $60 waived for parties of more than 25. Order off the menu, or work with the chef to develop custom pasta platters or a set meal.
10012 107 St., 424-0707

Just Desserts

Although you can also chow down heartily on a meal at either the **Upper Crust** *(10909 86 Ave., 433-0810)* or **Vi's for Pies** *(13408 Stony Plain Rd., 454-4300)*, the star attraction at both of these cozy spots is the desserts: thick homemade pies, creamy cheesecakes, and succulent squares.

Going for Gold

If there's one Olympic sport in which Canada has a stronghold, it's the culinary arts. Team Canada, which includes several prominent Edmonton members, has been cleaning up at the Culinary Olympics for years. In 2000 in Erfut, Germany, the team (led by team captain Clayton Folkers and manager Simon Smotkowicz from the Shaw Conference Centre and local delegation members such as Cam Dobranski from the Hardware Grill) took a Grand Gold, three golds, and one silver, for a fourth-place finish overall.

Dine and Dance

Doucette's restaurant *(10120 103 Ave., 423-9982)* has heralded the return of dining and dancing to Edmonton. In addition to an exhaustive Sunday brunch and a weekday business lunch buffet, Doucette's has a house band with an equally exhaustive repertoire, covering favourites from the 1930s to the present. All that, and on Sundays a children's activity centre to keep the little ones busy while you linger over one more mimosa or cappuccino after brunch. Free parking evenings and weekends in the Canada Trust Parkade.

Have Your Cake and Eat Onions, Too

Every city has its local specialties, often dictated by the bounty of the good earth or the provenance of its early citizens. Think Winnipeg cream cheese, Montreal smoked meat, or Charlottetown's famed lobster suppers. With little apparent rhyme or reason, Edmonton seems to have informally adopted the humble *choan yo bang* (more commonly known as a green onion cake) as its civic snack. Breadier than a pancake, greasier than a flatbread, and fluffier than any pita, a green onion cake hot off the griddle, whacked into four wedges and gingerly dipped in fiery red chili-garlic paste, is the foodstuff of choice from vendors at the city's summer festivals. Almost any local Chinese restaurant has them on the menu, and local manufacturer Delta Foods churns out thousands of these delicately layered, labour-intensive treats for sale in the frozen-food section of local supermarkets. To make them at home takes only a little flour, oil, salt, and green onions – and a lotta mixing, rolling, and elbow grease to get the right layered texture, which puffs up upon cooking. Some credit local restaurateur Siu To with popularizing the cakes, which are sold on the streets of his native China, at his Edmonton restaurants Happy Garden, Mongolian Food Experience, and the Genghis Grill over the years.

Lunch Lady Land

Thanks to a snazzy $200,000 renovation last fall, the **NAIT Dining Room** *(Southwest corner of 118 Ave. and 106 St., 471-8678)* no longer feels like a student cafeteria, but more like an elegant contemporary dining room. Lunch and dinner, prepared and served by culinary arts and applied food and beverage program students, are served Tuesday through Friday. Although service can be occasionally awkward or a little slow, the prices will keep you coming back: $11-$15 for dinner entrées ranging from bison and venison to chicken and salmon. Delicious desserts homemade by budding pastry chefs, too.

La Bohème

Five separate dining areas, including a wine cellar and the whimsical Renoir Café, are available for group bookings, with French and Moroccan food as the kitchen's specialties.
6427 112 Ave., 474-5693

Red's

This 1950s kitsch location would make a wacky setting for a family or class reunion, business meeting, or special event. Possibilities include a rumpus room, loft, attic, skybox, or pool room accommodating 25-400 people.
West Edmonton Mall, 481-6420

Sidetrack Café

Train engineer fantasies as a kid? Live them out by booking the old train car at the Sidetrack for groups of 10-40 – but only if you and your friends love great food and great live music.
10333 112 St., 421-1326

Dinner Theatre

If your dining companions leave something to be desired, or if you just like to add drama to your meal, Edmonton offers more dinner theatre options than perhaps any self-respecting foodie city should. They tend to be more about the fun than the food, but check out these dramatic options:

Celebrations Dinner Theatre

This friendly spot is geared to families, with plenty of audience participation and entertainment that leans toward action and musical comedy. You'll get a three-act play and a four-course meal with choice of entrées and desserts and children's selections. They'll also single out your party's special event, birthday, or anniversary.
13103 Fort Rd., 448-9339

Celtic Hall

Medieval is the name of the game here, where eating with your hands, singing, and dancing is not an option — it's obligatory. There's no dramatic performance per se, but more of a variety show that might include juggling, dancing, and jousting. Medieval feasts are offered twice a month.
99 St. and 32 Ave., 430-3663

fish to fry

Back Home Fish and Chips

If you come from somewhere that serves light, crisply battered halibut, tart homemade lemonade, and delicacies ranging from deep-fried pineapple rings to hearty seafood chowder, then this will indeed seem like "back home" to you. This unpretentious, checkered-tablecloth joint is of the cheap and cheerful variety (a "single" order of fish and chips, at under 10 bucks, is a huge, three-piece serving with a mound of fries). It manages to always be buzzing, despite the fact that several other restaurants have floundered in this street-level, busy corner location. Other seafood treats such as scallops, razor clams, and calamari are also on the menu.
12323 Stony Plain Rd., 451-7871

Lighthouse Café

If there's anyone in the city that knows seafood, it's the Billingsgate Fish Market. After a renovation and a cutesy, lighthouse-shaped addition to the north, they're cooking seafood delights as well as serving them raw at the adjacent market. The delicious fish and chips comes either with traditional halibut or a revolving catch of the day, and with choices of white or malt vinegar, ketchup, or creamy tartar sauce (and a little ramekin of yummy coleslaw on the side). Seafood specialties like coquilles St. Jacques, oysters Rockefeller, a lobster roll sandwich, lobster bisque, and clam chowder are on offer with pasta and fish entrées, and the house specialty drink is a gin shrimp caesar with a fat, pink crustacean hooked on the side. The food is so good and authentic, you'll have trouble leaving without a bag of fresh or frozen seafood, live lobster, or Maritime treats like King Cole tea.
7331 104 St., 433-0091

Claude Buzon, once the chef of the renowned Claude's on the River restaurant, has been whipping up creations of a different kind lately. Buzon's French wife, Fabienne, had the idea for a new enterprise after visiting her mother's chef's hat company in France: a reusable, adjustable, and biodegradable viscose chef's hat to replace the disposable paper ones that have always been an industry staple. Their company, Edmonton-based Chef's Hat Inc., now also makes kitchen-friendly ties, aprons, and chef's jackets, and sponsors many culinary teams, including the award-winning Team Canada and Team Alberta. The hats, sold under the trade name La Toque Demagny on the company's Web sites (www.chefshat.ca and www.chefs-hat.com), have found a following around the world.
10554 115 St., 420-6700

perfect patios

DeVine's

The most palatable view of the river valley in the city.
9712 111 St., 482-6402

Earl's Tin Palace

Watch the passing show on Jasper.
11830 Jasper Ave., 488-6583

Jack's Grill

A latticed urban oasis in Lendrum.
5824 111 St., 434-1113

The Runaway Spoon

High Street secret, leafy garden patio.
12417 Stony Plain Rd., 488-6181

Symposium

A bird's-eye view of Whyte Avenue.
10439 82 Ave., 433-7912, upstairs

Jubilations

West Edmonton Mall has one of everything else, so why not a dinner theatre? This is one of those places where the audience will get involved whether they like it or not, interacting with in-character servers and cast members. The food is loosely themed to the production, with a choice of entrées and desserts.
West Edmonton Mall Phase III, 484-2424

Mayfield Dinner Theatre

Despite a devastating fire several years ago and a reincarnation, Stage West is still going after 25 years. Many local actors who grace the Citadel and other prestigious stages can be found in the high-spirited productions, which are often also studded with C-list Hollywood stars (think blasts from the past like Joyce DeWitt and Ken Kercheval). The material leans toward musicals and comedies, and the buffet table groans heavy.
16651 109 Ave., 484-4051

Classic Diners

Edmonton takes the old-fashioned, chrome-and-formica diner formula and turns it on its head. In these eclectic interiors you'll find offbeat cuisine to match.

Da-De-O

This funky little joint is hep to the jive of both Old South and New West. Cajun and Creole specialties like po' boy sandwiches, jambalaya, and gumbo spice up this long, narrow diner, still replete with individual jukeboxes at the tables and booths. Cool jazz (and icy beer) help combat the heat generated by biscuits spread with jalapeño jelly.
10548a 82 Ave., 433-0930

romantic rooms

Along with great food and good company, the prerequisite to a romantic evening is that elusive quality known as *atmosphere*, which each of these local eateries has in spades.

DeVine's

The restaurant formerly known as Vi's on the River is no less lovely for the name change. In the summer, the view of the river valley from the charming patio of this old house is superlative, and at any time of year the French-influenced menu and homemade desserts are conducive to intimate sharing.
9712 111 St., 482-6402

La Bohème

A touch of continental flair and a spicy mix of French cuisine, Latin dance, and European hospitality distinguish this charming brick heritage building in the Highlands. Proprietor Ernst Eder recently introduced Moroccan food into the mix, and teaches tango lessons (the dance of love, you know). There are many candlelit corners in which to lose yourself in the eyes of someone special, and if you get carried away there's a bed and breakfast upstairs.
6427 112 Ave., 474-5693

Red Ox Inn

Reserve one of nine tables at this intimate restaurant, nearly buried beside a barber shop in a Strathearn strip mall, and prepare to be delighted by both the charming European ambience and the attentive service. If there's beef on the menu, grab it: the saucy things this kitchen does to a steak are aphrodisiac enough for anyone. The short but immaculate menu also typically includes seafood, poultry, and vegetarian entrées.
9420 91 St., 465-5727

food and fun

Julio's Barrio

Don't be afraid to get rowdy in this friendly 'hood, where you'll find a hot, young crowd and spicy Mexican food. Fruit margaritas by the jug are favourites here, as is the ranchero dip appetizer (a layered dip served with crisp, perfect tortilla chips). The Whyte Avenue location makes it a popular pre-bar crawl spot, but after the first jug of margs goes down smooth, tequila shots can't be far behind and you could easily make an evening of it here.
10450 82 Ave., 431-0774

Yianni's Taverna

The combination of delicious Greek food, bellydancing, and powerful retsina or flaming shots of ouzo has gotten many a group in trouble here. Its gaudy neon sign shines its siren call on the weekends to bachelor and bachelorette parties and rowdy groups of all denominations. A highlight of the evening is always when the waiters gather with Mediterranean insouciance to perform a traditional line dance. The *kefalotiri* (deep-fried, flamed cheese) and *dolmathes* (rice-stuffed vine leaves) are addictive. It's named for its venerable proprietor, Yianni Psalios, who also operates other Greek joints in town including **Koutouki** *(10704 124 St., 452-5383)* and **Ziveli**.
1202 Jasper Ave., 453-3912
10444 82 Ave., 433-6768

The Korner Lunch

This odd little building has graced the bend in the road at 95 Street and 111 Avenue for 40 years. The interior is as frozen in time as a straw in one of its perfect milkshakes. It's classic coffee shop kitsch, including the tantalizing bouquet of coffee, cigarette smoke, and deep-frying. The interior has been the setting for scenes in a couple of local flicks, including *Life After Hockey* and *Isaac Littlefeathers.*
11063 95 St., 429-7965

The Silk Hat

Dating back to 1912, this is likely Edmonton's oldest restaurant. Until the restaurant and kitchen had an overhaul in 1997, it looked (and tasted) like it, too. The lunch counter, naugahyde booths, burgers, and icy-thick milkshakes still speak of a bygone era, while the cappuccino on the menu and the CV of the chef speak to contemporary crowds.
10251 Jasper Ave., 425-1920

Smoky Joe's Hickory Smoke House

Old fashioned barbecue took over the old Ritz Diner space, keeping some traces of the auto-inspired decor: the rear end of a vintage car still protrudes from one wall, while a racy checkered-flag mural graces another.

After you try the hottest, most infernal chicken wings in town, you'll likely be waving a flag of another kind (white, that is). Safer choices are the chunks of various tender and delicious smoked meats — turkey, beef, pork — that you can order up by the quarter- or half-pound.
15135 Stony Plain Rd., 413-3379

Soda Jerks and Johnny Rockets

These two come from the same nouveau-diner, manufactured kitsch menu. Despite laying on the faux-'50s charm a bit thick, both offer counters and booths at which to enjoy great burgers, fries, and shakes.
570 St. Albert Rd., St. Albert, 460-7635
West Edmonton Mall, 487-5379

The French Connection

The Crêperie *(10220 103 St., 420-6656)*, which recently celebrated its 25th anniversary in its venerable Boardwalk location, has classic crêpes, filet mignon, and traditional French onion soup among its timeless selections. **Three Musketeers Crêpery** *(10416 82 Ave.)* is the south-side option for crêpe fanciers. **Plantier's** *(10807 106 Ave., 990-1992)* does nouvelle cuisine with stunning presentation, including its decadent desserts like *mi-cuit* warm chocolate cake and traditional *mille-feuille* pastry. Hidden away on the west end but not forgotten, **Gini's** *(10706 142 St., 451-1169)* serves fine French food in unlikely strip-mall surroundings. Everyone knows that the word *cajun* evolved as a nickname for the Acadian French who migrated to Louisiana, so honour that Canadian lineage with a visit to **Louisiana Purchase** *(10320 111 St., 420-6779)* for flawless jambalaya (the special on Monday and Tuesday nights) and gumbo, delicate crab cakes, and a stunning pecan pie.

Café Bliss

Although the word *café* gets tossed around indiscriminately these days, **Café de Ville** *(10137 124 St., 488-9188)* truly has the aura of a Parisian haunt. Start with a perfect martini (premium olive fanciers will be in ecstasy) at the tiny, four-seat bar, then ask for a table in front of the fireplace where you can savour small plates (perfect as appetizers or light meals), salads, pastas, and traditional entrees. Seal the deal with a café de ville, a heady concoction of brandy, Kahlúa, triple sec, rum, and Galliano. Late at night, a similar café atmosphere can be had at **Café Select**, where the kitchen is open until 2 a.m. and the bohemian atmosphere makes for a cozy end to the evening.
10018 106 St., 423-0419

It's Not Easy Being Green

Vegetarians will find satisfaction at the humble **Max's Light Cuisine** (7809 109 St., 432-6241), offering generous, filling entrées at prices under 10 bucks. Tucked into a strip mall across from Southgate Centre, **Savoy's Health Café** (11010 51 Ave.) not only has delicious vegetable samosas (to go at nine bucks for a doz), but custom-blends health teas and juices according to whatever ails you. Drop by on a Tuesday or Saturday, when they make a great plate of *dhossa*, a crêpe-like crispy round filled with a delicious, spicy potato and vegetable mixture. At the many **Booster Juice** outlets around the city, suck back a shot of wheatgrass – just one ounce of the juice offers the equivalent nutrient hit of a kilogram of raw, green vegetables. The Italian veggie panini provides a more filling accompaniment. (10 Edmonton-area locations.)

Better Than Brown Bag

For a homespun touch in the heart of downtown, try the cozy **Carole's Café** (10145 104 St., 425-1824) for soups, salads, sandwiches, and light entrées like the wicked whiskey shrimp. Across the river, a similar style of homey light entrees can be found at the family-run lunch joint **Twig 'n' Berries** (8430 103 St., 413-6282). There's a commercial bakery in the back, so the place always smells delish, and the dessert case is packed with hefty cheesecakes and pies. A perennial favourite is the laid-back **High Level Diner** (10912 88 Ave.), where the eclectic mix includes university professors and young bohemians. Legendary breakfasts and coffee, and hearty lunches (quiche, shepherd's pie, huge salads). A few blocks away, the **Turtle Creek Café** (8404 109 St., 433-4202) is a roomy, two-level California-style restaurant with great thin-crust pizzas, pastas, and desserts.

Perfect Pizza

Funky Pickle

This Whyte Avenue stall serves up a thick, gooey slice with bizarre topping combos and whimsical names, like the Funky Chicken (chicken, snow peas, red pepper, bean sprouts, cilantro, and sesame seeds), the Veggie Fiesta (red pepper, pineapple, cilantro), the Big Meaty (for meat lovers), and the Pig Kahuna (a dressed-up Hawaiian). An extra-large 18" pie goes for about $26; a slice is just a few loonies. They deliver, although it's at its late-night best gobbled standing up at the counter, slathered with parmesan and hot peppers, on the way home from the pub.

10441 82 Ave., 433-3865

destination rooms

Hardware Grill

Located in the venerable old W.W. Arcade hardware store location, this contemporary room now boasts private screened booths, cozy tables, and contemporary cuisine on the floor where paint, tools, china, and appliances used to jockey for space in the old Goodridge Block. The distinctly Canadian offerings often include a must-have cedar planked salmon, beef, and bison dishes. And unlike the eclectic old hardware store, it's not closed on Wednesdays.
9698 Jasper Ave., 423-0969

Jack's Grill

It's not exactly a secret – picky *Globe and Mail* restaurant critic Joanne Kates called it "culinary perfection." Owner and chef Peter Jackson is obviously a man who likes secrets, though: his restaurant moved from its somewhat obscure Saddleback Road location to a new spot tucked into the Lendrum strip mall, where the discreet Js on the heavy doors hint at what's inside. Elegant enough for a special occasion but unstuffy enough for a relaxed dinner, with a regionally influenced menu.
5824 111 St., 434-1113

Tony's Pizza

Get an authentic New York-style slice and watch the chefs toss the dough at the Manzotta family-owned restaurant on the edge of Little Italy. This isn't one of those thick, droopy North American pies: although the cheese and toppings are first-rate, the crust is just thin and crispy enough to do the requisite vertical fold down the middle, ensuring that you won't lose a drop of delicious sauce or a crumb of semolina-dusted crust. Just try to stop at one slice. Tony's, which has a pedigree that traces back to former incarnations in Italy and the Bronx, will also do a Sicilian-style layered square pie, but be patient and call ahead – they need several hours' notice.
9603 111 Ave., 424-8777

Two other favourite neighbourhood joints are **Rose Bowl Pizza** on the north side *(10111 117 St., 482-5152)* and **Parkallen Pizza** *(8424 109 St., 430-4770)* on the south.

Unheardof

Even the name is a secret. After two decades, this restaurant still reinvents its dinner menu every two weeks, and each is a gourmet delight. For quick bites to stay or to go, there's now the Unheardof Pantry around the corner on 96th, a perfect spot for dessert and coffee or lunch.
9602 82 Ave., 432-0480

Via Vai

Surprises await you in this new commercial development (a glorified strip mall) in the West End. A welcoming fireplace. An elegant dining room with quirky (unique light fixtures and floral arrangements) decor. A California-influenced menu with stunning presentation. Who would've thought?
11-9977 178 St., 486-5802

Bunch of Brunch

If it's the greasy-spoon experience you seek, you won't do better than the legendary gasthaus-meets-diner **Barb & Ernie's** *(9906 72 Ave., 433-3242)*, where the eggs Benny, potato pancakes, and plate-sized pancakes rule. The lederhosen-clad Ernie is famous for greeting women diners with a booming, "Allo, gorgeous!" The **Sweetwater Café** *(12427 102 Ave., 488-1959)* has a Tex-Mex flavour, with salsa-spiked and guacamole-soothed egg dishes and delicious, flaky cheddar biscuits. For the ideal hair-of-the-dog-that-bit-you, hit the **Sidetrack Café** *(10333 112 St., 421-1326)* the morning after the night before. The kitchen of this popular night spot turns in a solid performance at Sunday brunch, with either a comprehensive buffet (including a custom omelette station) or a greatest hits menu of all your favourites. If everywhere else is lined up around the block on a weekend morn, you can always resort to the locally founded **Albert's Family Restaurants** chain *(16 Edmonton locations)* for fast relief with the menus and coffee.

Authentic Asian

VIETNAMESE, KOREAN, MALAYSIAN, AND THAI

If it's a big bowl of Vietnamese *bun* or *pho* or a fat shrimp salad roll you're craving, head to **Doan's** *(7909 104 St., 434-4448)*, and don't miss the lemongrass chicken. **Tropika** Malaysian restaurant *(6004 104 St., 439-6699)* serves addictive chicken, beef, and pork satays that are half-price (dine-in only) from Monday to Thursday, along with delicious, fluffy roti bread. The **Bul-Go-Gi House** *(8813 92 St., 466-2330)* is an Edmonton institution, as much for the rumpus room decor (a car drove into one corner a couple of years ago, mercifully necessitating renovations) and after-dinner sticks of Juicy Fruit as for the classic Korean dishes like barbecued meats and kimchi. For Thai, **The King & I** is the trendy Whyte Avenue mainstay *(8208 107 St., 433-2222)*, but equally good is the west-end **Banh Thai** *(15726 100 Ave., 444-9345)*.

best burgers

Photo: City of Edmonton Archives (ET17-12)

Earl's

Give a little thanks to restaurateur Bus Fuller every time you chomp down on a hamburger in Edmonton: he brought Canada's first A&W drive-in hamburger franchise to the city in 1956, complete with carhops and foamy mugs of root beer resting on those trays that hooked on to your car window. Later, Fuller not only started an eponymous restaurant chain but in 1982 virtually invented the casual dining concept behind Earl's, the now-ubiquitous Western Canadian restaurants emphasizing high quality, simple preparation, and friendly service. Earl's still dishes up a decent burger, with a good, thick patty and a bun substantial enough to hold it all together. Purists might say that the thick, lean patty is *too* lean (as in, almost dry) but that would be a petty quibble indeed, especially given the thick, crispy fries and rich spicy gravy. So would be complaining that Fuller moved his empire to the coast some years ago.
Seven Edmonton locations, 448-5822

Garage Burger Bar & Grill

An authentic burger experience awaits you at this unpretentious spot, where any of their delicious burgs and a heap of darkly crisped, skin-on, spicy fries will set you back less than

five bucks. It's truly located in an old garage (the hand-cranked garage door and the motorcycle at the front speak to its lineage), which tells you that they're serious about grease – we mean that in the best possible way. A bacon and cheese burger means several strips of real, crispy bacon and a slab of authentic cheddar, just as it should be (but seldom is anymore).
10242 106 St., 423-5014

CHINESE

For dim sum, we like **Marco Polo** in Chinatown *(2nd floor, 9700 105 Ave., 428-3388)* for its fast turnover and groaning carts, but the **Golden Rice Bowl** *(5365 103 St., 435-3388)* has its own set of south-side devotees. Dine in under the glowing sign at the **Ling Nan** *(10582 104 St., 426-3975)*, Edmonton's venerable Cantonese restaurant, or take-out Chinese from the zero-atmosphere but nonetheless yummy **Happy Garden** *(6525 111 St., 435-7622)*.

Gusto Burgers

If your craving can wait out the 15-minute drive north to St. Albert, a Gusto will satisfy any hamburger aficionado. It humbly calls itself the #2 burger in the area (only because everyone else claims to be #1). It started out as a tandoori chicken joint back in the 1980s, but the meaty, inch-thick Gusto burger the owner dropped onto the menu proved so popular, it's now their bun and butter. The menu is truly unique – cheese is exactly 42 cents, gravy is 54 cents, and the Gusto with curry sauce is a real taste sensation. This family-owned restaurant ain't no mass-produced fast-food joint, as evidenced by the sign that says, "Every one cooked and sold with over a gustillion smiles." Hey, if this burger is good enough for NHL player Jarome Iginla, it's good enough for you. *20 Muir Dr., St. Albert, 458-1110*

White Spot

British Columbians in exile can rejoice that the saucy Triple O burger is now available at two Edmonton locations, a full-service restaurant *(3921 Calgary Trail, 432-9153)* and, of all places, a kiosk in the Jackson Heights Mac's convenience store *(4333 50 St., 465-5340)*. It's a rather ordinary, thin broiled patty heaped with fresh shredded lettuce and tomato, but that sauce … we're pretty sure the "Triple O" stands for the number of zeros it will add to your cholesterol count.

JAPANESE

Sushi lovers will want to visit **Sakura** *(West Edmonton Mall, 481-3786; 10518 101 St., 428-8883)* at the dreaded Mall, because it has Edmonton's first kaiten-style (or conveyor belt) sushi bar, from which you can pluck small plates of passing delights. The **Tokyo Noodle Shop & Sushi Bar** on Whyte Avenue *(10736 82 Ave., 430-0838)* is young, hip,

and a great place to enjoy a steaming bowl of ramen or a spicy tuna roll. The **Mikado** *(10350 109 St.)*, opened in 1972, is Edmonton's oldest Japanese restaurant, and in its new, slightly bizarre location (near Railtown, next to a Harvey's) offers a sushi bar and private tatami rooms along with its famous sushi pizza.

EAST ASIAN

The rich decor and live traditional music make **Khazana** *(10177 107 St., 702-0330)* the tandoori restaurant of choice for curries, kebabs, and an enjoyable night out. **New Asian Village** *(10143 Sask. Dr., 433-3804)* is the south-side fave.

Succulent Sandwiches

Badass Jack's Subs and Wraps

For a sandwich with a difference, try this Edmonton-based franchise, which prides, itself on making everything from scratch, including its tasty buns and in-store slow-roasted chicken and roast beef.
Eight Edmonton-area locations

Charles Smart Donair

There's no shortage of gyro and donair joints around, but this is the city's favourite.
8952 82 Ave., 468-2099

Dunn's Famous

You won't find a bigger sandwich than the piled-high stack of Montreal-style smoked meat at this slice of Montreal in the Delta Edmonton South hotel. The smoked meat briskets, pickles, and peppers arrive weekly from Montreal.
4404 Gateway Blvd. N., 434-6415

Tasty Tom's

This offbeat entrée is called the pocket dog: a European wiener, smokie, or bratwurst served in an unsliced half-baguette that has been hollowed out and toasted from the inside — no fuss, no drips from the homemade sauerkraut, ketchup, and mustard.
9965 82 Ave., 437-5761

Pass the Pasta

The holy trinity of Italian restaurants in this book is **Il Pasticchio** *(11520 100 Ave., 488-9543)*, **Il Forno** *(14981 Stony Plain Rd., 455-0443)*, and **Il Portico** *(10012 107 St., 424-0707)*. There's something here for every taste and budget: the first is a casual, hearty trattoria (don't miss its eponymous signature dish) from the founders of the university's La Pasta. The second is the reincarnation of a popular Crestview neighbourhood restaurant, now located in more elegant surroundings in a Jasper Gates strip mall, but still with the same authentic pizza and pasta (the pesto is killer). The latter is a decidedly upscale downtown room popular for its generous sharing platters of antipasti and pasta.

However, no tour Italia of Edmonton would be complete without mentioning the successful **Sorrentino's** restaurants, particularly the elegant downtown outpost *(10162 100 St., 424-7500 or four other Edmonton locations)* adjacent to Churchill Square which features a cigar room and is perfect for a pre- or post-symphony or theatre nosh. Every April, the restaurants celebrate an aromatic garlic festival with a menu specially created to feature the stinking rose. In addition, garlic lovers will want to take in the fumes at **That's Aroma** *(11010 101 St., 425-REEK)*, Edmonton's only garlic restaurant. And the inexpensive neighbourhood fave **Tasty Tomato** *(14233 Stony Plain Rd., 452 3594)* has a no-reservations policy that lines 'em up out the door.

Literature & the Arts

Reclusive authors, hot presses, cool jazz, and festivals, festivals, festivals liven up the local arts scene. Why was Emily Murphy living a double life? How dare Edmonton just say no to robber baron Andrew Carnegie? When did Edmonton nuns object to a big penis? Also, we've got the scoop on more cornflakes than you can shake a spoon at, the inspiration for the Beat poets, bad boys of the art world, and how to buy a Renoir, cheap.

Janey Canuck

By the time Emily Murphy moved to Edmonton with her Anglican minister husband Arthur Murphy in 1907, the woman who would become the first female magistrate in the British Empire and a renowned women's rights crusader (for her role in the Persons Case) was already the author of four popular books of personal sketches under her pen name: *The Impressions of Janey Canuck Abroad* (1901), *Janey Canuck in the West* (1910), *Open Trails* (1912), and *Seeds of Pine* (1914). She was also a frequent contributor of book reviews and articles to Canadian newspapers and magazines, and her 1922 book *The Black Candle* was based on a series of exposé articles on the drug trade originally written for *Maclean's* magazine. The articles and book were influential enough that we have Emily (a.k.a. Janey) to thank for harsh Canadian narcotics and liquor laws that weren't modified until the late 1960s. A feisty-looking statue of Murphy graces the entrance to Emily Murphy Park near the University of Alberta campus.

Just Say No to Books

In 1910, American robber baron Andrew Carnegie was in the throes of giving away millions of dollars to North American communities to build libraries. A library board was formed in the town of Strathcona on the south side of the river that, after two years of diddling around, looked the gift horse in the mouth by asking Carnegie for more money, claiming he had based his donation on old census data and that the growing city required a larger bequest for its library. Carnegie stuck to his greenbacks; they imperiously refused the entire amount. Calgary wasn't so picky, and had cash-in-hand from Carnegie to build the Memorial Park Library in 1910. After Edmonton amalgamated with Strathcona, it took until 1913 to scrounge up the funds for the **Strathcona Library** *(8331 104 St.)*.

The Beat Goes On

Edmonton-born artist Brion Gysin was a radical who counted the Beat poets among his contemporaries and created groundbreaking work that is still influencing other artists 70 years later. In 1932 at age 16, he hopped on a passing cattle car and left Edmonton, never returning. His life journey plays like a cultural and artistic *Forrest Gump*: he was in Paris in the 1930s with surrealists Max Ernst, Salvador Dali, and André Breton. He later immersed himself in the culture of Northern Africa with American author Paul Bowles *(The Sheltering Sky)*. He was a compatriot of Burroughs and Jack Kerouac at the so-called Beat Hotel in Paris in the late '50s. (Gysin was said to be a seminal influence on Burroughs' famous book *Naked Lunch*.) In the '60s, Gysin was tight with the Rolling Stones, Iggy Pop, and David Bowie, and toured with Patti Smith. He collaborated with Burroughs on works he called cut-ups, collages of text, photos, and newspaper clippings. He experimented with film and sound clips long before the word multimedia was coined, calling himself a "sound poet," and modern musicians from R.E.M.'s Michael Stipe to U2's Bono have cited Gysin as an influence. Gysin died in 1986, and in 2000 the Edmonton Art Gallery mounted a major career retrospective of his work, *I am That I Am*, that met with rave critical reviews.

Hop on the Bus, Gus

If you think rhyming couplets and your morning commute are mutually exclusive phenomena, look more closely at the poetry in motion sprinkled among the ads lining Edmonton Transit buses and LRT cars. Career poets and student writers alike are featured in the program, which started in April 1999 when the first National Poetry Month was launched. Edmonton didn't invent it – we're the third Canadian city, after Toronto and Vancouver, to put wheels to a public poetry initiative – but nonetheless it celebrates local writers and soothes harried local commuters.

Reclusive Authors

Many a best-selling and award-winning author toils behind closed doors in Edmonton:

Daisy Chang

This Edmonton immigration consultant is a household name in Asia, but her best-selling fiction is little-known in Canada. Perhaps because she writes in Chinese? Once a journalist and TV host in Taiwan, Chang immigrated to Canada in 1969 and began writing again in 1985. Today, her work is serialized in the *United Daily News*, Taiwan's top newspaper, with a circulation of more than a million.

Helen Forrester

Her birthplace of Liverpool is frequently the setting for the charming novels of June Bhatia (better known by her pen name), which are written from her flat overlooking Edmonton's river valley. The University of Alberta tapped her late physics professor husband for a faculty position in the 1950s, and she has lived and worked here ever since.

Pauline Gedge

How she has been dreaming up sun-soaked ancient Egyptian-themed novels from northerly Edmonton for the last 30 years we'll never understand — but her readers soak it up. She's sold six million copies of her books in 15 languages and commands six-figure advances, so she's doing something right.

Martyn Godfrey

The late children's book writer penned three worldwide bestsellers (including *Please Remove Your Elbow From My Ear* and *Can You Teach Me to Pick My Nose?*) and nearly three dozen other volumes, many of them award winners. Readings and writing workshops that the immensely popular author gave for kids were perennial local favourites.

Hipper Than Thou

The Edmonton Symphony Orchestra isn't just a bunch of stuffy penguins. In addition to getting out of the house (that house being the **Winspear Centre**, *9720 102 Ave., 428-1108*) for the five-day Symphony Under the Sky Festival every Labour Day weekend in Hawrelak Park, they've collaborated on a variety of hip and happening projects. A 1971 recording with the British band Procul Harum produced a best-selling album and the hit single *Conquistador*. (They reunited for two more concerts in 1992.) It has since performed with pop performers ranging from k.d. lang and the Reclines to chanteuse Holly Cole to the Chieftains and Spirit of the West. In 1999, the ESO produced its first annual rESOund Festival of Contemporary Music. It also offers the Young Composers Project for elementary and high-school aged students.

Good Pots

Their pots, vases, and bowls have become such collector's items over the last 25 years, we almost expect Martha Stewart to anoint them a good thing any day now. **Selfridge Ceramic Arts** *(9844 88 Ave., 439-9196)* is run out of the Mill Creek home of Carol and Richard Selfridge, who still make their own clay and glazes. They produce pottery items that are a whimsical mix of *objet d'art* and functional object. Their majolica and wood-fired stoneware has been exhibited in over 110 juried and invitational exhibitions all over the world, but flies just under the radar screens of the capital-A art world. Pieces that sold for a piffle in the 1970s now bring in thousands of U.S. dollars at sale and auction.

Nuns Protest Penis

Controversy broke out at the Grey Nuns hospital in 1998 when patients and staff complained that a recently-installed 1,000-kilogram sculpture looked like a giant penis. The work *Maundy* by Edmonton artist Clay Ellis (ironically, it's named for Maundy Thursday, the day Jesus bathed the feet of the poor) was installed by the Alberta Foundation for the Arts near the hospital's front entrance, in an area that was directly visible from the hospital's mental health ward. Sexual abuse patients being treated there said they found the work disturbing (although it had previously been shown without incident

elsewhere in Edmonton, Calgary, and Florida). The puzzled artist's response was, "I'm not sure what kind of angle they're viewing it from." The sculpture was then relocated to Grant MacEwan Community College, where one disappointed viewer drily commented, "It's not as big as I thought."

Buy a Renoir, Cheap

Pierre Renoir, the great-grandson of the famous Impressionist painter Pierre-August Renoir, is an artist who lives and works in Edmonton. This Renoir's works run more to sculpture and engraving than painting – and for good reason (not just Great-Granddad's imposing legacy, but the fact that his descendant is colour blind). Estranged from the rest of the Renoir family, Pierre has publicly criticized his family's attempts to capitalize on his late ancestor's fame. He is one of four sons of Paul Renoir, a grandson of the great painter, who moved his family of six to Edmonton in 1978 on the advice of Peter Pocklington, of all people (he had met the Renoirs in Europe while purchasing art). A family cheese factory and bottled-water venture were short-lived, and the other family members have since scattered. Pierre Renoir exhibits his sculptures and dry-point engravings locally, and in 1999 made a major donation from the proceeds of an art sale to the Northern Alberta Ronald McDonald House.

Stacy Schiff

Schiff won a Pulitzer Prize in 2000 for her book *Vera*, the biography of the wife of author Vladimir Nabokov. She lives half the year in Edmonton, and half the year in New York. (Nice work if you can get it.)

The U of A Posse

No less than three current University of Alberta professors have won Governor General's Literary Awards in the last decade: Rudy Wiebe in 1994 for his novel *A Discovery of Strangers* (and previously in 1973 for *The Temptations of Big Bear*), Greg Hollingshead (photo below) in 1995 for his fiction collection *The Roaring Girl*, and Ted Blodgett in 1996 for the poetry collection *Apostrophes: Woman at a Piano*.

Photo: courtesy NeWest Press

Walk the Walk

The 124 Street area several blocks south of Jasper Avenue has been designated the **Gallery Walk District**. Several galleries join to hold seasonal shows in the funky High Street area, which also includes great coffee shops, stores, and restaurants.

Bearclaw Gallery

10403 124 St., 482-1204

Bugera/Kmet Galleries

12310 Jasper Ave., 482-2834

Douglas Udell Gallery

10332 124 St., 488-4445

Electrum Design Studio

12419 Stony Plain Rd., 482-1402

Front Gallery

12312 Jasper Ave., 488-2952

Scott Gallery

10411 124 St., 488-3619

West End Gallery

12308 Jasper Ave., 488-4892

Healing Secret

Inside the University of Alberta Hospital is an art gallery with a therapeutic purpose. The **McMullen Gallery**, located just inside the east entrance of the Walter McKenzie Health Sciences Centre (8440 112 St., 492-5834), provides both art exhibitions and classical music recordings for patients, staff, and the public. In addition to changing bi-monthly exhibitions at the McMullen, more than 800 pieces of Alberta art are rotated throughout the rest of the hospital, providing a subtle link between art and healing.

Little-Man Syndrome

The **Faculté Saint-Jean** discovered a cache of eclectic art a decade ago in the basement of its old student residence: hundreds of prints of the larger-than-life French emperor Napoleon, many of them worthless, a few of them valuable. The only thing the diverse specimens seem to have in common is that they portray the famous little emperor. The collection hails from the unlikely origin of Las Vegas, where one Leo Toupin, a graduate of the former College Saint-Jean, apparently arranged for the donation in the 1950s or '60s. Campus legend has it that a couple of the Oblate fathers piled into a pickup and trucked the hundreds of framed pictures back across the border to Edmonton. When the prints were removed from their frames in the early 1990s, items found cached inside the backing included clippings, pictures, and documents including a set of French menus.

Our city's gifts to the world of music include two renowned pianists and a keyboard genius of another sort:

Violet Archer

She was a composer, teacher, and musician who studied with Hungarian composer Bela Bartok in New York and on scholarship at Yale University. She later taught at the University of Alberta and lived in Edmonton for 36 years before moving to Ottawa shortly before her death in 2000. Her extensive body of work includes more than 400 compositions, two operas, and many children's songs.

Marek Jablonski

It strummed the heartstrings of the city when, as a 17-year-old piano prodigy in 1956, this Polish immigrant didn't have the money to attend the famed Julliard School. Edmontonians banded together to raise the needed funds, and Jablonski's career later led him to standing ovations earned from the world's concert stages.

Nelli Antonio Peruch

This local virtuoso is a leading player and composer on that humble folk instrument, the accordion. He has even built a better instrument: in collaboration with the Italian accordion company Victoria, he has designed an accordion that dramatically increases the instrument's range of notes, making it suitable for playing classical and orchestral works.

Edmonton is the live theatre capital of Canada, with more theatre groups per capita than any other city. The **Citadel Theatre** is Canada's largest, with a gigantic reputation in the Canadian theatre community. The impressive glass and brick facility covers a whole city block and contains five separate performance spaces and an indoor botanical garden, the Lee Pavilion. Former actor and director Joseph Shoctor and pals first performed in the unorthodox space of the old Salvation Army Citadel in 1965, hence the name for the 1976 structure we enjoy today. Shoctor's grand experiment set the stage for a rich theatre scene in Edmonton that endures to this day. Here are some of the other players:

city of festivals

Unlike the "City of Champions" moniker the city saddled itself with during the heady, transient sports victories of the 1980s, this designation seems destined to stay. Nearly every month (and more frequently during the summer), Edmonton celebrates some aspect of culture or the arts. Here are the biggies:

Edmonton International Fringe Theatre Festival

The granddaddy of the festivals started as the brainchild of Brian Paisley on a lick and a promise in 1982 and has grown to the second-largest in the world, after the original Edinburgh Fringe. Today, Fringe Theatre Adventures produces not only a 10-day, 1,000-performance extravaganza that now attracts a half million people every August, but runs the Arts Barns (the old bus storage barns) as a year-round event venue, and operates a major fundraising campaign and sibling festivals like Beyond the Fringe and the Carnival of Shrieking Youth.
448-9000

The Works: A Visual Arts Celebration

Churchill Square becomes a giant outdoor art gallery each June. The festival has seen its share of avant-garde happenings since it began in 1985, including a performance piece by New York artist Marshall Weber, who spent 24 hours in a refrigerated trailer, surrounded by explorers' artifacts encased in ice, reading from *The Rifles* (a novel about the Franklin Arctic expedition by cult author William T. Vollmann). Californian Barry Schwartz also brought his weird blend of art and science to the Works: the self-taught electrical engineer channelled raw electrical power through specially insulated gloves, sending sparks soaring.
426-4673

Azimuth Theatre
What: Non-profit theatre promotes social change by tackling topics like domestic abuse and breast cancer and initiating post-play audience discussions.
Where: 300-11745 Jasper Ave., 454-0583

Catalyst Theatre Society
What: Produces original, experimental theatre that has also been a hit at the Edinburgh Fringe.
Where: 8529 103 St., 431-1750

Jagged Edge
What: Lunchtime performances appealing to all.
Where: 3rd floor Edmonton Centre, 10205 101 St., 463-4237

Northern Lights Theatre
What: Aims for "dark, poetic, and funny" scripts and productions.
Where: 11516 103 St., 471-1586

other festivals

Northern Alberta International Children's Festival

When: Late May/early June
What: St. Albert-based celebration of theatre, music, dance, and storytelling.
459-1542

River City Shakespeare Festival

When: July
What: Gonzo performances of Shakespeare in the park and eclectic and traditional stagings all over the city.
425-8086

Symphony Under the Sky

When: Labour Day weekend
What: Relaxed classical and pops in the open air and under the amphitheatre in Hawrelak Park.
428-1414

The Word is Out

When: Mid-September
What: Book and literary festival.
422-2663

play time

The Fringe Theatre Festival has been an incubator for many local playwriting talents, including these scribes:

David Belke

Work that Belke premiered at the Fringe has gone on to national recognition, including a Samuel French Award for his play *That Darn Plot*. Crowd favourites have included *The Maltese Bodkin*, a noir-ish thriller with Shakespearean elements.

Rapid Fire Theatre
What: Holds weekly improv theatre performances and Theatresports competitions.
Where: New Varscona Theatre, 10329 83 Ave., 448-0695

Studio Theatre
What: University drama students produce professional-calibre theatre at the city's lowest ticket prices.
Where: Timms Centre for the Arts, 87 Ave. and 112 St., 492-2495

Theatre Network
What: Develops and produces new Western Canadian plays.
Where: Roxy Stage, 10708 124 St., 453-2440

Walterdale Playhouse
What: Oldest operating amateur theatre group in Canada, founded in 1959.
Where: 10322 83 Ave., 439-2845

Workshop West
What: Develops and produces new Canadian plays.
Where: 11516 103 St., 477-5955

Marty Chan

Chan debuted as a playwright at the 1990 Fringe, and has been packing houses ever since with plays like *Polaroids of Don* and *Mom, Dad, I'm Living With a White Girl*. He has also written for television (*Jake and the Kid*, *The Incredible Story Studio*).

Photo: courtesy NeWest Press

Brad Fraser

The author of *Unidentified Human Remains and the True Nature of Love* and *Poor Superman* had early plays like *Chainsaw Love* and *Return of the Bride* produced at the festival in the 1980s.

Darrin Hagen

Best known as the main instigator behind Guys in Disguise, the longtime Flashback's drag troupe, Hagen has since enjoyed solo success, writing plays like *Tranny, Get Your Gun!* and *Tornado Magnet: A Salute to Trailer Court Women*, typically with him/herself in the glam lead roles. He's now a host on Access television and is also the author of *The Edmonton Queen: Not a Riverboat Story*, both the play and the book.

Stewart Lemoine

His company Teatro la Quindicina was formed in time for the 1982 Fringe, and has been producing offbeat, Noel Cowardesque comedies like the seminal *Cocktails at Pam's* ever since. Lemoine has a brilliant ear for witty dialogue and a feel for offbeat (Eastern Europe, remote islands) settings. His actors so thoroughly embody the characters he writes, it's hard to imagine another cast performing these plays.

ORGAN DONATION

Thanks to a retired chemistry professor, one of the finest pipe organs in the world will soon be constructed at the **Winspear Centre**. A $2 million donation in 2000 from Stuart Davis supplemented the half-million dollar endowment left by the Centre's namesake, the late philanthropist Francis Winspear. The 6,070-pipe organ will be handcrafted by Orgues Letourneau Limitée of St. Hyacinthe, Quebec and installed by 2002. The world-class organ will be the crowning jewel in the elegant Winspear Centre, a $45 million concert hall that opened in 1997, providing an acoustically superior 2,000-seat venue for musical performances. The concert hall is of a 19th-century design known as a "shoebox" plan: high, long, and narrow, it relies on simple, natural materials like concrete and wood, and near-perfect natural acoustics for its lustre.

pressing issues

Sage advice to small Western Canadian presses might be to gather their hard-earned dollars together and light a big bonfire at once, sparing themselves several years of time and heartache in the publishing industry. These Edmonton houses have defied the odds, fought the good fight, and (gasp!) even managed to turn a few dollars over the years.

The Books Collective

Renowned Edmonton speculative fiction writer Candas Jane Dorsey heads up this collective of several imprints: Hodgepog Books, River Books, Slipstream Books, and Tesseract Books. Genres range from children's to sci-fi to erotica.
214-21, 10405 Jasper Ave., 448-0590

Duval House Publishing

Duval House/Les Editions Duval focuses on First Nations language learning materials, and publications on environmental issues in Canada and the world.
18228 102 Ave., 488-1390

Hurtig Publishing

Hurtig Publishing is long defunct, buried by the Herculean effort of publishing the first and second editions of the *Canadian Encyclopedia* (the company and the title were sold to McClelland & Stewart in 1991). Charismatic owner Mel Hurtig was never one to shy away from a challenge: he opened Edmonton's first bookstore in 1957, and started his own publishing company a decade later. (He's also an outspoken nationalist and anti-Free Trade crusader who created and led the National Party in the early 1990s, but that's another story entirely.)

Mags and 'Zines

Check your local newsstand for copies of these fine Edmonton-produced magazines.

Alberta Venture
Alberta's only provincial business magazine; published 10 times a year.
201-10350 124 St., 990-0839

Legacy
Alberta's cultural heritage magazine, named Alberta Magazine of the Year in 1997 at the Western Magazine Awards.
9667 87 Ave., 439-0705

Mote
This culturally astute Web 'zine calls itself "a fanzine ... about local music, art, and film," but it has much more, like interviews, reviews, and opinions that are smart, informed, and totally entertaining. Find it at *MoreGoatThanGoose.com*.

New Trail
The University of Alberta's award-winning alumni magazine; published quarterly.
Office of Alumni Affairs, 492-9534

Lone Pine Publishing

Lone Pine is a breath of fresh air with its broad range of regional plant, animal, bird, and outdoors guides under its imprint. Started by Grant Kennedy and son Shane in 1980, the company now has offices in Edmonton and in Washington state.
10145 81 Ave., 433-9333

NeWest Press

A company that started in 1977 as an outlet for Western Canadian books and political commentary has since published more than 100 books of fiction, criticism, poetry, drama, and non-fiction, including history, politics, biography, and Native and social issues. It also created the *NeWest Review*, a literary journal now published out of Saskatchewan.
201-8540 109 St., 432-9427

Tree Frog Press

Children's books are the current focus of this press, founded by local author Allan Shute in the 1970s. (Back then it published the *Edmonton Access Catalogue*, a wacky alternative city guide and worthy precursor to the book you're holding.) Its volumes of poetry and fiction have won national and international awards.
10144 89 St., 429-1947

Wild Child

In 1995, Edmonton honoured one of its famous sons, controversial artist Attila Richard Lukacs, with a one-man show at the Edmonton Art Gallery. He didn't disappoint, supplying a full complement of the homoerotic, classically inspired paintings from his East Berlin period, including donkey-heads, skinheads, severed heads, and massive phalluses everywhere. Local audiences equally enthusiastically responded with a full complement of moral outrage and amateur art criticism. These days Lukacs, who was born in Edmonton in 1962 (the family moved to Calgary a year later), works out of New York. Of his Alberta childhood, he said, "My younger brother used to play hockey, and my older brother used to work out at my dad's hobby ranch. I stayed home and did needlepoint."

On Spec

Canada's premier magazine of speculative fiction; published quarterly.
PO Box 4727, 413-0215

Other Voices

Fiction, non-fiction, prose, poetry, and art; published twice a year.
PO Box 52059, 433-1834

The Rouge

The only Canadian magazine devoted to football — professional, university, junior; published monthly.
15235 64 St., 975-8424

Windspeaker

Canada's national Aboriginal news source; published monthly.
15501 112 Ave., 455-2700

Writers Block

Literary magazine that has published everyone from local to international authors; quarterly.
9934 33 Ave., 417-1135

The noble cause of beautifying Edmonton's downtown is underway, beginning with the Roy Leadbeater sheet-metal sculpture *Aurora's Dance*, erected in 2000 on the 104 Street promenade. Thanks to a nearly $3 million initiative called the Art & Design in Public Places Program, 14 more works will appear over the next five years. The $85,000 fence-like installation celebrates Alberta's heritage of industrial innovation by deriving shapes from engineering and technology widgets and gadgets. (Not surprisingly, the sculpture's unveiling came shortly after the opening of the Aurora Mine by Syncrude, the project's lead sponsor.) Its sharp angles and ragged edges prompted one local newspaper wag to speculate how long it would take before some Boyle Street wino accidentally impaled himself on it.

Aurora is Leadbeater's third public artwork in Edmonton's downtown, joining two others he previously completed for the Citadel. A further stroll downtown reveals other intriguing works like *The Big Rock* by Catherine Burgess and Sandra Bromley in Rice Howard Way *(100A St. and 101A Ave.)*. It's a seven-metre, 40-tonne boulder of pink Quebec granite, with fir trees and grasses planted on top. Vancouverites complained that the piece was a direct ripoff of Siwash Rock in Stanley Park, but the artists insisted it was inspired by the Southern Alberta badlands.

BREAKFAST OF MANY, MANY CHAMPIONS

In the wild and woolly days of 1969, when the word "happening" could be authentically employed as a noun instead of a verb, artist Les Levine staged a performance art extravaganza across the street from the Edmonton Art Gallery in Churchill Square. Its name reads like an FBI code word: *Corn Flake.* Levine proposed to blanket the square in a crunchy orange coat of Kellogg's Cornflakes, an event he characterized (in typical fickle-artist fashion) both as an "act of nothingness" and an "act of returning something taken from the earth." (Never mind that corn has never exactly been a staple crop in downtown Edmonton.) After negotiations to secure an adequate supply of cornflakes, Levine fell slightly short of the quantity needed to execute his grand scheme, covering what amounted to a corner of the square in cereal. Still, he proclaimed it a successful commentary on ecology, using artsy terms like "mysterious invisible action" or a "disposable state of consciousness" to describe the stunt. A thinking person would have trucked over to the giant Edmonton City Dairy milk bottle (now interred in Northlands Park) and offered free breakfast for all. Levine re-created the piece in 1999 in Windsor, Ontario, where the head of a local school breakfast program lamented that the 250 boxes of cereal tossed to the elements (and the seagulls) could have been put to better use.

No trip to Edmonton is complete without clowning for a photo next to the sculpture *Lunchbreak* in Churchill Square. The cast aluminum figure of a labourer taking a rest on a park bench was created by Seward J. Johnson in 1983. (A similar sculpture of a worker chowing down provokes constant double-takes from Phase Three food court patrons at West Edmonton Mall.)

A giant mural, *Bush Pilot in a Northern Sky*, painted by Canadian artist Jack Shadbolt in 1962, almost stopped traffic at the Edmonton International Airport. When the airport was planning renovations in 1999 it discovered that the six-panel mural on the departures level of the old terminal couldn't be removed with being damaged, and renovation plans had to be changed to accommodate the 13 by six-metre abstract work. If murals are your thing, venture as far west as Stony Plain where the downtown is brightened with a series of 19 murals depicting the area's pioneer and agricultural past.

Finger Prints

A dozen local artists who were passionate about the art form of print-making formed the **Society of Northern Alberta Print-Artists (SNAP)** in 1982, and since 1996 have been running a dedicated gallery in the old Great West Saddlery Building *(10137 104 St., 423-1492)*. It has hosted prominent international events like the International Print-artists Cooperatives Symposium, a gathering of like organizations from around the world. SNAP supports itself by renting two dozen artists' studios and through various levels of sponsorship and membership, including an innovative *Print Newsletter* sponsor membership for $100 a year that includes four limited edition fine art prints annually, one with each issue of the newsletter.

Pole Dispute

For years it seemed as if the Polish Centennial Memorial would *never* get built. In 1995, a century after the first Polish immigrants arrived in Alberta, a local committee held a juried competition for a commemorative piece of public art. Alberta artist Ken Macklin won the competition, but the board of directors of the Alberta branch of the Canadian Polish Congress put the kibosh on his abstract steel sculpture, saying it wasn't "Polish" enough and comparing it to an "old house with pieces dropped down in the yard." (Macklin later sued for breach of contract.) Ironically, a few years later a Chinese-Canadian artist, Chu Honsun, was awarded the commission. However, by that time public enthusiasm for having the sculpture displayed on the Legislature grounds, as planned, had waned amongst fears that an abstract piece would be out of place beside the ornate Beaux Arts structure. Consequently, when the Polish Memorial was finally erected in June 2000, it was located beside the **Polish Hall** *(10960 104 St.)* instead. The finished work is a four-metre column featuring cone-shaped pieces of steel and etched images of Polish historical scenes.

Best Bookstores

Looking for that hard-to-find volume? Try these local independent and specialty retailers:

Ascendent Books
Volumes on philosophy, self-help, alternative healing, and reincarnation share shelf space with cards, jewellery, and gift items (of the candles and incense variety) in this peaceful shop, which also has a small café in the back.
10310 124 St., 452-5372

Audrey's Books
More than 100,000 volumes are in stock at this large, relaxed downtown store. Sales help is always gracious and knowledgable, and special order services are available.
10702 Jasper Ave., 423-3487

Belgravia Books & Treasures
This neighbourhood gem is a jumble of gifts and new and used books, including many volumes on local history, spirituality, and philosophy.
7601 115 St., 436-4125

Keeping up With the Yardley-Joneses

Longtime newspaper cartoonist J. Yardley-Jones has retired from his ink-stained wretchedness but found a new calling in dappled watercolour paintings of Edmonton scenes. His popular street scenes and landscapes are available at Snowbird Gallery *(West Edmonton Mall, 444-1024)*. Carrying the family pen these days is Paul (better known by the moniker Spyder) Yardley-Jones, whose futuristic and fantastic doodles have enhanced the A-Channel's "Big Breakfast Show," Edmonton Art Gallery cartooning workshops, and a 1980 Pontiac station wagon in which Spyder's been known to tool around town.

Bjarne's Books

Specializes in antiquarian and rare books and first editions, with concentration in history, travel, art, and Canadiana.
10533 Whyte Ave., 43907133

Blessings Christian Marketplace

It calls itself Canada's largest full-service Christian supply store, with aisles of Bibles, books, music, and other church supplies and Christian gifts.
14315 118 Ave., 455-4467; 9058 51 Ave., 466-1223

Computer Book Source

The selection of computing and technology books and magazines here is a geek's dream, and through this outlet and a Calgary store they can source and ship almost anything in the digital realm.
10408 103 Ave., 429-1077

Edmonton Book Store

Given its proximity to the U of A campus, this shop does a brisk trade in second-hand university textbooks and other new and used volumes.
11216 76 Ave., 433-1781

It's a Man, It's a Woman, It's ...

Photo: courtesy Trish Barnes /ManWoman

Anyone who has vague memories of the hazy, crazy days of the early 1970s in the city will recall the auspicious debut of the artist known as ManWoman (a.k.a. Patrick Kemball) at Latitude 53 gallery in 1973. He has always been known as much for his long curly locks and heavily-tattooed physique (including an eternal flame between his eyes and as many as 200 swastikas on his bod) as for his art. Manny (as his friends call him) studied at the Alberta College of Art in Calgary before moving to Northern Alberta to live in a cabin near Warburg. There, in 1965, according to ManWoman's own biography, "On my 27th birthday, I went into a trance and my soul soared up into the godhead. For one year I was flooded with all the classic mystical experiences – heart openings, third-eye openings, flights of ecstasy." Whatever. Then he moved to Edmonton and began creating art, and the rest is Canadian pop art history. These days, Manny toils from his back-country Cranbrook home and recently authored the book *Gentle Swastika*, part of his lifelong quest to redeem the ancient good luck symbol from its Nazi connotations.

Photo: courtesy Rudy Wiebe

Edmonton has been the early stomping ground of many scions of CanLit. Many of them attended the University of Alberta, under the legacy of inspired creative writing teacher Frederick M. Salter, who first brought the Edmonton writing program to prominence in the 1940s and '50s (influencing award-winning Alberta writers Rudy Wiebe [photo above] and Robert Kroetsch). The crusading editor of *Chatelaine* for nearly 20 years, Doris Anderson studied under Salter and cut her journalistic teeth at the *Edmonton Bulletin*. W.O. Mitchell published *Who Has Seen the Wind* a few years after graduating from the U of A in 1943 and later returned as writer in residence. Aritha van Herk studied under Rudy Wiebe and now mentors young writers at the University of Calgary. Governor General's Award-winning poet Lorna Crozier (in 1992, for the poetry collection *Inventing the Hawk*) did a master's degree there, and acclaimed novelist and magazine writer Katherine Govier studied there in the late 1960s. And among the science fiction writers spawned are Candas Jane Dorsey and best-selling author Sean Stewart. *Shoeless Joe* (later adapted into the film *Field of Dreams*) author W.P. Kinsella was also born in Edmonton in 1935, but the renegade writer claims no ties to the U of A. Acclaimed Canadian novelist Margaret Atwood also spent a year teaching at the U of A early in her career.

Kid Stuff

If you want to read an amateurish piece of work by Jane Austen or Charlotte Brontë, the imprint to look for is the Edmonton-founded Juvenilia Press. University of Alberta Austen scholar Juliet McMaster founded the Press in 1994 as an outlet for printing early works written by classic authors when they were under the age of 20. The series now includes work by Lady Mary Wortley Montagu, Malcolm Lowry, George Eliot, and CanLit grand dames Margaret Atwood and Margaret Laurence. In the late 1990s, the press moved to Sydney, Australia upon McMaster's retirement. No, you don't have to be under 20 to work there.

Greenwood's

Still going strong despite the mega-bookstore that opened just a few blocks down Whyte Avenue, this comprehensive family-owned store has a kids' offshoot, **Greenwood's Small World**, just around the corner, that has cool toys and gifts along with books, books, books.
10355 82 Ave., 439-2005

Laurie Greenwood's Volume II

Laurie Greenwood decided she'd like her own store, and took over this location. Her popular Tuesday book review spots on CBC's *Radio Active* (just before the five o'clock news) are almost as influential as an Oprah endorsement.
12433 102 Ave., 488-2665

Map Town Maps and Travel Books

The city's biggest selection of maps resides here, along with travel books, GPS receivers, and other items for the globetrotter.
10344 105 St., 429-2600

Our fair city has not fared all that well in the literary canon. Nary a glamorous best-seller has been set here, although many authors have paid homage to the River City in their work — inevitably fixating on the weather. After an apparently miserable stint at the University of Alberta, the young Margaret Atwood wrote the short story "Polarities," in which a young woman academic just happens to go mad one winter. (Memorable dialogue includes: "The city has no right to be here. I mean, why is it? No city should be this far north: it isn't even on a lake or an important river, even.... It doesn't look like anything, it doesn't *have* anything, it could be anywhere. Why is it here?")

Edmonton-raised Timothy Taylor set the story "The Resurrection Plant" in his hometown, and from his tone and his current home in Vancouver, we deduce that he likes the coastal climate better. "When does it warm up here?" whines a transplanted child in the story. "I'm going numb."

Surely the most innovative literary depiction of Edmonton occurs in Sean Stewart's *The Night Watch*, set in an apocalyptic Edmonton circa 2074, when the High Level Bridge takes on mythical status as the dividing line between the pagan Magic forces on the north side of the city and the virtuous Southside.

What we *really* need is a local writer to give the city some sex appeal — and by that we don't mean this infamous line from Brad Fraser's serial-killer play *Unidentified Human Remains and the True Nature of Love*: The character Kane says, "Beverly? You're from Beverly and you're a homo?"

Orlando Books

Feminist and lesbian/gay literature mix with a well-chosen selection of literary fiction, poetry, cultural studies, and politics volumes at this progressive store, which also has a selection of rainbow-sporting (gay-friendly) merchandise.
10123 Whyte Ave., 437-4080

Power Engineering Books

With the largest selection of technical books and code and standards manuals, this is your one-stop shop for all things techie.
7 Perron St., St. Albert, 458-3155

Queen's Printer Bookstore

You never know when you'll need a Hansard transcript of Legislative proceedings ... okay, you'll never need one, but doesn't it restore your faith in democracy to know that they're here? (Along with official legislation and other Alberta government publications.)
11510 Kingsway Ave., 427-4952

Ukrainian Book Store

Along with Slavic dictionaries and Ukrainian-language books and music, you'll find traditional costume and *pysanka* (Easter egg) supplies and gifts.
10215 97 St., 422-4255

hoof it

From traditional folk and classic ballet to avant garde modern, break a leg on the Edmonton dance scene.

Alberta Ballet

Although technically based in Calgary, this renowned company was founded in Edmonton in 1966 by modern dance pioneer Ruth Carse and performs here several times a year. It also hosts travelling companies in its performance space, the Jubilee Auditorium.
Suite 470, 10123 99 St., 428-6839

Brian Webb Dance Company

The head of the dance program at Grant MacEwan, Webb has long been a central figure on the Alberta dance scene. Trained in New York in the 1970s, Webb and company produce challenging modern dance, frequently collaborating with other stellar groups.
John L. Haar Theatre (Jasper Place Campus, Grant MacEwan Community College), 10045 156 St., 497-4416

Mile Zero Dance

Founded in 1985, this contemporary dance troupe (which was dormant for a few years, but seems to be back on its toes) experiments with non-dance artists – such as writers, poets, and avant-garde musicians – in its productions.
10565 114 St., 424-1573

Shumka

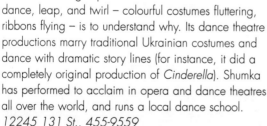

Photo: Ellis Brothers Photography

The Ukrainian word from which they take their name means "whirlwind," and to see this group dance, leap, and twirl – colourful costumes fluttering, ribbons flying – is to understand why. Its dance theatre productions marry traditional Ukrainian costumes and dance with dramatic story lines (for instance, it did a completely original production of *Cinderella*). Shumka has performed to acclaim in opera and dance theatres all over the world, and runs a local dance school.
12245 131 St., 455-9559

Literary Readings

A diverse spectrum of literary events – from highbrow to lowbrow, and everything under the rainbow (particularly at Orlando) – happens regularly at local venues. Watch for special events at Audrey's, Greenwood's, and Laurie Greenwood's Volume II.

124th Street Fiction Reading Series
The Writers Guild of Alberta hosts quarterly events on Saturday nights at Steeps teahouse.
12411 Stony Plain Rd., 422-2663

Open Stage Poetry Readings
Tuesdays at 7 p.m. at the Back Room Vodka Bar.
10324 82 Ave., 490-1414 or 477-0102

Orlando Books
Friday nights in the Bloomsbury room upstairs.
10123 82 Ave., 432-7633

The Tuesday Night Poetry Series
Sponsored by the Stroll of Poets Society, this event is held at several Edmonton cafés and bistros over a 12-week period each year.
www.icentre.net/stroll

Vinok Worldance

Folk dancing from all cultures is fodder for this group's productions, which can run the gamut from First Nations to Spanish to Chinese traditional dance. The result is multi-media, folkloric presentations that often incorporate historical sources and storylines.
454-3739

Kompany Dance & Affiliated Artists Society

Popular and accessible dance and musical theatre performances have been the hallmark of this lively song and dance troupe for the last two decades.
870-10150 100 St., 944-9115

Three Dead Trolls in a Baggie

At first, audiences considered this troupe's name disgusting – then they saw the comedy and got really offended. For several stellar years in the late 1980s and early '90s, the Three Dead Trolls (there were never three, but usually four and sometimes two) were Edmonton's answer to the *Kids in the Hall*: irreverent, inventive, and inured to comedy with "a tendency to embrace the idiots of the world instead of laughing at them," in the words of girl troll Kathleen Rootsaert. Rootsaert, Wes Borg, Joe Bird, and Paul Mather met at the Sidetrack in 1987 and started making beautiful comedy together, leading to popular Fringe shows (like *Skippy Gets A Boner*), memorable songs ("The Toronto Song" remains a perennial Alberta radio fave), and even a short-lived CBC television series (it bombed). Neil Grahn later replaced Mather, and in later years Dana Anderson was a sometime player. Post-Trolls, Rootsaert has created a successful acting career, notable for appearances in plays from Stewart Lemoine's and her own pen. Grahn went on to host the popular CBC program *Rough Cutz* and now writes and directs the internationally syndicated comedy travel show *The Tourist*. And the red-haired, impish Wes Borg proves that it's hard to keep a dead troll down: the 1999 Fringe hit *PileDriver!*, starring Trolls Bird and Borg and local vamps Guys in Disguise in a touching true tale about gay wrestlers in the '70s, was his latest play to enjoy a hit Toronto run in April 2001.

MASTER STROKES

Special security, lighting, and window coverings were installed in the **FAB Gallery** on the U of A campus in 1995 to host a very special exhibition. *Rubens to Picasso: Four Centuries of Master Drawings* brought together 150 drawings and studies by 64 of the most prominent artists in history, including Cezanne, Degas, Matisse, Monet, Picasso, Rubens, Seurat, and Van Gogh. The oeuvre was drawn from three anonymous private collections (at least one of them rumoured to be of local origin). Because of their delicacy, many of the drawings are rarely shown, and the six-week Edmonton show in the fall of 1995 represented an exclusive engagement for the exhibition, curated by Victor Chan and masterminded by former Department of Art and Design head Desmond Rochfort (now president of the Alberta College of Art and Design).

What you want, baby we got it. From housewares to sex toys, prospecting supplies to kitchen sinks, and outlet stores and bargains galore. Whether you need an antique tea cup, a feather boa, or a good used suit, you'll find it listed in these pages.

Penny-Pinching

In Edmonton's early days, the penny wasn't even considered real currency. Legal tender in other parts of the Dominion, red cents didn't pass muster this far west, where shopkeepers and customers preferred to round up or down to the nearest five cents, willingly paying the price for the convenience of not handling the trifling coins. Until 1914 that is, when James Ramsey opened a high-volume department store downtown. His gimmick? Not a clubby points scheme or a friendly greeter at the door, but simply prices that were lower – or seemed lower – than everywhere else. You see, canny Ramsey introduced to Edmontonians the now-familiar innovation of pricing items ending in nine, dramatically handing back the penny change to every skinflint customer that passed through his doors. He ordered $100 worth of the previously neglected coins, which had to be brought in from out of town. How refreshing to note that our progressive society has taken nearly a century to come full-circle, with leave-a-penny-take-a-penny dishes ubiquitous in today's local stores.

The Cat in the Hat

For 63 years in business, hatter John Kitsco, proprietor of **Mr. John's Hat Shop and Men's Wear**, remained an icon of style. Meticulously turned out, flawlessly dressed in suit and tie, Kitsco manned his Whyte Avenue storefront, which was one of only two remaining old-school hatters in North America when it closed in 2000. Along with carrying high-quality manufactured hats, the shop also hand made custom chapeaus, such as the fancy toppers worn by the Speaker of the Legislature and Alberta's lieutenant-governor. Other luminaries who were hatted by Mr. John include former American president Gerald Ford, Henry Kissinger, the Ghermezian brothers, and the late Edmonton philanthropist Francis Winspear.

bargoons

Blue Skys

This manufacturer's outlet sells its high-quality line of anoraks, parkas, and cozy fleeces at prices around 40 percent below retail. Since they're the official supplier to the Canadian National Figure Skating Team, you may be able to pick up the odd sample piece sporting a national team logo, allowing you to look – and save – like a champion.
10575 114 St., 425-1440

Creative Packaging

The storefront retail operation of Classic Packaging Wholesale has store-quality wrapping and packaging goods, including gorgeous gift wrap and ribbon in bulk rolls, paper and plastic bags of any colour and description, and dozens of little sacks and boxes perfect for wrapping everything from jewellery and clothing to homemade chocolates and cookies. They also offer classes for the all-thumbed in producing quick and beautiful wraps and elaborate wedding and party decorations.
10520 170 St., 484-2912

Dots

Racks of high-quality sportswear separates by Sigrid Olsen, Mexx, and Mac & Jac deeply discounted from their regular retail prices grace the front of its cavernous downtown warehouse store. The further toward the back of the store you go, the greater your chances of finding something that might be suitable for wear at a costume party.
10235 112 St., 426-2959; Heritage Mall, 435-6093; West Edmonton Mall, 483-9115

Big Box on the Prairie

Do you like to get your shopping experience in bulk? Then the massive big-box and outlet complexes that have been cropping up in areas like Mayfield Common, South Park (no relation to the cartoon) Centre, and South Edmonton Common are for you. There, you'll find national retailers peddling their wares at discounted prices in outlet-style stores:

Danier Leather
3803 Calgary Trail, 433-7601; Mayfield Common, 444-2389

Globo Shoes
174 Mayfield Common, 486-0435; 3803 Calgary Trail, 430-1411

Jean Outlet
130 Mayfield Common, 483-7957; 3803 Calgary Trail, 461-9203

Pennington's Wearhouse
3803 Calgary Trail, 437-9685; Londonderry, 473-6271; Mayfield Common, 489-2851

Roots Outlet
3803 Calgary Trail, 430-6363

Winners
Five Edmonton-area locations, including St. Albert and Sherwood Park

Names in Lights

Before commercial signage became the drab exercise in homogenous corporate branding that it is today, local businesses were defined by their signs — the bigger, more elaborate, and brighter-glowing neon, the better. You can still catch the neon glow at these locations:

Commercial Hotel

10329 82 Ave.

Da-De-O

10548a 82 Ave.

**Don Wheaton
Chevrolet Oldsmobile**

10727 82 Ave.

Hub Cigar

10345 82 Ave.

Royal Hotel

10220 96 St., 424-3107

Silk Hat

10251 Jasper Ave.

Yianni's Taverna

10444 82 Ave.

Labels for Less

The discount clearance outlet for Henry Singer Men's Wear and Blu's Women's Wear has designer suits and separates, usually slightly off-season, at 50-90 percent discounts off regular prices.
Lower level Edmonton Centre, 425-9273

The Nut Man Outlet

Find all those snack-size bags of yummy sweet and salty treats without dealing with that annoying guy who stops at your office every month.
5113 99 St., 439-7757

Off Broadway

A mish-mash of low-priced women's sportswear and various home textiles, including sheets, towels, and kitchen linens. The eagle-eyed shopper can occasionally spot a pedigreed piece of clothing with its label partially clipped to hide its designer provenance.
Bonnie Doon Shopping Centre, 463-4401

Russell Food Equipment

Buy the same supplies and equipment that local restaurants have for your very own kitchen. There's no reason to keep stealing glasses from your neighbourhood gin joint when you can buy the exact same ones here for mere coins. And if you've always had your eye on one of those big industrial bagel toasters, its yours for less than a G.
10225 106 St., 423-4221

Selma Bos Outlet

It's only open twice a year, but local fashionistas flock here to buy the factory-direct collections of local designer Selma Kuchmak under the Selma Bos label. Two seasons of her sophisticated business and casual wear are available from the second-floor outlet at different times of year: spring (opens in March for about 10 weeks) and autumn (open Labour Day weekend to the end of November).
2nd floor, 9932 81 Ave., 433-4954

When Pigs Fly Outlet

Just around the corner from the popular Whyte Avenue eclectica emporium (10470 82 Ave., 433-9127). You'll find all kinds of novelties, housewares, and gifts here at a minimum 50 percent off their regular prices.

X-S Wares

An Alberta chain offering loads of stylish, urban living accessories by companies like Umbra and Harmon in a no-frills setting – at bargain prices. The selection of comfy, overstuffed furniture includes unique pieces like chaise lounges and jumbo ottomans in up-to-the-minute colours and fabrics. If you can't find the perfect wedding or shower gift among the reams of pottery and pictures frames here, give up and send cash.

Heritage Mall, 413-7273; 5420 Gateway Blvd. N., 5345 103 St., 702-1282

One-stop Shopping

You know those busy Saturdays, when you need to rent a video, buy a CD, get some groceries, and maybe pick up a few household items (like a stockpot, or maybe a bongo drum)? Do it all at one of the city's many East Asian groceries, where the array of merchandise is staggering. There's no equal for fresh, whole spices (like cloves and nutmeg for potpourri or mulling spices) and a huge array of Caribbean, Indian, and Asian foods and ingredients, including exotic hot sauces. You might also find gorgeous silk sari fabric, reams of elaborate fabric trims, jewellery and bindis, and hair extensions of various colours and descriptions. We favour the **Spice Centre** *(9280 34 Ave., 440-3334)*, located in a strip mall that also includes a couple of sari shops and an excellent Indian restaurant, **Maurya Palace** *(9266 34 Ave., 468-9500)*.

CHRISTMAS IN JULY

Every day is like Christmas at **Kringle's: A Christmas Tradition** *(10422a 82 Ave., 433-6635)*, the year-round Christmas store that's redolent of evergreen and mulled cider every month of the year. It has collectors' Christmas ornaments, fancy hand-blown glass balls, Christmas villages, nativity scenes, and a bountiful selection of cards and wraps. If you don't see what you're looking for, ask one of the friendly "elves" on staff for assistance. Kringle's also has a sister store, **Kringle's at Home** *(12511 102 Ave., 447-2808)* that offers more timeless home decor items.

COSTUME BALL

Shirley Potter's *(10536 102 Ave., 429-1556)* dancewear and costume shop is a riot of colours, textures, and wacky stuff. Feather boas, hats (from tiaras to bowlers), theatrical makeup, and costumes (for rent or purchase) ranging from medieval knights to zoot-suited swingers to gorillas hang side-by-side upstairs; downstairs is a complete dance-supply store — from pointe shoes to tap shoes — and hundreds of bolts of flashy and colourful fabrics, sequins, and ribbons. In the basement is The Crypt, where only brave horror-film aficionados (or those seeking creepy costumes or a source of fake blood) should venture.

if you love this planet

It's hard to be a friend of the earth while retaining your status as a credit-card-carrying consumer. These local shops provide green alternatives and recycled products that might help ease that mindless-consumer conscience:

Architectural Clearinghouse

You might drive by this Gateway Boulevard yard stacked with old timbers, windows, and doors thinking it's a junkyard. Architectural Clearinghouse salvages and collects used building materials from construction and demolition sites and resells them at deep 30-50 percent discounts. Inside is a large collection of cabinet hardware, fixtures, and even carpet. They'll also come pick up your discarded home building items for free.
5920 103 St., 438-222

Earth's General Store

Environmentally friendly personal care items (from toothpaste to sanitary napkins to diapers), household cleaning supplies, natural-fibre clothing (like a great unbleached cotton terry robe for $60), and food products like nuts and fair-trade coffee are staples at this groovy store, which also posts local information on topics from cycling to recycling.
2nd floor, 10832 82 Ave., 439-8725

Good Earth Clothing Co.

A selection of linen, rayon, and cotton clothing ranges from breezy resort wear to Indonesian tie-dyed sarongs to sophisticated knit separates, most in an extensive range of sizes.
10443 124 Ave., 482-3039

True North Hemp Co.

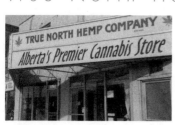

The smell of patchouli assaults the nostrils as you enter Edmonton's biggest and best head shop, stuffed with hemp clothing, cosmetics, oils and candles, edibles, and a huge selection of pipes and bongs for, you know, whatever one might need those kinds of things for.
10760 82 Ave., 437-4367

vintage

The Junque Cellar

All eras and styles of retro furniture crowd into this cozy basement, with 1970s stereo and TV consoles next to the chrome and formica dinette sets from the '50s. Vintage clothing and jewellery co-exist with international items like contemporary picture frames, batik, and chunky wool sweaters.
Downstairs, 10442 82 Ave., 433-9963

Orbit

A huge selection of vintage clothing includes racks of screaming muumuus and gaudy Hawaiian shirts and some wicked retro ties, scarves, and handbags. Lots of collectibles, like lunchboxes and toys, and the odd piece of furniture are part of the well-picked array here. The same people own a funky contemporary clothing store, **Mars and Venus**, just around the corner on Whyte.
8241 014 St., 491-0296

Next-to-New

FOR MEN

Get the look for less with consignment — that is, gently used — suits and business fashions for men at **Dress to Suit Boutique**. You'll often find labels like Hugo Boss, Armani, and Versace lurking on the racks of suits, shirts, jackets, pants, and ties. They're fussy about quality, so the clothing's condition is like new.
10141 100A St., 426-2172

FOR WOMEN

Changes

Calling itself the "classy consignment company," this store has upscale sportswear, grouped by colour, and a good selection of consignment footwear. The odd new piece or designer sample is mixed in, at prices far below regular retail.
10558 82 Ave., 439-3129

record stores

Looking for vinyl, imported club mixes, local artists, and various and sundry obscure recorded music? Visit one of these indie shops:

Blackbyrd Myoozik

New and used rock, country, folk, jazz, electronica, classical, and world beat.
10442 82 Ave., 439 1273

Carrefour Librairie-Bookstore

The place to go for French-language recordings, books, and vids.
8527 91 St., 478-2120

Freecloud Records

Vintage vinyl and out-of-print records (45s 78s, and LPs) including pop, rock, country jazz, R&B, punk, alternative – well, everything.
10764 101 St., 429-1476

The Gramophone

Alberta's best selection of classical CDs and videos (and pretty good opera and jazz sections, too). If you can't find it here, they're glad to oblige with special orders.
8724 109 St., 428-2356

Groove Asylum

New and used dance music, rap, reggae, techno, alternative, and more.
10514 Jasper Ave., 497-7615

Sound Connection

One of the biggest used record stores in the city, with lots of rarities and imports in the mix. Also sells videos and band merchandise (posters, T-shirts).
10838 124 St., 425-8721

Snaggs

An out-of-the-way neighbourhood store with a selection of reasonably priced designer consignment, including a regular rotation of labels like Gap, Anne Klein, Donna Karan, Calvin Klein, and Louben.
3018 106 St., 436-2778

Vespucci

They've cornered the high end of the consignment market, regularly stocking fancy gowns or suits with posh designer labels.
12539 104 St., 433-856

FOR KIDS

BoyGirl Rewear

This store sells and consigns better-quality used kids' togs, and since it's located just a hop and a skip from affluent Glenora the pickings tend to be sweet indeed.
12606 Stony Plain Rd., 453-2935

Tickety-Boo

Located in a tony neighbourhood, this shop has plenty of little Gap, Club Monaco, Roots, and Esprit cast-off duds at discount prices.
5675 Riverbend Rd., 432-2000

fashion

Blu's Women's Wear/ Henry Singer Men's Wear

The brother and sister stores in this Alberta chain are located side by side in Manulife Place, both selling suits and sportswear from leading designers (like Armani, Calvin Klein, and Ermenegildo Zegna for men and Anne Klein, Armani, and Emanuel for women). Shoes by Blu's has high-fashion women's footwear; there's a stand-alone Henry Singer at West Edmonton Mall and a Blu's at Southgate.
Manulife Place, 423-6868, 425-4544

Concrete Clothiers

Local designer Deidre Hackman is the designing genius behind this progressive fashion outpost, which carries original designs for both men and women.
10047 102 St., 428-0450

Etzio/Avenue Clothing

Both are must-stops on any Whyte Avenue fashionista's stroll. Funky jewellery and accessories mix with wardrobe basics and upscale seasonal separates. Find Esprit and DKNY at Etzio *(10338 82 Ave., 433-5292)* and lines like Mexx and Louben at Avenue *(10318 82 Ave., 433-8532)*.

Thrift Stores

Value Village (Whyte Avenue, west end, and downtown locations) is the supermarket of thrift stores, but you'll often find that the smaller outlets are less picked-over (and, inevitably, a little smellier — hey, it's a trade-off). Any of these stores can usually arrange for pick-ups or drop-offs of your unwanted items, too.

Alberta SPCA Thrift Store
15126 Stony Plain Rd., 444-4450

Beacon Thrift Store
4112 118 Ave., 479-1230

Bibles for Missions Thrift Store
15210 Stony Plain Rd., 489-6958

Bissell's Thrift Shoppe
9232 34 Ave., 440-1883
8818 118 Ave., 471-6644

Gravity Pope

Shoe fetishists can while the day away here trying on Fluevogs, Doc Martens, Roadhogs, Clarks, and the latest fashion footwear from Kenneth Cole and Elle. There's also a small clothing boutique featuring lines like Free People, Roxy, and Quicksilver at the back of the store. *10442 82 Ave., 439-1637*

Goodwill

To make a donation or arrange a pick-up, call 944-0211
8759 51 Ave., 944-0243
10304 108 St., 944-0382
1260 137 Ave., 944-0401
15020 Stony Plain Rd., 944-0563
10455 80 Ave., 944-1041
11714 34 St., 944-0059

IODE Shoppe

8941 82 Ave., 466-4241

Lou Gehrig's Disease Society Thrift Store

4427 118 Ave., 477-2182

Salvation Army

To make a donation or arrange a pick-up, call 437-6861
2003 Tudor Glen, St. Albert, 458-7638
9616 101A Ave., 425-9908
2849 Mill Woods Rd., 469-8291
10131 Princess Elizabeth Ave., 477-1599
5115 99 St., 432-6751

Sam Abouhassan

The elite name in men's clothing in Edmonton has dressed Wayne Gretzky and other NHL stars with refined custom design and tailoring. *Commerce Place, 429-7998*

TK Clothing Co.

Casual and professional fashions that are contemporary but elegant are the hallmark of this High Street boutique. Among the brand names are Anne Klein, Eileen Fisher, and Votre Nom. There's also a custom bedding shop, **All Tucked In**, literally tucked into the back of the shop. *10127 124 St., 488-7277*

Who Cares

A funky Jasper Avenue store that carries clothes and jewellery geared to fashion-forward twenty- and thirty-somethings, including brands like Logic, Powerline, Dex, and Quick Reflex spread over two levels. *11222 Jasper Ave., 429-2273*

home furnishings

Chintz & Company

Think chintzy as in decorator-size bolts of the flowered fabric, not necessarily as in "cheap." Overstuffed furniture, upholstery trims and ribbons, and housewares ranging from unique cutlery and pottery to beautiful tablecloths and napkins are stuffed into this rich-looking store. A good selection of picture frames, pillows, and seasonal decorations and garden ornaments, too. Design consultations and custom textiles are available.
10502 105 Ave., 428-8181

Exclusive Lamps and Lampshades

Exquisite lampshades, from Victorian-style to leopard print, are hand made by Joanna and Eva Jakubik at this High Street shop. They take custom orders and also do recovering and repairs of shades and lamps.
12413 Stony Plain Rd., 414-1692

Hothouse

By name and by nature, this Edmonton-based company is hot. It first made its mark with clever contemporary furnishings (a CD rack made from recycled tires, a wine rack shaped like antlers) that have appeared everywhere from American sitcom sets to posh publications like *The Robb Report*. Now they've opened a home and gift store just off Whyte Avenue, where

Cosmetics

Carmela's Profumeria
Rationing your favourite eau de cologne because you can no longer find it in Canada? This boutique sources hard-to-find European and discontinued perfume and scent lines.
12531 102 Ave., 455-3336

Lux
Cosmetics connoisseurs will appreciate the elite and hard-to-find beauty products that Jennifer Grimm and Louise Skinner have gathered under one roof at Lux. Beeswax products from Burt's Bees and the Bliss Spa line are among their wares; they regularly post celebrity endorsements from *In Style* and other magazines next to the products they carry.
10120 124 St., 1-877-451-1423

Vu•Du
Get a high-quality skin-care product and a little life lesson from every product by Philosophy, one of the lines carried here. They also have Smashbox cosmetics and the Bloom aromatherapy line of body care and cosmetic products, including Happy Nappy diaper cream and other baby products. A small salon/spa in the

back offers makeup and esthetic services (waxing, facials, manicures, tinting) and Pamper Party packages that include a full treatment menu plus a light meal and wine for you and your gal pals.
10522 82 Ave., 434-7032

Body Shops
For a Body Shop-like experience without the horrors of a shopping mall, try the made-in-Canada alternative **Pure Radiant Energy** *(10740 82 Ave., 988-7873)*, a Vancouver-based franchise that offers a no-frills, high-quality skin and hair care line and smelly delights like deli soap (by the sliver or by the slab), bubble bath, and shower gel. Or if you can brave the overpowering smell, enter the new U.K. sensation, **Lush** *(10624 82 Ave., 437-9427)*, for decadent massage bars and bath bombs.

Hothouse's own furnishings and accessories blend nicely with innovative furniture lines like Calligaris from Italy and whimsical giftware items (everything from inflatable Christmas trees to feather boa-trimmed slipcovers for vases).
8004 103 St., 434-2184; 10155 102 St., 428-6260

Konto Weekend Store

Visit Konto's regular showroom for home or office furnishings any day of the week, but on weekends check out the low-priced clearance items at the Weekend Store next door. Pine furnishings, home accessories, and slightly damaged items are discounted and many pieces are cash and carry.
6120 99 St., 437-1535

Old Hippy Wood Products

There are now four Edmonton-area locations and five other Alberta stores (and, curiously, one in Japan) carrying this well-made, solid-wood furniture in pine, birch, cherry, maple, and oak. This is the real deal: top-grade lumber attached by dado joints and then hand-finished. Select from a huge catalogue or dream a custom design. Chill, man: Old Hippy doesn't use any endangered rainforest wood products.
10019 81 Ave., 448-0985;
10810 170 St., 448-0872;
7941 Argyll Rd., 448-2514;
112-150 Chippewa Rd., Sherwood Park, 449-0020

Pure Design

This Edmonton-based company made a splash recently with its collection of Douglas Coupland-designed tables, including the clever face-off circle of the *Hockey Night in Canada* table. It also carries designs by international luminaries like Karim Rashid. Find it at local stores or watch the company's website *(www.pure-design.com)* for news of new product lines or its annual warehouse sale, where design junkies descend in hordes for deals on scratch 'n' dent and discontinued items.
16646 111 Ave., 483-5644

kitchen and housewares

Bosch Kitchen Centre

Serious cooks have long known about this obscure south-side storefront, tucked into a semi-industrial strip-mall area. There's high-end cookware, small appliances, and gadgets of every description (boiled egg-slicer, anyone?), and in the back room a mouth-watering stash of high-quality cooking and baking supplies: fresh nuts and dried fruits, quality chocolate, spices, and even hog casings for home sausage-making. A full range of cooking classes, too. *9766 51 Ave., 437-3134*

Call the Kettle Black

Fun and functional stuff for the kitchen abounds at this High Street store, including cookware, barware (we like the vermouth spritzer for making martinis), and table linens. *12523 102 Ave., 448-2861*

Garlic and More

Whether you're scaring off vampires or a cold, the stinking rose is found in abundance at this Bonnie Doon store. It has a huge selection of garlic-enhanced spreads, dips, and sauces (including a whole wall of hot sauces at the back of the store), but also carries lots of kitchen gadgets and decor accents. *Bonnie Doon Shopping Centre, 448-1919*

G. Dennis

If you have nearly $200 to spend on a single copper and aluminum-clad skillet, come on down. G. Dennis not only has cool gadgets and gorgeous dinnerware and barware, but carries a selection of gourmet packaged foods and condiments and has a demonstration kitchen in the back for cooking classes and displays. This may be the best bridal and gift registry in town for gourmets. *10746 82 Ave., 438-4117*

Crafts and Souvenirs

There's no reason to return from a trip to Edmonton with nothing but a crappy West Edmonton Mall t-shirt to show for it. An item made by a local artisan speaks volumes about the city and its arts community. The **One of a Kind Cameo Craft Show and Sale** happens every November at the Shaw Conference Centre *(9797 Jasper Ave., 988-8914)*. In early December, shoppers flock to the **Butterdome Craft Sale** — Western Canada's largest — for unique items, at the Universiade Pavilion on the U of A campus. There's also a year-round craft market at **Treasure Barrel** in Old Strathcona under the Virginia's Soap Deli sign *(8216 104 St., 439-9372)*.

Alberta Craft Gallery Shop

This store within the Alberta Craft Council is a huge repository for glass, jewellery, pottery, and wood, fabric, and metal crafts. There are some traditional two-dimensional artworks, too. If you see work by artists you really like, you can usually get in touch with them directly to find out more about their work.
10186 106 St., 488-6611

Graelin's

With possibly the city's broadest selection of locally made pottery, as well as carvings, silkscreens, and various Ukrainian-inspired craft items, Graelin's is a must-see High Street stop.
10123 124 St., 482-3105

Molson Boutique

It may not be handcrafted, but nothing says I love you quite like beer-inspired merchandise. Stop at this store adjacent to the Molson brewery for hats, sweatshirts, bags, glassware, and more. It's the only Molson boutique in Canada.
12006 104 Ave., 482-8817

antiques roadshow

Antique Malls

Multiple vendors stake out booths in these giant antique and collectible emporiums, so you might find quaint prairie antiques (butter churns, pickle crocks) beside a stall selling vintage 78s or one peddling Formica dining sets. A huge selection of large and small furniture items, and individual vendors are often willing to haggle.

Strathcona Antique Mall
7614 103 St., 433-0398

Rocky Mountain Antique Mall
7025 103 St., 485-0020

Artifacts Trading Co.

There's a beautiful selection of jewellery here, mostly in silver and with semi-precious stones like amber and lapis. An eclectic mix of exotic items like masks and fine Japanese sake and tea sets sit side-by-side.
8222 103 St., 447-1111;
three other Edmonton locations

Chickies

French country-style house and garden antiques are the specialty of the house, literally located in a ramshackle-looking old house in a gentrified pocket of the Highlands.
11204 65 St., 479-1928

From Times Past

Owner Johanne Yakula sources antiques and small collectibles (ranging from vintage glass Christmas ornaments to china tea cups) for this High Street store from local estates and consignments, and lovingly displays them, often with the embellishment of a handwritten tag detailing their provenance, in this charming High Street shop.
Lower level, 12505 102 Ave., 448-9671

Paris Market

The old Mercer Warehouse (reportedly complete with a black-robed ghost and *Exorcist*-style meat hooks in the basement) has now been converted into a slice of the Left Bank. Angela Larson and Christine Miller have turned this exposed-brick, colourfully painted space into a charming market with booths for antiques, vintage clothes, fabrics, and crafts like mosaics. A little cappuccino bar provides welcome respite. Open weekends only.
10363 104 St., 424-2511

Salvation Army Antiques and Collectibles

A cut above the typical Sally Ann outlet, this location specializes in furniture, clothing, jewellery, and collectible cast-offs that qualify as bona fide antiques, or at least as funky vintage. Prices are also a cut above normal for thrift, but far below antique-store levels.
5115 99 St., 432-6751

Tiffany's

Film and television set-dressers long ago discovered Tiffany's Antiques and Decor (also known as Tiffany's Birdshop), a treasure trove of props, commercial signs, nostalgic memorabilia, and odd architectural bits and pieces. The 111th Avenue store is the original.
9314 111 Ave., 479-5356;
10135 82 Ave., 434-2414

Craft Supplies

Earthly Goods

This quilting supply shop was recently ranked among the top 10 quilting stores in North America. Thousands of colour-grouped bolts of fabric line the walls of this shop, along with sample quilts and crafts for inspiration. The knowledgable staff can advise on classes and supplies.
5848 111 St., 433-7179

Wool Revival

It's a knitter's paradise, with everything from traditional wools and cottons to fancies like sequined, chenille, and velvet yarns. Tons of patterns, too, and helpful advice from expert staff.
6513 112 Ave., 471-2749

Stogies

Smoke 'em if you've got 'em, or get 'em at these fine humidors:

Burlington-on-Whyte
10468 82 Ave., 439-8519

Hub Cigar
10345 82 Ave., 429-0144

La Tienda
8426 109 St., 439-5108

stationery

Evergreen Stationers

Probably the largest selection of loose (by-the-sheet or by-the-ream) papers and envelopes, including lovely vellums and embossed papers, in the city. Tons of invitation samples line the walls and the display cases, providing inspiration for design-your-own invitations or templates for ordering them custom-made. A big selection of guest books, pens, handmade paper, wrapping paper, and unusual stationery supplies (like wax and gummed seals) and unique greeting cards. *3855 99 St., 468-2734*

Notables

Bag it, box it, or wrap it with supplies from Notables, which also carries greeting cards, custom and boxed stationery, and an invitation ordering service. They also have a showcase full of supplies specific to Jewish holidays, such as Hanukkah candles and commemorative bar mitzvah items.
12418 102 Ave., 488-4625

garden and outdoors

Apache Seeds

This old-fashioned neighbourhood gardening store is like a relic from the past, with its chalkboard of daily specials and new arrivals posted outside, its huge collection of indigenous Alberta seeds, and its wide variety of pots and planting media. Open year-round.
10136 149 St., 489-4245

Blooming Prairie

Local grower Katie Benschop believes in selling primarily native Albertan grains, seeds, plants, and flowers. That means the selection at this south-side garden shop leans toward wildflowers, herbs, and ornamental plants (think seed pods, grasses, and sheafs of grains dyed pretty shades). Dried-flower enthusiasts will literally have a field day here (the store's motto: "We save summer"), where a wild-looking crop sprouts across the lawn.
9535 76 Ave., 431-1451

Hole's

Located on what used to be the Hole family farm in St. Albert is now one of the biggest greenhouse operations in Western Canada. (The matriarch of the family is Lois Hole, former chancellor of the University of Alberta and now the Lieutenant Governor of Alberta.) You'll find a wealth of seeds, plants, trees, shrubs, and information, along with a full-service floral shop for bouquets and arrangements (they do weddings, too). Lois Hole's ever-growing series of popular gardening books is for sale here, too.
101 Bellrose Dr., 419-6800

Lee Valley Tools

Serious gardeners and woodworkers can spend hours in this West End shop browsing ingenious tools, toymaking parts, decorative and cabinet hardware, and garden ornaments.
10103 175 St., 444-6153

Wild Bird Marketplace

All things winged are the focus of this quaint Highlands-area store, which stocks a huge selection of bird feed and seeds, birdhouses, garden ornaments and windchimes, and books on birding.
6419 112 Ave., 474-2075

Sex

NASTY

Rodeo Drive *(10725 124 St., 474-0413)* sponsors an annual fetish fashion show, and that's all you need to know about its proclivities. A relative newcomer to Edmonton is **B&D Emporium** *(9652 Jasper Ave., 428-5847)*, but longtime fans of its Inglewood store in Calgary will find all the same fine-quality personal appliances and latex clothing they've become accustomed to.

NICE

Romantic Interlude staff are so open and friendly it's easy to forget they're trying to sell you giant dildos and six-inch lucite high-heeled shoes, among other goodies. This is the type of clean, well-lighted sex shop that strolling couples (or singles) don't feel embarrassed to enter. Now, *exiting* with one of those gigantic bad boys in hand might be another problem entirely....
10434 82 Ave., 431-9812; 11828 103 St., 479-8749

sporting goods

Bedrock Supply

Prospecting equipment like gold pans and sluices, lapidary (rock-polishing) supplies, and jewellery-making tools and semi-precious stones and beads. Also a selection of crystals for New Age types, and even metal detectors for the scavengers among us.
9617 63 Ave., 434-2040

Dorjac Canada

If you like poking around in boxes and piles of stuff looking for bargains, Dorjac's was built for you. It does mostly wholesale trade in sporting goods to teams and schools, but there's plenty of hockey equipment and balls of every description floating around this warehouse, which doubles as a retail storefront. Not everything's priced (ask the staff), but most stuff is a bargain.
17356 108 Ave., 484-7581

Fila Outlet Store

A huge selection of Fila shoes and clothing — everything from tennis skirts to bathing suits — at 25-50 percent off regular prices. Youth and kids' sizes, too, and great end-of-season clearance sales.
5431 103 St., 414-1310

Wholesale Sports

There's usually nothing but mud-spattered trucks and SUVs in the parking lot of this north side hunting, fishing, and camping emporium. Heavy-duty sleeping bags and tents (including ice-fishing tents in the winter), outdoor clothing, guns and knives, camping tools and supplies by brands like Zeiss, Kelty, Eagle, and Trekk are here, and none of 'em at those fancy downtown prices. You'll find the high-end stuff, too, like Leica binoculars for a cool two grand.
12505 97 St., 477-3737

FUN AND GAMES

The funky little **Elephants Never Forget** *(12515 102 Ave., 453-5121)* store on High Street provides two levels of mischievous fun for big and little kids. Sure, some of the gifts, games, and toys could be deemed "educational," but they're so much fun you'll be able to sneak them past even the most suspicious kid. The **Edmonton Space and Sciences Centre Gift Shop** *(11121 142 St., 452-9100)* has a fascinating array of truly bizarre stuff, including freeze-dried food like astronauts eat and space pens that write upside-down and underwater. Teach kids those important life lessons with a pet from **Dad's Fish Room** *(9912 81 Ave., 433-FISH)*, which bills itself as "the store for the true aquarist" and carries rare fish and aquarium plants and supplies. Located in a charming house in Old Strathcona, its atmosphere is much more pleasant than the average pet store.

What, you may ask, has Edmonton's imprint on the international movie and music scenes been? We're glad you asked. In these pages, find out about the early days of SCTV, when Hollywood came to town, our beauty queens, prodigal sons and daughters, and Grammys, Oscars, and Pulitzers.

SCTV Takes Off, Eh

In 1981, Edmonton's ITV station scored a coup by bringing the virtually unknown Second City comedy troupe here to film a few seasons of the fledgling series *SCTV*. Shortly after, the CBC picked up the series for national broadcast, but being good bureaucrats they wanted to ensure the proper quota of Can-con was indoctrinating unsuspecting Canuck audiences. In response, cheeky comics Rick Moranis and Dave Thomas invented hoser alter-egos Bob and Doug McKenzie as "an exercise in mediocrity" and mock-Canadiana, as they later recalled. The segments were such a hit, they spawned the 1983 movie *Strange Brew*, which premiered in Edmonton a week before opening in other cities. Ironically, ITV later cited *SCTV* as a positive example of original, entertaining Canadian content in its CRTC applications. Post-*SCTV*, other alumni of the era such as John Candy, Andrea Martin, and Eugene Levy went on to varying degrees of Hollywood and comedy success.

Fashion to the Stars

Greg Polkosnik is the world's foremost expert on fashion astrology – well, okay, he's the world's *only* expert on fashion astrology. The Edmonton author (who often signs off as Mr. Greg P.) is the author of *Cosmically Chic: Discovering Your Fashion Style Through Astrology*, in which he characterizes various astrological signs by their style of dress and dispenses pithy advice, like: "The Cancer style is probably the most classic style in the zodiac. You can dress well at any age because you dress in a manner that is quite timeless." Call it flaky, call it what you like, but Mr. Greg P. has carved out a unique little niche for himself, and has already been hired by *Harper's Bazaar* to write a regular column for the fashion magazine.

Giants of Jazz

Photo: courtesy Tommy Banks Music

New Orleans may be the birthplace of jazz, but Edmonton is a place where many music greats have settled over the years. The famed Yardbird Suite, which moved to its current south-side location in 1984, has been around in various incarnations since the late 1950s. The jazz scene in the 1960s and '70s was sparked by the big band led by pianist (and now Canadian Senator) Tommy Banks (photo above), who also hosted a popular eponymous television variety show from 1968-83. (Ironically, both Banks and his longtime colleague, Juno-winning bebop saxophone player P.J. Perry, were born in Calgary but later came to Edmonton.) The late saxophone player Earl Seymour played in Banks' band for years before leaving for Toronto in the late 1970s. (He later played on the Blood, Sweat and Tears album *Nuclear Blues* in 1980, and toured with popster Neil Sedaka.) Composer and pianist Bill Emes was a hub of the local jazz scene until his untimely death from hepatitis in 1997, and in his day accompanied vocalists like Big Miller and Sheila Jordan. The Big man himself was a blues crooner who had performed with jazz greats like Duke Ellington, Count Basie, and Miles Davis. (He died in 1992 during rehearsals for a musical, *No Small Feets*, based on his life story.) Today, musicians like saxophonists Perry, David Babcock, and Kent Sangster, guitar player Bobby Cairns, and trumpeter Bob Tildesley are some of the stalwarts of the local scene.

Jazz City Festival

A late-June institution for 20 years, this festival threw its aegis around its floundering Calgary counterpart in 1998 to revitalize it. Jazz luminaries appearing over the years have included Chick Corea, Sonny Rollins, Chet Baker, Betty Carter, Dizzy Gillespie, Ray Brown, Stan Getz, Wynton and Branford Marsalis, Ornette Coleman, Diana Krall, J. J. Johnson, and Nicholas Payton. Edmontonian Marc Vasey is the passionate jazz aficionado behind this international-calibre show. 432-7166

Other Festivals

Blueberry Bluegrass and Country Music Festival
When: July
What: Grass-roots music festival in Spruce Grove.
963-4181

Cariwest Caribbean Carnival
When: August
What: A Caribbean Mardi Gras of parades, food, and music.
421-7800

Comedy Arts Festival
When: January
What: Kicks you out of the January doldrums with just-for-laughs improv and performances.
437-8828

Edmonton International Street Performers Festival
When: July
What: Mimes, magicians, jugglers, and crowd-pleasing performers of all stripes.
425-5162

First Night Festival

When: New Year's Eve

What: Indoor and outdoor family fun at an alcohol-free celebration.

448-9200

Giovanni Caboto Day Festival

When: Late June

What: Be Italian for a day in Giovanni Caboto Park in Little Italy.

424-4869

Heritage Festival

When: August

What: Food and cultural displays and performances outdoors in Hawrelak Park.

488-3378

Klondike Days

When: July

What: All the traditional trimmings like a parade, midway, and exhibition. Includes the popular **Taste of Edmonton** in Churchill Square.

423-2822

Local Heroes International Screen Festival

When: Late March

What: A celebration of indie filmmaking found locally and around the world presented by the National Screen Institute.

421-4084

Edmonton Folk Music Festival

This annual feel-good fest is dear to the hearts of many locals, especially the couple who got engaged a few years ago when the groom-to-be unfurled a tarp on which was inscribed a very big, very public, proposal. (They now live in Calgary and have two kids.) It's easy to let romance overtake you when you're sitting cupped in the natural amphitheatre of Gallagher Park after sundown, surrounded by flickering candles, mellow music, and good karma, man. Mega-stars appearing since 1980 have included Joan Armatrading, Joan Baez, Donovan, Long John Baldry, Elvis Costello, Emmylou Harris, Laura Lush (photo above), Jay McShann, Sarah McLachlan, and T-Bone Burnett. Longtime producer Terry Wickham has a talent for selecting just the right mix of world, roots, and true folk music.
429-1899

En Français

For more than 50 years, Alberta's only French radio station has been broadcasting from Edmonton, to the delight of the province's many French-Canadians. The CBC station's call letters, CHFA, are said to stand for "Courage, Heroism, Fierte (pride), and Amour (love)." Those words are apt, considering the struggle to get the station on the air. The right-wing government of then-premier Ernest Manning fought to keep French radio off the airwaves in 1949. However, more than 200,000 francophones (including 200 recently returned war veterans) signed petitions in favour of the station, which was finally approved by Prime Minister Mackenzie King (who was coincidentally in an election year). The station held its launch at the Garneau theatre on November 20, 1949, with about 700 joyful francophones in attendance; 50 years later, it celebrated its anniversary in the same location.

The *Edmonton Journal* didn't just report on a hostage situation that happened in 1973, it participated in it. A harmless looking elderly man entered the newspaper's library one August morning and proclaimed that he had a bomb, shutting down the paper for more than three hours. What *Journal* staffers didn't know was that the man, James Henry Cameron, was a war veteran who was terminally ill with leukemia and had left a message that amounted to a suicide note for his wife. (It spoke of a "daring venture" and apologized for the parking ticket their vehicle would surely incur in the duration.) One of his hands was buried inside a can, from which wires ran to a heavy briefcase. He demanded publication of his 2,000-word personal manifesto on the front page of that day's *Journal* – or he would blow up the building. Suspecting a hoax, police and newspaper management negotiated with Cameron for hours until canny *Journal* staff produced a few hundred copies of a dummy edition of that day's paper, with the manifesto prominently reproduced. Unsatisfied, Cameron demanded an opportunity to conduct broadcast interviews, but was foiled by a radio reporter whose tape recorder, hidden in her purse, caught Cameron candidly telling her the bomb threat was fake. The prankster was quietly escorted out by police, and when his briefcase was opened they discovered the bomb was fake, too: the case contained 27 paperback books. Four weeks later, Cameron died.

READ ALL ABOUT IT

One of Canada's premier brass bands for 15 years was the Edmonton Newsboys, a group of youngsters (most still in their teens) first assembled in 1914 by a newsstand owner, John Michaels, who wanted to keep youths off the street and out of trouble. The Newsboys were popular locally, playing at parades, celebrations, and most of the Edmonton Grads' basketball games. The nadir of their success game in 1924, when the Prince of Wales selected them as the only Canadian band invited to the British Imperial Exhibition. By the 1930s the band had dissolved, but local schoolteacher Vernon Newlove found its old instruments and used them to start the Edmonton Schoolboy's Band, which continued the musical legacy.

NEWS HUB

Hub Cigar *(10345 82 Ave., 439-0144)* is a holdover from the days when a gentleman could while away a morning or afternoon smoking, discussing the day's news, and perhaps shooting some snooker with cronies at a storefront newsstand. It still has the same creaky floor and news cred (it stocks nearly 10,000 papers and magazines from all over the world), but an impressive new humidor keeps cigar aficionados coming back for more. Browse as long as you like — in the winter, that won't be long, since the 1910 structure is poorly heated and insulated — but be aware that the very modern accoutrements of a video surveillance system will catch you peeking at those dirty magazines.

Photo: Provincial Archives of Alberta (J38272)

In Edmonton's early days, media other than paper were used to deliver the daily news. During the early days of the First World War, so hungry were people for news that the *Edmonton Journal* sent a sign painter to the Dominion Cigar Store mid-day to paint the day's news headlines on the side of the building.

At one time, you could hear daily news downtown without turning on the radio. Pete Jamieson was Edmonton's unofficial town crier for more than 40 years, beginning in 1935 when the manager of the Dreamland Theatre asked the usher to stand outside with a sandwich board and a megaphone to drum up business. Jamieson took to the megaphone as well as he did to beer (a fixture at downtown pubs, he was fond of saying beer was a good throat lubricant), and was soon hiring himself out to a variety of Jasper Avenue merchants to sweep their sidewalks and announce their news along with the day's weather and headlines. Through the 1960s, he favoured a dapper Cary Grant-ish look, with a pencil-thin moustache and jaunty hats (he rotated more than 200). By the '70s Jamieson had grown a bushy white beard, had a wardrobe of flamboyant fashions, and favoured a megaphone plastered with Edmonton Eskimos stickers. In the late '70s, the waning days of Jamieson's daily strolls of downtown, the National Film Board produced a short documentary about him called *Never a Dull Moment*. Jamieson, who never married, spent the last years of his life in a nursing home and died in 1991 at the age of 83.

mad for movies

Edmonton is one of the most avid movie-going cities in Canada. The flick fans attending 126 Edmonton and area screens help give Alberta the highest per-capita movie attendance in the nation, according to Statistics Canada, and in 1999 the Silver City in West Edmonton Mall was Famous Players' top-grossing venue in Canada. There's enough range to suit every taste and budget: there's the stadium seating and curved screens of Cineplex Odeon's 16-screen **South Edmonton Common** complex *(1525 99 St., 436-8585)*, where ticket prices top out at $12. A short drive north, **Cinema City 12** *(3633 99 St., 463-5481)* is still the best deal in town, with $2 admission for a wide selection of second-run movies before 6 p.m., $2.50 for shows after 6 p.m., and $3 for midnight shows that are popular on the teen scene. There are also two local IMAX theatres, at the **Edmonton Space and Sciences Centre** *(1121 142 St., 451-3344)* and **Silver City** *(West Edmonton Mall, 444-2400)*. There's the **Paramount** *(10233 Jasper Ave., 428-1307)* for ear-splitting sound and big-screen impact, and numerous art-house and repertory screens for the black turtleneck set.

Edmonton Film Society

Housed in the Provincial Museum's auditorium, this group is dedicated to keeping the Hollywood of yesteryear alive. It presents regular screenings on Monday nights at 8 p.m., with four eight-film series a year. Each series is organized around particular themes (such as Warner Brothers in the 1940s), and each movie is kicked off by a short lecture. It also provides a video rental service for members.
12845 102 Ave., 453-9100

The Garneau

A 1940 jewel that still maintains its lustre, this south-side movie theatre was the first in Alberta to install a select number of double seats – a quaint innovation known as "two's company" seats – for moviegoing couples. The furniture that was used for years in the theatre's lobby were remainders from what was used for a Hotel Macdonald reception for King George VI and Queen Elizabeth in 1939. It is considered one of the

Beauty Queens

The immortal words inscribed at the Playboy Mansion are, "Through these doors walk the most beautiful women in the world." Well, a few have resided in Edmonton over the years, too. Where are these Edmonton-connected beauty queens now?

Miss Canada 1998
Juliana Thiessen married Logan Day, the son of the current Canadian Alliance party leader, at an Edmonton Presbyterian church in 1999. Then-Alberta treasurer Stockwell Day performed the ceremony himself. The publicity-hungry Day (that's Junior, not Senior) had publicly proposed to Thiessen in December 1998, while swarmed by media attention in the foyer of the House of Commons.

best examples of the early modernist style of architecture in Edmonton, and since a major renovation in 1998 has been playing first-run art-house and quirky independent films to packed houses once again. A boxy little "penthouse" on the roof once housed a private office for the manager, but today holds little more than a massive exhaust fan. One of the best deals yet, since the top ticket price is only eight bucks.
8712 109 St., 433-0728

Metro Cinema

Promoting film and video as an art form, this group shows a mixed bag of mostly contemporary independent, international, and Canadian cinema at the Milner Library. Screenings are Thursday through Sunday, with discounted admission for members (yearly membership is $7 and includes one film).
7 Sir Winston Churchill Squ., 425-9212.

The Princess

Built by early Edmonton businessman John McKernan in 1913, this grand dame has hosted vaudeville shows, "talkies," adult movies, repertory films, a pool hall, a shoe repair shop, a tailor, and even a ghost over the years. Defunct as a theatre from 1958-70, the old movie house was taken over by the Old Strathcona foundation in 1978 and became a successful repertory theatre for more than a decade. The Princess beat the big theatre chains to the punch by installing gigantic, plush seats back in 1987 (the old, red Princess seats are still collectors' items around town). The theatre, purchased by private owners in 1997, still uses real butter on its popcorn, but has changed its format to first-run art-house fare. A smaller screen in the basement has been dubbed **Princess II**.
10337 82 Ave., 433-0728

Drive-Ins

At one time during the 1970s, Edmonton was the drive-in capital of Canada with, at 10 screens, more than any other city. Given that it doesn't get dark until as late as 10 p.m. in the summer, and that it's too bloody cold to consider a drive-in during the winter, Edmonton

was a decidedly odd place for the format to flourish. The first was the Starlite, which opened in 1949 somewhere out in the wild west of the city (just east of the Mayfield Inn site). It was followed by the likes of the Skyvue and the Belmont (the first curved drive-in screen in the province) and the wide-screen Twin Drive-In in the north end. Today, there's not a single drive-in left in the Edmonton area — bad news for the current generation of horny teens.

brushes with greatness

Edmonton's lustre has never exactly matched Hollywood's on the entertainment map, but we've had our star-studded encounters. Here are just a few of these sexy, sordid, and sorry tales:

Shut Up and Shoot

Hockey star Wayne Gretzky failed to parlay his aptitude on the ice onto the small screen in the early 1980s, when he made a guest appearance on the soap opera *The Young and the Restless*. Obviously rigid with nervousness (or maybe just embarrassment) and nearly tongue-tied, the Great One played a small-time hood and barely managed to choke out his single line, "I'm Wayne, from the Edmonton operation."

Babe to Watch

TV's *Sheena* and former *Baywatch* babe Gena Lee Nolin, she of the blonde hair, bright-white smile, and big ... (no, not *that* former *Baywatch* babe, the *other* one) made a well-publicized appearance in Edmonton in February 1998 to help promote Safari's Bistro. The restaurant was owned by the family of Nolin's husband, Greg Fahlman, who grew up in Edmonton, met Nolin at a Las Vegas video software trade show in Las Vegas in 1991, and married her in her pre-*Baywatch* days in 1993. The restaurant quickly failed; no word on the marriage.

Many Alberta listeners know Holger Peterson as the host of the long-running weekly blues radio show *Natural Blues* on CKUA, but Peterson has made another lasting contribution to the local music scene with the record label he formed in 1976. **Stony Plain Recording** *(Box 861, Edmonton, 468-6423)* releases of locally recorded material by blues pianist Jay McShann, guitarist Duke Robillard, and vocalist Clarence "Big" Miller have helped put Edmonton on the roots music map. Talents as diverse as Long John Baldry, Steve Earle, Emmylou Harris, Celtic band Spirit of the West, New Orleans musical legend Professor Longhair, local favourites Junior Gone Wild, and country/folk singer Ian Tyson have recorded on the Stony Plain label, which is still going strong.

POLKA KINGS

If you've ever been to a prairie family reunion, wedding, or anniversary, you've heard *The Bird Dance*. And if you've heard *The Bird Dance*, chances are you heard the version done by legendary Edmonton dance band The Emeralds. Together for more than 30 years, the band has sold four million records and has toured all over the world, playing for dignitaries like Prince Andrew and former prime minister Brian Mulroney. Polka, waltz, swing, foxtrot – these guys play it all. Although local legend has it that The Emeralds (named for the May birthstone nearly all the members share) invented *The Bird Dance*, but in fact it's not so. The band's manager heard the novelty tune on a trip to France in 1982, and quickly had the boys back home record a version that caught on all over the world – now who will take responsibility for inventing this goofy dance?

The Bird Dance

1. Make a "chirping beak" motion with thumb and fingers.
2. Flap your elbows like "wings."
3. Shake your "tailfeathers" and clap your hands four times.
4. Link "wings" with your partner and "fly away."

Everything but the Kitchen Sink

A legend in his own mind, if nowhere else, Sam Kitchen was a sometime cowboy, mountain guide (he once led the Prince of Wales to the top of Signal Mountain), and movie stunt double who made his home in Edmonton for many years. When 20th Century Fox camped out in Wainwright to film *The Thundering Herd* in 1923, Kitchen helped herd thousands of buffalo for the cameras and was the star's stand-in for dangerous shots. He also assisted on *The Country Beyond* and the Marilyn Monroe Western *The River of No Return*, both filmed in Alberta. Kitchen lived in Edmonton from the 1950s until his death in the '70s.

Am I Canadian?

Actor Jeff Douglas was an unknown until he donned hoser duds and filmed his famous rant for Molson's popular "I am Canadian" commercial in 2000. Douglas struck such a chord of nationalism that his words were recited by no less than Heritage Minister Sheila Copps and were cheered when the commercial was played in movie theatres. Douglas was mobbed at a series of live appearances across the country, and predictably soon split for the greener pastures of the biz in California. However, he was supposed to redeem his hoser cred in April 2001 with a run at Edmonton's Citadel Theatre playing the Bard's Romeo. Alack and alas, it was not to be: Douglas pulled the plug on the role in mid-February, not wanting to interrupt the buzz he was generating in L.A.

Six Degrees of Sutherland

Everyone knows that Donald Sutherland and son Keifer are a one-two punch team of Hollywood B-actors, but

who knew they were descended from Western Canadian political royalty? Keifer's mother is Shirley Douglas, the Toronto-based actress daughter of Saskatchewan politician Tommy Douglas, widely regarded as the father of modern Canadian medicare for programs he put in place in 1958. Deeply concerned about Alberta's proposed Bill 11 in

2000 (legislation that many felt would open the door to two-tier, and eventually private, health care), Douglas asked her famous son to attend a huge public rally in front of Alberta's Legislature, where he gave a passionate keynote speech and received a standing ovation for comments like, "They have slowly bled it from us to service private interests and to eventually line their own pockets and they are not going to get away with it."

The Gig is Up

Any self-respecting survey of bizarre celebrity deaths includes an entry on actor Gig Young, whose last theatrical appearance was in Edmonton in 1978. Young, who was born Byron Barr in Minnesota in 1913, took his unusual stage name from a character he played in the 1942 film *The Gay Sisters*. He appeared in fluffy romantic fare like *Tunnel of Love* and *Teacher's Pet* with stars like Doris Day in the 1950s. After Young won an Oscar for Best Supporting Actor playing opposite Jane Fonda in the 1969 film *They Shoot Horses, Don't They?*, his career went downhill – to the extent that he found himself doing dinner theatre at Edmonton's Stage West in October 1978. The play Young starred in at Stage West was *Nobody Loves an Albatross*, and after its successful local run he even spoke of trying to take the production to Broadway.

Young, who had been recently diagnosed with skin cancer, was reportedly distraught with jealousy despite his marriage three weeks before to his fifth wife, a beautiful 31-year-old New York magazine editor named Kim Schmidt. On October 19, within a few days of returning to New York from Edmonton, the dead bodies of Young and Schmidt were found in their posh apartment across from Carnegie Hall in an apparent murder-suicide. Young appeared to have shot Schmidt once in the head with a .38-calibre revolver before turning the gun on himself.

PULITZER PRIDE

In 1938, two enterprising journalists pursued a local story that earned them the first-ever Pulitzer Prize to be granted outside the U.S. The previous year, the popular Social Credit government in Alberta had proposed legislation known as Bill Nine, a law that would have forced reporters to reveal their sources, forced newspapers to publish government-prepared news stories, and allowed government officials to halt publication of any news story deemed unfit. Although the bill was eventually defeated by Lieutenant Governor J.J. Bowlen (who was kicked out of Government House for his impertinence in the matter), *Edmonton Journal* managing director John Imrie and associate editor Balmer Watt had launched an early print campaign against the bill. The *Edmonton Journal* received a bronze plaque and a special citation in the journalism category of the 1938 Pulitzer Prize, "for its editorial leadership in defense of the freedom of the press in the Province of Alberta, Canada."

k.d. lang

In her early days – the days before lesbian chic, before the anti-meat campaign, before the inexplicably lower-case name – k.d. lang was just a gal named Kathy Dawn who wore crazy cowpunk getups and did a mean Patsy Cline. Born in Edmonton, she grew up in the small town of Consort and her first band was in fact called the Reclines, in homage to the country songbird. With her wild get-ups and high-intensity onstage antics, crazy wigs, and step-dancing, in the 1980s lang quickly became a local audience favourite and critics' darling: her band played a concert with the Edmonton Symphony Orchestra, and an Alberta Ballet production, *Lifted By Love*, was choreographed to her music. She has sold millions of records worldwide, won several Grammy Awards, acted in several independent films, and composed the soundtrack for *Even Cowgirls Get the Blues*. lang now lives in the U.S. (most recently, in California), although she maintains a home in rural Alberta. (You can take the girl out of Alberta....)

Richard Buckner

In an adulatory profile of indie folk singer Richard Buckner in *GQ* magazine, writer Sarah Vowell wonders, "So what's he doing in Canada?" The answer is that it's all about love, baby. Always a favourite at the annual Edmonton Folk Music Festival, Buckner met a local woman who captured his heart and is now his wife. Consequently, when Buckner's not on the road he spends time in Edmonton, often frequenting Mosaics vegetarian restaurant, a gathering spot for his local hangers-on. Buckner, who is originally from Northern California, has released four albums of sparse, esoterically beautiful songs (the most recent, *The Hill*, a musical interpretation of Edward Lee Masters' *Spoon River Anthology* poetry) that have won critical raves.

TPOH

The bespectacled, lanky-haired Moe Berg screaming the lyrics to the hit song *I'm An Adult Now* is the epitome of geek rock. The St. Albert native's smart, quirky lyrics earned his band The Pursuit of Happiness (known to fans by the acronym TPOH) the enviable tag of a "thinking man's rock band" from *Rolling Stone*. Songs like *She's So Young* and *Two Girls in One* have Berg's trademark catchy melodies and clever lyrics, but what TPOH may end up being remembered for in the annals of Canadian history is a 1995 novelty song called *Gretzky Rocks*, which features lines like: "When I lived in Edmonton/He made us a city of champions/With Jari and Semenko by his side/He filled our frigid city with pride." Although based in Toronto now, the band is still together and released *Sex & Food: The Best of the Pursuit of Happiness* in 2000. Berg is also an author whose first book of fiction, *The Green Room*, was published in November 2000.

SNFU

One of Canada's most famous punk bands got its start in Edmonton in 1981, when five Edmonton lads got together to play the kind of thrash music trickling across the Atlantic from the U.K. During the 1980s, a worn – and preferably soiled, perhaps with sweat shed from notorious front man Chi Pig – SNFU concert shirt was the best kind of Edmonton street cred money could buy. Fifteen years and eight albums later, the now Vancouver-based band is considered a seminal influence on almost every other punk-inspired Canadian band that came after. Anyone who's seen Bruce McDonald's 1996 mock-documentary *Hard Core Logo*, based on Michael Turner's novel about the reunion tour of a defunct punk band, has got to wonder about the similarities: outrageous lead singer (in the film, named Joe Dick), a road trip between Edmonton and Vancouver, tensions between lead singer and lead guitarist (original SNFU guitarist Brent Belke left the band in 1998), and it even starred Edmonton-raised Callum Keith Rennie ... go figure.

Secrets of the Theatres

Thistle Rink

For a few brief shining years, an ugly, Quonset-hut style round-roofed building on 102 Street north of Jasper Avenue was the largest covered building in Edmonton. Built in 1901, for a dozen years it was a multi-purpose venue for everything from rowdy hockey games to political rallies to theatrical performances. It hosted the inaugural ball when Alberta became a province in 1905, and the province's first Legislative Assembly was held there before moving to McKay Avenue School in 1906. All that history went up in flames in October 1913, when the building was destroyed in a spectacular fire. The 101st Regiment Edmonton Fusiliers, which used the rink as an armoury, inadvertently gave the old building a 21-gun salute when it burned down: more than 20,000 rounds of ammunition were discharged during the raging blaze.

Pantages Theatre

As part of a North American circuit that attracted top performers, Edmonton's Pantages Theatre on Jasper Avenue hosted major performers like Sarah Bernhardt, Buster Keaton, Stan Laurel, the Marx Brothers, Will Rogers, and Fred Astaire from the time of its opening in 1913. Vaudeville baby Mickey Rooney was once carried onstage at the Pantages as an infant by his father, comedian Joe Yule. After the death of vaudeville around 1930, the Pantages caught a second wind as a movie theatre renamed the Strand. It was from the Strand that charismatic grass-roots politician William "Bible Bill" Aberhart broadcast his weekly Sunday night sermons in the 1930s. Although it was declared a Provincial Historic Site in 1976, the Pantages/Strand building was torn down in 1979.

The Citadel

Today, the word Citadel is synonymous with one of the finest live theatre complexes in Canada. The theatre's name was quite literal in 1965 when a group of local theatre types, including actor and former Broadway producer Joseph Shoctor, moved into the old Salvation Army

Last Act

A sad incident marred the usual feel-good atmosphere of the 1998 International Street Performers Festival: on July 13, a performer collapsed during his act in front of 250 spectators, who thought it was part of his schtick and left him laying on the ground for several minutes before seeking medical help. The performer, 45-year-old Australian Wayne Condo, later died of a heart attack. During his popular comic act, Condo interacted with audience members, at one point seeming to sniff a man's armpit and keel over backwards. The audience member had already endured Condo's good-natured needling and pranks such as sticking a toilet plunger on the man's bald head; after Condo fell over, the man stuck the plunger on Condo's head in a comic attempt to "revive" him, and also draped a cloth over Condo's face. The rest of the audience watched and laughed, even shouting remarks and encouragement. Tragically, several children were among the spectators who saw Condo's attempted resuscitation by medical personnel and later learned of his death. The festival provided on-site bereavement counselling to stunned members of the audience. An outpouring of sympathy from Edmonton audiences went out to Condo's widow and two young children in Melbourne.

An Eye Opener

Bob Edwards was an old-time legendary newspaperman who made his reputation in Calgary in the early part of the 20th century with his *Eyeopener* newspaper, a muckraking scandal sheet that believed "it is a mistake to spoil a good story by sticking too closely to facts." Less well-known is the fact that Edwards spent most of the year of 1900 living and working in Strathcona (then a separate town from Edmonton), where he edited a newspaper called the *Alberta Sun*. A character in the Edmonton chapter of Edwards' life was Jim Halliday, a tailor who just happened to be Edwards' roommate above a south-side cigar store. Edwards once staged his friend's death by hanging a stuffed suit of clothes from their window – then recorded people's reactions for his newspaper.

Local legend has it that there was a well outside the roomies' lodgings that began to take on a decidedly dank cast in the summer of 1900 – so much so that local merchants and residents went fishing down the well to discover the source. When a woman's dead body was drawn out, the normally unshockable Edwards was said to be so upset at the sight that he drank his whiskey without water from that day on.

Right-Handed Writer

What started as a Christian conservative news magazine in the 1970s grew into one of the major contemporary voices of Western Canadian discontent, thanks to a rabble-rousing journalist named Ted Byfield. *St. John's Edmonton Report* magazine was originally published out of the St. John's boys' school Byfield helped found in Selkirk, Manitoba; over the years the renamed *Alberta Report* magazine groomed writers including playwright Frank Moher, *National Post* editor-in-chief Kenneth Whyte, and *Saturday Night* deputy editor Mark Stevenson. (Former *Globe and Mail* editor-in-chief William Thorsell also hails from Edmonton, but from more rarefied roots: he was an academic and administrator at the University of Alberta before rising through the editorial board ranks of the *Edmonton Journal*.)

Byfield's exacting journalistic standards (he himself had won a National Newspaper Award in the 1950s) were legendary, as was the self-taught journalist's distaste for j-school graduates. Byfield's magazine has demonstrated anti-abortion, anti-government, and anti-gay (the "Can Gays be Cured?" cover line is legendary) biases. However, it also predicted the eventual rise of the Reform Party (now the Canadian Alliance) and has been a barometer of contemporary Western conservative thought on issues like Quebec separatism. Although his son Link now runs things at *Report Magazine*, the septuagenarian's columns continue to regularly incite readers' ire.

Citadel *(10030 102 St.)*. After moving to its current digs on Churchill Square in 1976, the Citadel witnessed many explosive moments, acting and otherwise. The opening night audience of a 1987 production of a musical revue called *Jerry's Girls* was evacuated because of a false bomb scare; the real bomb was the show itself.
9828 101A Ave., 425-1820

The Rev

A decade after the hoity toity theatre types vacated the old Citadel, promoter Oliver Friedmann opened a music club there that has been on the cutting edge of the touring music scene in Edmonton since 1989. First known as the Bronx, and most recently as the Rev, the club has held early concerts by then-unknown artists like Nirvana, Green Day, and Big Sugar. Plagued in recent years by noise and nuisance complaints from its staid downtown neighbours, the Rev and its basement dance-club companion Lush were threatened with closure by the city in December 2000, but were saved by mediation that promised to appease nearby residents and businesses.
10030 102 St., 424-2745

City Media Club

The City Media Club died in 2000, along with the demise of the hard-drinking, ne'er-do-well journalist types that once populated establishments such as the earlier Edmonton Press Club, once located at 10203 97 Street. Located for years under the IGA store at 8910 99 Street (where Fiddler's Roost is today), Media Club performances were occasionally punctuated with the sounds of dropping cans or screeching grocery carts upstairs. Its hallmarks were top-name live bands (the likes of Tex-Mex band Los Lobos, and Canadian favourites Doug and the Slugs and Murray McLauchlan) and a stuffed blue marlin hanging on the wall. The club moved to the basement of the CKER Radio building *(6005 103 St.)* in 1994, but never regained its former popularity.

The Gem

Described in the late 1970s as a "bucket of blood" by a city alderman, the Gem was once a 500-seat Art Deco-style movie house and has also been a Chinese theatre, a soft-core porn house, a grungy music hall, and a disco. When it hosted travelling rock bands in the early '70s, the Gem was truly a diamond in the rough, with nearly 200 police investigations — including for robbery and murder — over four years. It still stands dilapidated on Jasper Avenue, the oldest theatre in the city (built in 1914), its interior in tatters, and its future uncertain.
9622 Jasper Ave.

CKUA Music Library

Photo: Charlene Rooke

If you've ever listened to eclectic CKUA radio programs like the *Celtic Show*, the *Old Disc Jockey*, and *Natural Blues* and wondered where the veritable cornucopia of musical treats comes from, the answer is from a 100,000+ item collection housing as many as 1.5 million different musical selections. The music spans five floors of CKUA's digs *(10526 Jasper Ave., 428-7595)*, where it moved in 1959. It's estimated to be among a handful of the best music collections in North America, priceless for its eclectic mix of classical, jazz, and pop music and novelties like 16" vinyl versions of wartime radio broadcasts sent to the troops overseas. The nearly 2,000 linear feet of LPs, 78s, and CDs is growing by leaps, as not only current releases but donated collections from listeners and estates roll in the doors. David Ward, the curator of the collection, marvels. Of the some 15,000 listener-donated items waiting to be catalogued, he says, "They pay to listen to us then they give us their records." A computer index has recently joined the old-fashioned card catalogue in helping keep track of the collection, which sadly doesn't include tapes of early on-air performances from future stars like Joni Mitchell, Robert Goulet, k.d. lang, and Jann Arden and visiting musical greats like Frank Zappa. "If we'd kept all the things we'd ever aired, we'd have a truly priceless collection," Ward says.

The Day the Music Lived

Crisis hit Edmonton-based Alberta radio station CKUA in 1997, when gross public financial mismanagement silenced the frequency for 36 days after 70 years on the air. As its call letters would indicate, CKUA started as an offshoot of the university in 1927, the first station of its kind in Canada to broadcast university extension programs across the province. (The first transmitter was on the south side of Pembina Hall.) Over the years it morphed into an alternative to commercial radio, with a unique combination of earnest talk and global music, retaining its public service as the province's emergency warning system – an important role it played in the 1987 Edmonton tornado disaster. The provincial government had cut the station loose in 1994, with nothing but three years of transition funding and an appointed, high-paid foundation board to guide it (unsuccessfully). Annual public funding drives since 1997 have created a structure the station calls "listener-supported radio," funded by donations, commercials, and corporate sponsorship. It's still the coolest little radio station in the West.

CULT CELEBRITIES

Only in Edmonton could a goofy, bespectacled naturalist who sings little nature ditties and waxes poetic about bugs, wildflowers, and other normally unsung treasures of nature become a star. He's John Acorn, better known by the title *Acorn the Nature Nut,* the name of his Discovery Channel series produced by Edmonton's Great North. Acorn is a bona fide biologist (with degrees in entomology and paleontology) who also strums a mean *I Could Be Your Tall Lungwort, Baby.* The show has developed such a cult following amongst kiddie and adult audiences alike that it's now shown in the U.S. (on PBS and cable channels) and as far away as the Middle East, the U.K., and Asia. Acorn, who began his career as a park interpreter at a northern Alberta provincial park in the late 1970s, has also authored nature books and hosted the bird watching series *Twits and Pishers.*

Other unlikely cult media celebs include longtime Shaw Cable yoga host Gerda Krebs; Klondike Eric (aka Eric Neville), a figure dear in many adults' hearts from their childhood years watching and visiting the kids' variety show *Popcorn Playhouse;* and former CKUA radio broadcaster Gaby Haas, "Canada's Mr. Polka," who for a time held three Guinness World Records for the longest-running radio program in the world, *Continental Musicale.*

Hollywood North

In typical Hollywood fashion, for purposes of storytelling we have taken liberties with the phrase "filmed in Edmonton" to include a broad geographic swath extending from Red Deer up to Fort McMurray, or thereabouts.

Angel Square (1990)

Charming children's Christmas flick set circa 1945 includes picturesque shots of the Old Strathcona Gazebo Park and features many local actors. Directed by Anne Wheeler; parts of her *Bye Bye Blues*, *Loyalties*, and other productions were also filmed in Edmonton.

Birds of Prey (1985)
Sentimental Reasons (1984)

These early films by director Jorge Montesi pre-date his successful career as a director of made-for-TV movies and series like *Highlander* and *NYPD Blue*, on which he also had a small recurring role (as Father Kankarides) in the early 1990s.

Blood Clan (1990)

Just your average movie about a simple prairie girl who resorts to cannibalism to get her way. Renowned Canadian actor Gordon Pinsent and British actor Robert Wisden co-star.

Hit Radio

By its very presence at the site of a crime, a local radio station may have inadvertently brought a police standoff to a tragic end in 1958. On an early August Sunday morning, a reclusive paranoid named James Alix was fighting his own personal war. Alix, clearly delusional, believed he was fighting the French Army and had dug trenches around his west-end home, a converted boxcar. He fired shots that struck a neighbour's car that morning, and when police arrived on the scene he had literally bunkered down for a battle. The police tried peaceful means first: they tried to flush Alix out of the trench with a fire hose, but in the process Alix shot the fire chief in the arm.

At that point, the mobile cruiser of a local radio station arrived on the scene and, sensing a scoop, began live broadcasts. After that, rubberneckers began to arrive at the Jasper Place-area home by the thousands (as many as 5,000, some reports say). The tense situation took on the atmosphere of a carnival as children frolicked and spectators lined the streets. Canisters of tear gas intended for the gunman blew back toward the police and crowds, posing even more of a problem.

Finally, a local councillor named Richard Butler volunteered to help defuse the situation, and revolver in hand crept through tall grass toward where Alix hunched in the trench. A quick volley of gunfire ended with Butler dead and Alix wounded in the arm; Alix was captured and charged with murder but was later declared insane and committed to the Oliver Mental Hospital. A coroner's inquiry reported that the "operations of the police were extremely hampered by the presence of thousands of sightseers due to radio broadcasts of transpiring events."

famous sons and daughters

Tommy Chong

The 1970s stoner movie king was born here in 1938 to Chinese and Scottish-Irish parents. His family later moved to the Calgary area where, ironically, one Cheech Marin had come from Los Angeles to study pottery with a local artist. The two didn't hook up as a comedy team until 1970 in Vancouver, at Chong's brother's nightclub, Shanghai Junk. They then took their act to L.A.'s Troubadour club, and the rest is hazy history.

Bobby Curtola

In the 1960s he was a teen idol who crooned his way to the top of the charts with songs like *Hand in Hand With You* and *Fortune Teller*. Since then, he's done everything from singing advertising jingles (for Coke and IGA supermarkets), playing lounges in Vegas, and starting his own businesses (manufacturing the ill-fated Sea Czar beverage, and now a chain of retro rock 'n' roll truck stops). Born in Thunder Bay, Curtola married an Edmonton woman in 1975 and for years the family made its home in the suburb of Spruce Grove.

Michael J. Fox

Born in Edmonton but raised in Burnaby, the diminutive actor is best known for his television roles in *Family Ties* and *Spin City*, and for his public battle with Parkinson's disease, which recently caused him to take a hiatus from acting.

Draw! (1984)

Charismatic senior actors Kirk Douglas and James Coburn graced local sets including Fort Edmonton Park during the filming of this traditional Western about an aging desperado and his aging ex-sheriff arch-nemesis.

The Edge (1997)

Anthony Hopkins won't soon forget his visit to Alberta: after filming an icy scene in Canmore he was hospitalized for hypothermia, and later had to have an operation in Calgary for back pain. Underwater scenes in which Hopkins struggles to free himself from a crashed airplane were filmed at the Kinsmen Sports Centre pool. Hopkins' talented co-stars in the film include a grizzly bear named Bart and a slightly less hairy Alec Baldwin.

The Song Spinner (1995)

Larger-than-life Broadway star Patti LuPone spent three weeks in Edmonton in 1995 filming a made-for-TV movie on the ITV sound stage, where a spooky medieval set was built to represent the film's Castle Shandrilan, the centre of a silent kingdom to which LuPone and a youngster struggle to return joyous sound.

Heart of the Sun **(1997)**

The Road to Saddle River **(1994)**

Solitaire **(1991)**

Local actor and director Francis Damberger has filmed parts of his acclaimed, Prairie-influenced films around Edmonton. *Solitaire* is a family Christmas reunion drama; *Saddle River* is an offbeat comedy about Western life; *Heart* tackles the dark history of the Alberta government's forced-sterilization program.

Hello Mary Lou: Prom Night II **(1987)**

This teen screamer works on the premise of a 1957 prom queen who met her fate coming back for revenge 30 years later. Distinguished actor Michael Ironside suffers along as the queen's former high-school sweetheart.

Isaac Littlefeathers **(1984)**

Running Brave **(1983)**

Both stories about Native athletes who encounters discrimination on their paths to success. Parts of the latter, starring heartthrob Robby Benson as American Olympian Billy Mills, were filmed at athletic facilities on the U of A campus. Original director Don Shebib took an "Alan Smithee" (i.e., refused to be credited as director) on this pic when Disney demanded sweetened-up, politically toned-down changes.

Robert Goulet

Born in Massachusetts to French-Canadian parents, Goulet moved to Edmonton at age 13, had his professional singing debut with the Edmonton Symphony Orchestra in Handel's *Messiah* at age 16, and made his radio debut on CKUA. The crooner's career has thrived for four decades in concerts, films, recordings, and Broadway appearances (including his famous role as Lancelot in the Julie Andrews production of *Camelot*), and his deep baritone is world famous.

Paul Gross

The hunky actor best known for his long-running role as an upstanding Mountie on television's *Due South* grew up in southeastern Alberta but came to Edmonton in the 1980s to pursue theatre at the University of Alberta. Originally an aspiring playwright, Gross' *The Deer and the Antelope Play* won the Clifford E. Lee National

Playwriting Award in 1983, and he went on to win numerous theatre awards for acting and writing in Toronto. Gross remains a local favourite: he occasionally makes appearances in support of the university's drama school and his recent musical appearance with David Keeley at the Winspear Centre was a hot ticket.

Jill and Jacqueline Hennessy

These dishy Edmonton-born twins are best known for playing dishy twins in the creepy Jeremy Irons thriller *Dead Ringers*. Jill also starred on *Law and Order* in the mid-1990s as Claire Kincaid.

Arthur Hiller

Born and raised in Edmonton, the former president of the Director's Guild of America and the Oscar-granting Academy of Motion Picture Arts and Sciences has directed more than 30 feature films, including *The Out-of-Towners* and the Golden Globe-winning *Love Story*, along with episodes of TV series like *Alfred Hitchcock Presents* and *Gunsmoke*. The former CKUA and CBC employee hung out in Edmonton with Leslie Nielsen and acted small roles at his parents' Yiddish theatre before striking it big in Hollywood.

Bruce McCulloch

Born in Edmonton, this famed *Kids in the Hall* performer and film director *(Dog Park, Superstar)* mainly grew up in Calgary but attended grades 11 and 12 at Edmonton's Scona High School.

Leslie Nielsen

The silver-haired comedian best known for his slapstick *Naked Gun* movies was born in Regina but was sent to be schooled in Edmonton after his family moved to Canada's north. He was the snooker champ of the Vic Comp graduating class of '42 and staged a homecoming in 1996, playing the serious role of American trial lawyer Clarence Darrow in the one-man show *Darrow* at the Citadel. Nielsen is also known for his early television roles on shows like *The Virginian*, *Hawaii Five-O*, and *S.W.A.T.*

Catherine Mary Stewart

Best known as nurse Kayla Brady on *Days of Our Lives* and for her cupcake role in *Weekend at Bernie's*, the starlet was born and raised in Edmonton and started out wanting to be a dancer, eventually going to London to pursue a hoofing career. (Who would have known she wasn't a classically trained

Silence of the North (1981)
Ordeal in the Arctic (1993)

Northern Alberta doubles as the tundra of the frozen north (gee, that's a stretch) in both these films. In the former, Ellen Burstyn and Tom Skerritt are homesteaders who struggle against the elements. In the latter, Richard Chamberlain, Melanie Mayron, and hometown girl Catherine Mary Stewart survive a tragic plane crash in the north.

Silent Cradle (1997)

Shortly after she cracked up and went wandering around Hollywood barefoot and with amnesia, Margot Kidder filmed a made-for-TV movie here about illegal trade in bootleg babies, co-starring Lorraine Bracco and John Heard.

Small Sacrifices (1989)

The city was abuzz when former *Charlie's Angel* Farrah Fawcett came to town with sweetheart Ryan O'Neal to film this made-for-TV melodrama about a woman who kills her children. The set was briefly frozen at the Charles Camsell Hospital when an actual code emergency came in and filming had to be halted. Farrah and Ryan filmed a bedroom scene in the south-side home of a delighted U of A employee, who got a free home interior paint job out of the gig.

Snow Day (2000)

Probably the biggest Hollywood production to hit Edmonton, thanks to production manager and hometown girl Grace Gilroy. Chevy Chase starred in this comedy about the hijinx that ensue when a school in upstate New York is closed because of a snow storm.

The War Bride (filmed in 2000; set for release in 2001)

This Canada-U.K. co-production stars Oscar-winning actress Brenda Fricker (*My Left Foot*) as the hostile mother-in-law of a newlywed British war bride; Canadian actress Molly Parker (*Kissed*) is her handicapped daughter. Look for Fort Edmonton Park in several scenes.

actor?) Her first movie part was in the locally-made ski comedy *Powder Head*, and after her movie career (flicks like *The Last Starfighter* and *Night of the Comet*) waned, she appeared in TV mini-series like *Hollywood Wives* and *Sins*.

Anne Wheeler

This pioneering Canadian director has been honoured with the Order of Canada for her diverse career producing, directing, and writing everything from National Film Board documentaries to commercial films (including *Bye Bye Blues* and *Angel Square*) to TV fare (*The Diviners* and episodes of *DaVinci's Inquest* and *Cold Squad*). Many of her projects have been filmed in Edmonton.

Nathan Fillion

When Steven Spielberg tapped Edmonton actor Nathan Fillion for the eponymous role in *Saving Private Ryan* (he was the first, incorrect, Private Ryan located by the Tom Hanks character), the actor put his soap opera days as Joey Buchanan on *One Life to Live* far behind him. Since then he's appeared in *Blast From the Past* and Wes Craven's *Dracula*. His first movie role was in the locally produced *Ordeal in the Arctic* in 1993.

Callum Keith Rennie

He's made a career out of playing slacker hotties in smart, edgy films like *Last Night*, *eXistenZ*, *Hard Core Logo*, and TV shows like *Twitch City*. Born in England but raised in Edmonton, Rennie started acting locally at the late age of 25. He is probably best known for his least-edgy role, playing Chicago detective sidekick to Paul Gross' straitlaced Mountie in the final season of *Due South*.

Nightlife

What's cooking in Edmonton at the midnight hour? We've got belt-buckle bars, titty bars, classy cocktail lounges, and pubs of all nationalities. And if you're one of those teetotallers who thinks Prohibition never should have ended, shake your moneymaker on local dance floors or check out live music, improv comedy, and late-night munchies, including those mysterious pickled eggs at the Strath….

Prohibition

While the prohibition of alcohol in Alberta (1916-23) didn't spawn the gangster and crime scene it did in the U.S., officials encountered a few enterprising bootleggers. One memorable incident involved a man travelling by train from St. Paul with a *lot* of excess luggage. His suitcases were filled with crocks of illicit moonshine, and only when one of them fell during a train change in Edmonton did the distinctive smell tip off police.

Secret Cubbyholes

Although it's practically the most acceptable form of social intercourse around today, "mixed drinking" between men and women was actually *prohibited* within Edmonton for many years (giving rise to the popularity of just-out-of-bounds watering holes like St. Albert's lost and lamented Bruin Inn). In the post-Second World War era, returned servicemen hosting young ladies at dancehalls and nightclubs like the Trocadero or Club Roosevelt got creative with Alberta's arcane liquor rules. A small cubbyhole or wooden box secreted under the table was just big enough for a bottle of spirits, which a crafty patron could sneak into the club, and sneak out of hiding whenever a drop was needed to liven up the evening.

cocktails for two (or more)

Edmonton's bar scene was distinctly pubby until a few years ago, when several more upscale cocktail lounges started cropping up. Here's the pick of the crop.

Back Room Vodka Bar

The choice seats are the sleek chocolate-brown booths at this sophisticated, mellow spot. Entertainment factor: the not-too-obtrusive spinning of several house DJs sometimes draws a small knot of dancers.
2nd floor, 10324 Whyte Ave., 436-4418

Devlin's

Behind the velvet drapes, cigarette-phobes will love the effective smoke-sucking system in this dim, intimate lounge. Cheapskates will adore the happy hour specials (most drinks and a selection of food around half price). Everyone else will fall for the unpredictable mix of music and those little TV screens embedded in the floor.
10507 82 Ave., 437-7489

Halo

The city's first New York-style dance club and lounge is a modern, sophisticated space downtown for the wannabe *Wallpaper** crowd.
10538 Jasper Ave., 423-4256

The Library

This venerable lounge has a great selection of scotches and comfortable club chairs in which to enjoy them. The quality of the eats, coming from a top-notch hotel kitchen, is far above the usual pub grub.
Hotel Macdonald, 10065 100 St., 424-5181

Lola's

A plush martini bar where out-of-drag queens, fag hags, and erotic art on the walls are not uncommon sights. Decent humidor, too.
8230 103 St., 439-4876

Late-Night Munchies

All dressed up and no place to go after the bars close? There's no need to resort to the shrink-wrapped horrors of convenience store mystery meats with these late-night eats around:

Boston Pizza

This Cliff Claven-endorsed pizza chain was founded as the Boston Pizza and Spaghetti House in Edmonton in 1963 by Gus Agioritis. The Whyte Avenue location stays open until 3 a.m. on Saturdays to satisfy that pizza-bread jones.
10854 82 Ave., 433-3151 and 18 other locations

Café on Whyte

Boasting 24-hour service in a Bread Garden-style environment — and nothing on the menu of baked goods and prepared entrées costing more than $6.99.
10159 82 Ave., 437-4858

Café Select

With its warm and elegant atmosphere, this slightly boho café makes a great post-theatre or -movie spot. The kitchen stays open until 2 a.m. every night.
10016 106 St., 423-0419

Funky Pickle Pizza Co.

Thick, cheesy pizza and daily special topping combos (like the Pig Kahuna, a variation of a Hawaiian), served by the piping-hot slice or by the pie. Lined up out the door on weekends.

10441 82 Ave., 433-3865

Humpty's

9555 82 Ave, 437-0727 and five other Edmonton locations

Keegan's

8709 109 St., 439-0370 and two other Edmonton locations

These two greasy spoons are the solution for 24-hour hunger. Nothing hits the spot like a big, messy plate of Keegan's poutine in the wee hours.

Mr. Tube Steak

This sleek cart is perpetually parked along Whyte Avenue after dark, and there's no late-night craving or heartache that a big, hot sausage won't satisfy. *Whyte Avenue around 105 St.*

Steel Wheels Rock & Roll Pizzeria

Conveniently located right across from the south-side Club Malibu (or The 'Bu to those in the know). Do you care what pizza tastes like at this time of night? You do not. It could be a disc of cardboard with sauce and cheese atop it, and you would wolf it down gratefully.

8430 103 St., 439-9978

Secret Watering Hole

What may be the best little watering hole in the West is hidden behind the timber faux-fort walls of **Molson House** *(10449 121 St.)*, the log structure adjacent to the Molson brewery. But it takes more than authentic ID to get into this joint: Molson House holds a private hospitality room where the brewery entertains clients and groups. The whole thing is done up in highly kitschy frontier decor (skins and heads on the walls, log-hewn everything) that gives a bit of a nod to the long history of the brewery (originally the Edmonton Malt and Brewing Company), which has been there since the wild and woolly days

of 1913. If you're ever invited, go – and take a cab so you can avail yourself of an hour or two of bottomless brew.

Whyte Avenue

Every couple of years, a controversy kicks up over the commercialization of Whyte Avenue. Just as regularly, upstanding (and, one suspects, teetotalling) citizens complain that too many bars now populate the Ave. Granted, Chapters, Starbucks, and 7-11 stores have moved in, but they haven't exactly crowded out the independents like Greenwood's Bookshoppe, the Block 1912 coffee shop, Hub Cigar, and Divine Decadence. Yes, there are more bars than you can shake a stick at on the blocks between 105 and 103 Streets (does anyone get the pseudo-English Elephant & Castle and Sherlock Holmes pubs hopelessly confused?), but nightlife is, in part, what has helped revitalize Whyte over the years. That said, it's not uncommon to see gangs of rowdies and the odd late-night scuffle – particularly around university mid- and end-of-term times.

During Historic Edmonton Week every summer, you can do walking tours of Old Strathcona through the Old Strathcona Foundation that cover historic buildings like the Strathcona and Commercial Hotels *(433-5866)*.

The Strath

You ain't been drinkin' in Edmonton until you've sat down to a table full of draft at the venerable **Strathcona Hotel** *(10302 82 Ave., 439-1992)*. As a holdover of an old liquor law that decreed beer could only be sold by the glass in beer parlours, draught (which you can also order by the pitcher) comes in tiny juice-size tumblers that necessitate the ordering of many, many glasses – most people order in fours. (Good thing they're less than a buck each.) While you're at it, chow down on a couple of pickled eggs from the big jar on the bar (if you dare) or challenge fellow barflies to peanut races. The mix of patrons – from Whyte Avenue hipsters to old-timers to college kids getting a taste of the elusive "real world" – is as eclectic as the mix of tunes on the jukebox.

The Strath started out respectably, hosting Strathcona's first public school in 1892 and the Westminster Ladies College during Prohibition. Not much has changed at the old wooden hotel over the years, although the boards that covered the tavern windows (another arcane Alberta liquor control law) for years have long been removed and a bank of noisy, flashing VLTs has been added in recent years. Things that never change: the carpet, the abruptness of the waitresses, and the size of the bouncers.

RAINBOW A GO-GO

Only a subtly glowing red "R" and a rainbow motif doormat announces the location of **The Roost** *(10345 104 St., 426-3150)* in a nondescript brick building downtown. Edmonton's pre-eminent gay nightclub opened in 1977, and was once named the "Best Gay Nightclub west of Toronto" by *FAB* magazine. It's a private club with a members and guests only admission policy – since the music and dancing here are among the best in the city,

straights clamour to get in, too.

Boots and Saddles *(10242 106 St., 423-5014)* and **Buddy's Pub** *(11725B Jasper Ave., 488-6636)* are the other main gay bars in town, and **Secrets Bar and Grill** *(10249 107 St., 990-1818)* is a lesbian hangout.

If only a good drag show will camp up your weekend, watch for performances by Guys in Disguise, the grand dames of the local scene. The Fly Boys are the latest pretenders to the crown, and you can also occasionally catch a local troupe of Village People impersonators.

Belt-Buckle Bars

Cook County Saloon

Please, a little respect: this rustic-looking saloon and stage was named the Country Club of the Year at the 2000 Canadian Country Music Awards (unsurprising, perhaps, since the awards were held in Edmonton). Country stars of the likes of Patricia Conroy have hit the boards for live performances at this 700-seat club, which packs 'em in with recorded music most weekends. Just a two-step and a jump from the Whyte Avenue scene.
8010 103 St., 432-2665

Longriders

Another urban cowboy hangout on the other side of town holds two-stepping lessons every Wednesday and hosts live bands every weekend.
11733 78 St., 479-7400

Cowboys

Highlights here are a Thursday ladies' night, a broad selection of live and DJ'd music (which definitely leans toward country), and a fierce mechanical bull.
10102 180 St., 481-8739

The undisputed king of Edmonton strip clubs is **Chez Pierre** *(10040 105 St., 423-2707)*, since 1971 the best place to snatch a peek and a meal (or is that the other way around?) in the downtown core. Flamboyant Belgian nightclub impresario Pierre Cochard (that's his rakish image looming large, painted on the side of the building) built his reputation on lunch specials that included corned-beef sandwiches and a 20-minute striptease, making for a quick and satisfying nooner.

It was the first bar in Edmonton to go topless and then bottomless, to feature male strippers, and to host the Miss Nude Edmonton competition. Busted over the years for contravening various liquor regulations more times than you can shake a pastie at, the club was occasionally without a liquor license, but usually packed as a result of the media controversy the busts (both kinds) generated.

Incredibly, for many years the undisputed star of the shows was Cochard's wife Darlene, who would strip at the club at noon and night, and mind the couple's children in between shows.

live music

Alternative

Nearly 1,000 bands (including an almost-famous Nirvana and Green Day and Canadian bands like Sloan) have passed through the doors since **The Bronx** was opened in 1989 by Oliver Friedmann, still the owner after all these years. In 1997, Friedmann sharpened the club's edge by renovating the joint, renaming it **The Rev**, and turning parts of the building and the basement into the dance clubs **Lush** and **Therapy** (10030, 10028, and 10030a 102 St., 424-2745). **New City Likwid Lounge** (10161 112 St., 413-4578) also hosts an eclectic mix of live bands on the weekends.

Blues

Got a serious case of the blues? Head to the Commercial Hotel (10329 82 Ave., 439-3981), where **Blues on Whyte** features top-notch local and touring acts nearly every night of the week. Down in Mill Woods, **The R&B Club** (9271 34 Ave., 490-5469) is a relatively new venue bringing in a variety of rockin' and swingin' bands Fridays and Saturdays.

Folk

Popular jam nights rule the roost at **Fiddler's Roost** (8906 99 St., 439-9788): Mondays it's a country jam, Tuesdays are for fiddlers, and Thursdays are open jams. **The Full Moon Folk Club** (Bonnie Doon Hall, 9240 93 Ave., 438-6410) is one of several Edmonton non-profit operations run by music-loving folk. The Full Moon's house band opens every evening, warming up the crowd for local and visiting acts. Mercifully smoke-free, the Full Moon serves a mean bowl of chili, too. The **Northern Lights Folk Club** hosts shows at the Queen Alexandra Community Hall (10425 University Ave., 439-1273), and the **Uptown Folk Club** at Queen Mary Hall (10844 117 St., 463-3957).

GOT TIX?

If you're unfussy about the evening's plans and want to sample the local arts scene, make a last-minute trip to **Tix on the Square** (3 Sir Winston Churchill Sq., 420-1767). Run by the

Edmonton Arts Council, it's an authorized Ticketmaster outlet, information centre, and clearinghouse for day-of and rush ticket sales. It's open from 9:30 a.m. to 6 p.m. every day, and tickets for musical, theatre, and cultural events are frequently available for same-day performances at up to 50 percent off the regular price. The Arts District location puts you within blocks of venues like the Winspear Centre, Citadel Theatre, Stanley Milner Library, and Edmonton Art Gallery, and a short LRT ride to the south-side scene. It also acts as a regular advance-ticket box office for major concerts and events and for local and out-of-town community arts groups. Tons of flyers, publications, and posters promote current and upcoming events, and there's an adjacent café in which to browse them. They also sell a selection of merchandise for community arts, culture, and festival groups.

GET SIDETRACKED

If you have but one shot to go out on the town in Edmonton, you simply can't go wrong at the Sidetrack any day or time of the week. The venerable **Sidetrack Café** *(10333 112 St., 421-1326)* — yes, there really is an antique train car in the back, and ask your server about the ghost — celebrated its 20th year in March 2001. While the cozy club is best known for the high-calibre live music acts it features, the kitchen has some chops of its own. The piled-high nachos are among the biggest and best in the city, and offerings like burgers and steaks are always solid (great breakfasts, and a lavish Sunday buffet, too). There are some serious grooves worn in the wooden dance floor, the work of acts ranging from Sarah McLachlan to Bo Diddley to k.d. lang. The music ranges in style from folk and blues to rock and pop and everything in between, with local acts sharing the spotlight with national and international ones. Weekends tend toward danceable music, and there's a comedy/variety show on Sundays.

Jazz

The volunteers of the Edmonton Jazz Society — the oldest jazz society in Canada — run the **Yardbird Suite** *(11 Tommy Banks Way, corner of 102 St. and 86 Ave., 432-0428)*. Since 1973 it has been the definitive place to see top Canadian and international jazz performers. Various levels of membership in the EJS get you sweet discounts on individual performances or on a full season of shows. Tuesday night jazz and blues jams were the norm for a while, but call ahead to be sure. Dinner, drinks, and some smooth jazz at one of the intimate tables at the street-level **Zenari's on 1st** *(10117 101 St., 425-6151)* make a perfect Friday night out. The best local acts and dishy comfort food pleasantly steam up the windows on a chilly evening. No cover, but a minimum charge is applied to orders. **Four Rooms Restaurant** in Edmonton Centre *(137 Edmonton Centre, 426-4767)* brings local jazz acts to this contemporary, elegant setting on weekends. **Tin Pan Alley** *(4804 Calgary Trail, 702-2060)* has the slogan "pasta by day, party by night." This restaurant and music club features jazzy acts weekly; check listings for details.

There's no better place to be on St. Patrick's Day than the **Irish Sports & Social Club** *(12546 126 St., 453-2249)*, which reportedly draws the most authentic pint in town. Gotta be Irish, though: members and guests only. A popular Whyte Avenue destination is **O'Byrne's Irish Pub** *(10616 82 Ave., 414-6766)*, owned by two actual Irishmen, the Byrne brothers Denis and Paul. A handsome interior (pressed-tin ceiling, dark woodwork) and the creation of several different spaces and rooms over two levels give the pub a homey, cozy feeling, and the food is surprisingly good pub grub (like an Irish breakfast of black pudding and soda bread, or

traditional Irish stew). There's a Celtic jam on Tuesday nights and an open mic night on Sundays. If you don't mind that pop culture pseudo-Irish feel to a pub, try offerings like downtown's **The Druid** *(11606 Jasper Ave., 454-9928)* or **Ceili's Irish Pub and Restaurant** *(10338 109 St., 426-5555)*.

For an authentic pub experience without all the Green Isle kitsch, head straight for the **Black Dog Freehouse** *(10425 82 Ave., 439-1082)*. This is the real deal: solid selections and service behind the bar, a wildly eclectic, slightly scruffy-looking Whyte Avenue crowd, and such a comfortable atmosphere that bar-stool imprint might just become permanent. Great rooftop patio in the summer; rec-room style softer digs in the basement. In the Castledowns area, the cozy neighbourhood **Crown and Anchor Pub** *(15277 Castledowns Rd., 472-7696)* has the requisite authentic British telephone booth and engraved brass bar plaques and pewter mugs for its regulars. Located in an old bank building, the pub's offices are now safely tucked in the vault, and the back room is football (i.e., soccer) heaven, with games on the telly and jerseys on the wall. Try a traditional ploughman's lunch or a steak and kidney pie.

Sporting Pursuits

If you're only happy when you're keeping score, get out of couch potato mode and check out these local facilities:

Northlands Spectrum

Once the most fashionable activity in town, a night at the track is still a fun night out. Edmonton boasts a century-old racing tradition and one of the finest facilities in the country. Renovated in 1995, Northlands now includes Colours restaurant and the Uplinks sports bar, Spinners casino, and simulcast racing and betting links with tracks all over the world.
115 Ave. and 73 St., 471-7379

Overtime Broiler and Tap Room

They've tried to disguise the fact that this is essentially a sports bar with posh decor that runs to teak and tile and an ambitious menu that offers pub-food standards and elegant entrées. But what gives away the true nature of *Older*time (local nickname for this aging cougar-bar) are the television sets flanking the room — dozens of them, including (reportedly) small screens above the men's room urinals — seemingly tuned to every point-scoring ritual on the planet.
10304 111 St., 423-1643

Playdium

Open until 2 a.m. on weekends, this games room isn't just kids' stuff. Soar over the Grand Canyon in a virtual glider, battle an opponent one-on-one in interactive games like Street Fighter or Combatica, or enjoy typical video arcade and sports bar offerings.
West Edmonton Mall, 444-7529

Red's

Designed to resemble a retro rec room, Red's is a huge, two-storey chamber of amusements, with a bar and restaurant, billiards and bowling, a game room with all the latest video and interactive amusements, and even a bandstand and dance floor that has hosted everything from live music to comedy and hypnosis shows.
West Edmonton Mall, 481-6420

Schank's Athletic Club

Schank's is a copy of its Calgary counterpart: a restaurant and bar with beer on tap, sports on the screen, and a host of video and sport (that is, if you consider NTN trivia, bowling, and mini golf to be true sports) amusements.
9927 178 St., 444-2125

shall we dance?

If you can't shake your moneymaker at one of these local dance hotspots, then give up — it's probably broken:

Tango and Salsa

The owner of **La Bohème** B&B and restaurant *(6427 112 Ave., 474-5693)*, Ernst Eder, is an aficionado of the classic Argentine tango that originated in Buenos Aires in the 1800s. He and partner Tamara not only conduct weekly classes ($10 per person), but host a Friday night *milonga*, or tango party (for both watchers and dancers) that gets cooking around 10 p.m. Or try **Mezza Luna** *(10238 104 St., 423-LUNA)*, which hosts free Latin dance lessons every Wednesday at 9 p.m. For a melange of *salsa, merengue,* and *cumbia* beats, visit **La Habana** *(10238 104 St., 424-5939)*, a family-run club that attracts dancers of all ages.

Retro

A disco ball graces the dance floor at the front of the long, narrow room that is **Suite 69** – a portent of the 1970s and '80s retro tunes that will shake you all night long on weekends. If you remember these tunes from the first go-around, you're probably a little too old to be hanging out here....
8232 103 St., 439-6969

Top-40

Barry T's Grand Central Station *(6111 104 St., 438-2582)* is an old warhorse on the nightclub "meet" market scene. Nightly drink specials and theme nights like ladies night (Wednesdays). Located in an old train station just off Whyte Avenue, a downstairs corner of **Iron Horse's** *(8101 103 St., 438-1907)* capacious restaurant and bar space becomes a dance floor on weekends (and opens onto a great patio in the summer).

Alternative and After Hours

Parliament *(10551 82 Ave., 434-5366)* earned its street cred as Rebar before changing names in 2000. Today they play a mix of house and techno music over two (usually packed) floors. Clubs like **Therapy** *(in the alley, 10028 102 St., 903-7666)*, **Evar After** *(10148 105 St.)*, and **Sublime** *(10147 104 St., 905-8024)* don't even open their doors until the hours when most of us are already sound asleep in bed (11 p.m. to 2 a.m.). Rave on.

bowling

Forget ordinary five- and 10-pin — the rage these days is glow-in-the-dark bowling for grown-up kids. Trip the light fantastic at these local lanes:

Bonnie Doon Bowling Lanes

Forty-eight lanes of five-pin bowling, including neon and bumper bowling.
Bonnie Doon Shopping Centre, 466-9047

Callingwood Lanes

Neon bowling, a playroom, and a licensed lounge makes these lanes suitable for kids of all ages.
#300, 6655 178 St., 444-2695

Edmonton Bowling Centre

Five-pin with computerized scoring, cosmic bowling with laser light show, and a billiards lounge.
3223 Parsons Rd., 463-2695

Comedy

Chimprov

Rapid Fire Theatre stays true to its name in this sometimes-inspired, sometimes-insipid improvised comedy night, every Saturday at 11 p.m. (except the last Saturday of the month — apparently the chimp is otherwise engaged that night).
Varscona Theatre, 10329 83 Ave., 448-0695

The Comedy Factory

From Thursday to Sunday, catch rising stars and the troupe of talented Comedy Factory Improv Players.
3414 Gateway Blvd. N., 469-4999

Die-Nasty

Edmonton's weekly live, improvised soap opera is still going strong in its 10th season. Luminaries like Joe Flaherty, Mike Myers, and Nathan Fillion have been known to drop in, and there's a marathon 53-hour improv production held one weekend every autumn. Addicts can get a Die-Nasty membership card ($25) that reduces the weekly $8 admission to $5.
Varscona Theatre, 10329 83 Ave., 448-0695

Theatresports

Invented by Keith Johnstone for a University of Calgary drama class in 1977, this kooky competition has always flourished on Alberta soil. Hey, if it's good enough for *Kids in the Hall* Bruce McCulloch and Mark McKinney, it's good enough for you. Let the games begin, every Friday night at 11, presented by Rapid Fire. *Varscona Theatre, 10329 83 Ave., 448-0695*

Yuk Yuk's Komedy Kabaret

The local chain-store purveyor of giggles and belly laughs has shows almost every night of the week (except Sunday and Monday). Tickets are available for shows only or a dinner-and-show package price. Watch for amateur nights to see truly reckless heckling in action. *Bourbon St., West Edmonton Mall, 481-9857*

Fraser Bowling Centre

Bumper bowling and Globowl; league play and casual games. *2603 151 Ave., 478-5955*

Fun House

More than bowling, there's billiards, arcade games, mini golf, and other family-oriented fun here. *9103 31 Ave., 450-2695*

Gateway Lanes and Recreation Centre

Three dozen automatic-scoring 10-pin lanes, virtual reality golf, laser tag, billiards, an arcade, and bumper bowling. *3414 Gateway Blvd. N., 435-1922*

Pins and Cues

Ten-pin with automatic scoring, bumper and cosmic bowling, arcade and billiards, and an in-house Pizza Hut. *Westmount Shopping Centre, 451-3000*

Notoriety

So you think Edmonton's a nice, normal place? Think again, because cults, ghosts, witches, UFOs, ancient burial grounds, murder mysteries, sex scandals, and extortion scams all flourish here. Not to mention the red-baiting, the red-light districts, and infamous local figures like Pocklington and the Ghermezians.

The Great Escape

When it opened in 1995, the $5.4 million Edmonton Institution for Women in the west end was lauded as a new-school women's prison, with less punishment and more rehabilitation. The complex, which resembles a low-rise townhouse or condo development, originally had just a two-metre chain-link fence separating the prison yard from the industrial lands of 184 Street. In 1996, seven women – a quarter of the prison's population – went over the fence, including three women housed in a special "high-security" unit who reportedly walked through an unlocked door: the first incidents of women ever escaping from maximum-security custody in Canada. Corrections Canada spent nearly half a million dollars to retrofit the prison with additional security; today, the 78-bed institution no longer houses maximum-security women inmates.

Nightmare Ride

The Mindbender roller coaster in West Edmonton Mall's Fantasyland turned into a nightmare ride on June 14, 1986 when the back car of the German-made coaster derailed, injuring 18 people and killing three. The coaster had last been inspected by provincial officials in December 1985 and found safe. However, it was rumoured that months before the fatal accident mall officials had begun using sandbags instead of live employees in test runs of the roller coaster after a near-derailment during a trial run in March 1985 with five staffers aboard. Families of the victims, who complained that they weren't even told about the accident until after mall officials had talked to the coaster manufacturer to determine liability, fought for years for compensation from the mall's insurers, with many getting only funeral expenses and $3,000 in wrongful death benefits from the province.

Mary, Mary, Quite Contrary

While people sometimes dream of running off to join the circus, apparently elephants yearn for the opposite. In 1926, 14 elephants from the Sells-Floro Circus bolted after a yappy little dog spooked them while they were being unloaded from a CPR train one Sunday afternoon. Eight were immediately captured, but six made a run for it, including a 4,000-pound mama named Mary who staved off capture the longest. Mary left destruction in her wake, knocking down a trainer who attempted to capture her, tossing a policeman over a fence, and charging straight through the Cushing Brothers' Lumber Company office. She was captured at five the next morning, when another elephant was brought to her hiding spot near 116 Sreet and 107 Avenue to trumpet and lure her out.

Witchy Women

Up until 1985, a small renegade community flourished in Edmonton's Riverdale area, largely without the attention (and entirely without the modern sewer-system hookups) of the rest of the city. Derisively referred to as Dogpatch (after the hick setting of the comic strip L'il Abner), the area had residents who would haul water from a communal well, shuffle back and forth to their primitive outhouses, ride motorcycles (the Warlords gang had a house there for a while), and cast spells. Yep, spells – as in witchcraft. A shack known as the Black House was apparently home to a witches' coven, a neo-pagan sect given to burning ceremonial fires, chanting, and scratching giant pentagrams into the ground. The group was variously known as the Dogpatch Gnostic Church or the Universal Gnostic Church. The Dogpatch neighbourhood's outlaw existence ended in 1986, when tons of excavated earth from the current Telus Convention Centre site were dumped on the unsightly settlement, which the city had evacuated the previous year.

STAY NINE?

At most colleges and universities a 4.0 is a perfect grade point average. But at the University of Alberta, that same 4.0 will get you a flunking grade. Since the 1960s, the university has used a nine-point (stanine) grading system, which is quite unusual among North American schools. Students complain they suffer because the system is not well understood or easily compared at other institutions. The original thinking behind the system was that it allowed raw marks, such as percentage scores on tests and assignments, to be compared with other students' performance and then given an appropriate stanine grade. The university is considering alternatives like the four-point system or letter grades used at other schools.

MORDECAI'S VERSION

Edmontonians' hatred of the late Mordecai Richler stems back at least to the 1980s (and even further, for those who aren't fans of his writing).

In September 1985 of that year Richler, under the auspices of a profile of local hockey hero Wayne Gretzky in a Sunday *New York Times* sports supplement, gratuitiously slammed the city. Among the epithets he flung at bewildered Edmontonians were "grim religoius zealots" and "intrepid streetwalkers"; the city itself was likened to "the boiler room of Canada" without a "first-class restaurant anywhere in town." Mayor Laurence Decore and prominent locals like publisher Mel Hurtig immediately hurled offensive volleys in response, and the *Edmonton Sun* went so far as to publish Richler's Montreal home number for its readers' convenience.

Hurtig, in a letter published in the *Edmonton Journal*, wondered whether Richler was just nursing hurt feelings. Could it be he was retaliating against Edmonton for the scorchingly bad reviews local critics gave to a musical stage production of his novel *The Apprenticeship of Duddy Kravitz* (yup, you heard right — a musical) the year before?

You'd think the University of Alberta would have learned its lesson. Although the university had previously granted honourary degrees to serving politicians like Alexander Rutherford and John Brownlee without any hubbub while they were still in office, the practice backfired in 1941. The university offered an honourary doctorate to then-premier William Aberhart (photo above), but by a narrow vote later retracted the offer. The embarrassing incident was widely viewed as a show of political bias, and prompted the resignation of the university's president. Lesson learned, right?

When in 1996 the university opted to offer an honourary degree to premier Ralph Klein (photo below), the decision seemed especially odd. Some charged that the offer of the honourary doctorate to Klein — a high-school dropout — was simply an attempt to curry political favour. And in light of nearly $200 million worth of funding cuts that the Klein government had made to post-secondary education, professors, students, and the public were understandably enraged. Students demanded that the premier "de-Klein" the degree, and threatened to pitch rotten eggs and boo him if he appeared at convocation to accept it. He turned the offer of the degree down, saying, "I didn't ask for this."

no guru, no method

These days, many people head to India to bliss out on yoga and meditation. Who knew that you could pursue "alternative" spiritual enlightenment with the notorious Edmonton guru of your choice?

Brother John

His followers regard him as the human embodiment of truth, love, and light. They follow him to meetings around the world to stare in adoration and ask questions about their faith. They give him money, and some even give him their daughters. He's John de Ruiter, a former Edmonton pastor who has developed a worldwide following of devotees, and the kind of guru who offers a "shopping" link on his personal website for handy purchase of his books and tapes. Originally a Lutheran preacher, de Ruiter started his own sect (with himself, not Jesus, as the central spiritual figure) in the 1980s. His new-age preaching attracted followers like the von Sass family, whose lovely daughters, Olympian Katrina and former model Benita, have both been linked to de Ruiter romantically – despite the fact that he was married with three children at the time. Former TV host Jeanne Parr and her son, actor Chris Noth, have also been named among prominent followers. De Ruiter's followers once gathered at the Akashik Books in Old Strathcona, but have since moved to their own digs. *13128 St. Albert Tr., 487-8781*

Swami O'Byrne

Photo: courtesy Osho International Foundation

Once an upstanding judge's son, Edmontonian Michael O'Byrne became the leader of a commune known for attracting rich North Americans for peace, meditation, and sometimes group sex. (Did someone say "cult"? Nope, not us.) Osho Commune International is a multi-million-dollar organization based in Pune, a city located southeast of Bombay. There are more than 500 Osho Centres all over the world, and devotees can spend thousands on the pilgrimage to their mecca. O'Byrne – who first became known by his Sanskrit name, Swami Anand Jayesh – was, until his own death in

The Rich

Are they really so different from you and me? Edmonton's millionaires and billionaires aren't showy, ostentatious types: old and quiet is usually the definition of big money in this town. Yet millionaires make up just over two percent of our civic population, according to 1995 Statistics Canada figures. Here are a few of the usual suspects:

Allard Family

Boston-trained surgeon Charles Allard was the founder of a business empire that included real estate, industrial, and sports holdings, and a chain of media outlets. His children, including Cam, Tony, Peter, and Chuck Allard and daughter Cathy Roozen, were seeded throughout the businesses including Western International Communications Ltd. and Cathton Holdings. The Allards were ranked 47th in the *Financial Post Magazine's* list of 50 richest Canadians in 1996, before WIC was purchased by Shaw Communications and CanWest Global in 1999.

Bill Comrie

Brick by brick — and one annoying television commercial after another — Brick Warehouse furniture magnate Bill Comrie has built his fortune. His no-money-down-no-interest-until brand of retail madness is spreading across the country, expanding the chain he started in Edmonton in the 1970s. *Canadian Business's* "Rich List" ranked the onetime B.C. Lions owner 96th in the country in 2000, with an estimated worth of $285 million.

Ghermezian Family

The sons of a Persian rug merchant, Nader, Eskander, Bahman, and Raphael Ghermezian built the world's biggest mall and hold an interest in the only competition, the sprawling Mall of America near Minneapolis. In the late 1970s, the family was the largest private landowner in Alberta; despite financial troubles over the refinancing of West Edmonton Mall in recent years, the family business empire seems to be going strong.

Hole Family

The family-run engineering and contracting company Lockerbie and Hole is now in its third generation of presidents, with J.D. Hole at the helm. Brothers Jim and Harry also run Frobisher Ventures, a venture capital company. Jim Hole was a onetime chair of the board of the Edmonton Oilers organization, after the team was purchased by a group of 37 investors in 1998.

1990, the succesor to the late, notorious Rajneesh. Rajneesh (photo on previous page) – later known as Osho – was the commune's founder, who was once charged with 35 felony counts in the U.S., lived in a white Italian marble house, and owned an immaculate Rolls Royce Silver Spur II. Known for its cushy "Club Meditation" lifestyle, the commune welcomes nearly 10,000 fee-paying visitors annually. O'Byrne's brother D'Arcy and fellow Edmontonian Eli Shtabsky are said to also be involved in the worldwide operation.

Professor Fails the Test

This country's murder laws seem to have slipped the mind of a University of Alberta law professor who murdered his wife in 1987. Maurice Sychuk was sentenced to life in prison for killing Claudia Sychuk after what was likely an alcohol-fuelled argument when they returned from a New Year's Eve party at the posh Petroleum Club. (Their son found her body.) Sychuk was later discovered by the RCMP in a rural area near Devon, apparently in the middle of a suicide attempt. After a decade in prison, he had the law on his side, though: the model prisoner was released on parole in January 1998 on the condition that he would seek psychological counselling and avoid drugs and alcohol. His release set off a furor in the Edmonton community, which wondered if the former professor had *really* learned his lesson.

Double Murder Mystery

Was it electrocution or was it murder? When two employees of a Sherwood Park plant were found dead on October 1, 1994, the RCMP initially declared them victims of a bizarre industrial accident. However, upon *slightly* more thorough investigation, a medical examiner discovered each man had been shot three times in the head, execution style. Plant manager Tim Orydzuk and his helper James Deiter met at the plant on a weekend morning and never returned; Orydzuk's wife Stephanie later became suspicious at her husband's absence and discovered the bodies there. A suspect, James Dix, was tried but found not guilty when his trial revealed a bungled undercover investigation that included the usual litany of wiretaps, unreliable informants, and borderline coercion. The case is still on the books as unsolved; the murderer has never been found, and the motives and circumstances surrounding the deaths are still a mystery.

Just Like Bill and Monica

A scandal rocked the Alberta premier's office in 1933 when the father of a young woman barely out of her teens sued Premier John Brownlee for seducing his daughter. (The suit was based on an obscure point of law that allowed a girl's father to recover damages in such a case.) Brownlee had met the young woman, Vivian MacMillan, in 1930 in her hometown of Edson when she was just 18. Smitten with her, he later offered her a job in Edmonton as a government clerk in the attorney-general's office. Regular lustful jaunts out to the country in his car apparently weren't enough for Brownlee; he soon convinced MacMillan to move out of her lodgings and installed her in his family home as a "helper" for his wife. (His romantic signal to MacMillan for a nighttime tryst: flushing the toilet.) A new boyfriend finally encouraged MacMillan to escape the liaison some months later, bringing the whole sordid matter to a messy end.

The father, Allan MacMillan, was awarded $5,000 and the young woman herself $10,000 in damages by a judge in 1934; Brownlee maintained his innocence but promptly stepped down as premier and dropped a counter-suit against his former paramour. Appeals tied the matter up in court for the next six years, but in the end, Vivian MacMillan was the victor. Brownlee not only ruined his own political career with his scandalous resignation but heralded the end of five years of rule by his party, the United Farmers of Alberta, which never recovered its former stature in the province. Brownlee passed away in 1961; MacMillan died in 1980.

Dave and Cliff Lede

From the humble origins of Bill Lede's Leduc construction company Ledcor Industries has risen a second-generation fibre-optic fortune: his sons Dave and Cliff created 360Networks, a high-tech company valued at more than $2 billion when it went public in April 2000. (Mind you, that was before the dot-com crash....) They made the *Forbes* 2000 billionaire list, were valued at $4.6 billion and seventh-richest in the nation by *Canadian Business* in 2000, and ranked 12th in Canada on the *National Post's* list of wealthy Canadians in 2001.

Sandy Mactaggart

The co-founder of Maclab Enterprises, a company that owns and manages residential properties, office buildings, and shopping centres, is said to own a collection of vintage Rolls Royces, an ancestral home in Scotland, a retreat in the Bahamas, and a yacht to go with it. He's also a former chancellor of the University of Alberta, a noted philanthropist, and has been appointed an officer of the Order of Canada.

Raymond Nelson

The founder of Nelson Lumber started a company that grew to become the leading manufacturer of prefabricated homes in the country, doing more than $85 million in business in 1998. Nelson's personal worth was once estimated at more than $50 million.

Bruce Saville

Since the 1980s, Saville has built a high-tech business (which originated from a long-distance billing system for Edmonton Telephones) with annual revenues estimated as high as $40 million. By ponying up $7 million, Saville became the lead player in a community consortium of investors that bought the Edmonton Oilers in 1998 – but he resigned as a team director in 2000 immediately following Glen Sather's departure from the Oilers.

Bob Stollery

The multi-millionaire former chair of PCL Constructors has been a major donor to the Edmonton Community Foundation and other local philanthropic causes, including the Stollery Children's Health Centre.

Instant Millionaires

The lucky numbers are 6/49 for locals like Cecil Underwood and Gary Kulak. Former vacuum cleaner salesman Underwood scored a $10 million lottery win in 1992 and became a boxing promoter and racehorse aficionado. A $5 million jackpot built the bank account of former construction worker Kulak in 1997 – and he was the fourth Edmontonian that year to score seven-figure winnings.

Sin City

In Edmonton's frontier days, brothels ran in a barely-tolerated fashion along Kinistino (now 96) Street. The total number of local prostitutes was estimated as high as 500 in 1914, when the population was less than 20,000 – shocking but possible, considering the large proportion of single men lured west by land and industry.

Organized brothels faded around the 1920s, but the prostitution problem endures. Following a rash of prostitution offences in residential neighbourhoods in the early 1990s, Edmonton police started a Prostitution Offender Program – popularly known as "john school." Men caught soliciting sex have their choice between the one-day seminar and a court date, and john school is the more discreet option. It costs about $400 a participant, which goes to support the activities of a local anti-prostitution group. Lectures on points of law, paternity suits, and STDs are meant to scare the bejesus out of the johns, who are re-arrested at a rate of less than one percent.

You're Ugly, Your Mother Says You're Ugly

What does some guy in Gainesville, Florida know about beauty? Nuthin', we say. A Gainesville urban planner recently named Edmonton's former Calgary Trail (now Gateway Boulevard) one of the 10 ugliest streets in North America. Jim Colleran spread his evil gospel via *www.platetizen.com*, a website for city planners, and had reportedly compiled the rankings based on votes from the site's members. To add insult to injury, he later told the *Edmonton Journal* the street was "auto-oriented hell" and "numbing and entirely hostile to anyone who isn't on wheels." In retaliation, the paper not only ran an article touting recent improvements to the north- and south-bound strips, but also printed Colleran's personal e-mail and invited irate readers to contact him.

Killer Twister

While Edmonton is no stranger to bad weather, seldom has it been as bad as a July 27, 1987 tornado that killed 27 people, injured hundreds of others, and caused millions of dollars in damages. The twister began as violent thunderstorms moved in from the southwest and formed a funnel cloud that touched down just south of Beaumont. It then moved north, ripping roofs off houses in Mill Woods and leaving wreckage in its path in the eastern industrial area, where 13 people were flattened inside buildings, and large machinery and industrial equipment flew around like toys. Nearly 500 homes were damaged in the Clareview residential district in the north of Edmonton, and 37 were completedly destroyed. The worst devastation happened at the Evergreen trailer park, where nearly a quarter of the homes were destroyed. Today, 27 trees are planted at the site in memory of the victims of "Black Friday."

The Hunt for Red Edmontonians

The Communist Party of Canada, formed in 1921, found many sympathizers in the Edmonton area. More than 1,000 took part in an Edmonton May Day parade in 1925, including many from the ranks of the disgruntled unemployed. As a result of this show of strength, military guard was increased around Edmonton's armouries and a list of suspected communists was compiled by police. Covert undercover agents (including one southern Alberta prostitute) were even used to ferret out red sympathizers. A Depression-era labour demonstration in Edmonton in June 1931 was ended by armed troops that were said to be quashing a communist uprising. A major hunger march was planned for December of that year, but fearing chaos, officials turned down the request for a parade permit. Nonetheless, 10,000 people came out in force to demonstrate peaceably in Market Square – and were attacked by mounted police with heavy wooden batons. Draconian measures? So high did red fever run at the time, some organizers spent months in prison for what now seem like relatively inconsequential demonstrations.

WOULD YOU LIKE FRIES WITH THAT?

A rapist who attacked a 10-year-old Edmonton girl was undone by his bizarre habit of sucking ketchup directly out of small fast-food packets. Perry Fairley abducted the child while she was riding her bike near the LRT tracks at 81 Street and 114 Avenue in 1987 and drove her to a rural area, where he violently sexually assaulted her for two hours. The traumatized child couldn't pick him out of a lineup, and despite his resemblance to a police composite sketch Fairley wasn't convicted until 1989. The clincher was his weird ketchup addiction, which irrevocably tied him to the crime and earned him the moniker the "Ketchup Rapist." He served nine years and four months in prison and upon his release moved to New Brunswick, where his reputation and colourful nickname preceded him and earned him a chilly Maritime welcome from local residents.

THE MAN WHO LOVED WOMEN

They called him "Bluebeard" Watson, and perhaps that was the feature that attracted women to James Watson like flies to flypaper. Watson married a total of 31 women in his lifetime — and confessed to murdering 14 of them when he was arrested in Los Angeles on April 20, 1920. He had lived in Edmonton from 1914 to 1919 in two downtown homes, and had offices at various times in the Macleod and Tegler Buildings.

In April 1998, Harry Hole — a prominent Edmonton businessman and a member of the well-known Hole's Greenhouses and Gardens clan — received a letter that demanded $2 million U.S. or threatened harm to Hole's grandchildren. The letter instructed him to place the money in a suitcase and leave it at a certain time under the old caboose in End of Steel Park at Saskatchewan Drive and 103 Street. Hole informed the police, who planned to trap the extortionist. At the appointed time of 2 a.m. on April 13, 1998, they watched the park, but nobody came to retrieve the suitcase of money. Police tried again the next night, and Donald Witwicky, a St. Albert acquaintance of the Hole family, was arrested after he stopped and inspected the suitcase. Witwicky insisted he had been an innocent passerby who merely noticed the suitcase and stopped to check it out; he was tried but found not guilty in 1999 after four months in custody.

Witwicky had a troubled history: he apparently suffered from depression after losing the use of one arm in an accident, and had become addicted to video lottery terminals. He had served on a St. Albert school board and worked for an Edmonton school board, but left both after being investigated for financial irregularities when large sums of money went missing. He later declared bankruptcy, lost his house, and spent time in a treatment program for gambling addiction. Witwicky declared his innocence in the whole Hole matter even after the not guilty verdict, when he told the media he considered the Holes his "friends" and said, "I believe that justice has been served."

Fear of Public Sidewalks

They claimed city sidewalks just weren't safe enough for the extended Ghermezian clan of West Edmonton Mall fame – brothers Eskander, Nader, Raphael, Bahman, and their families – that lives in three large houses on the upscale west-end Wellington Crescent. They claimed threats of terrorism, child abductions, and hostage-takings. (Public accusations of bribery and false dealings in refinancing West Edmonton Mall, and constant protests by animal rights activists against the captivity of dolphins and other wild creatures in the mall, add credence.) The Ghermezians had to seek zoning approval to build covered walkways linking the three monster houses, resulting in a housing complex so big and unattractive several area residents appealed to the city in 1995 to lower their taxes based on reduced property values. (The residents lost.)

Reading Pocklington's Mind

As if provoking violent labour disputes, being kidnapped in his own home, selling the best hockey player in the world, and generally becoming the most reviled man in Edmonton wasn't enough notoriety for Peter Pocklington, he also become entangled in a bizarre lawsuit with a Toronto psychic in the 1980s. Peter C. Newman once reported that Pocklington "believes implicitly in the power of the psychic realm" and "is convinced that he leaves his body on nocturnal flights." Also deeply suspicious, the businessman was referred to a Toronto psychic named Rita Ellen Burns in 1977. Burns would consider the names of companies that were prospective investments and give her impressions of their possible success. Although a verbal deal had apparently been struck for her commission (a steep 10 percent), Pocklington reportedly made millions from her advice but didn't follow through with his promise; she sought $7 million in a 1984 lawsuit, but Pocklington won and didn't end up paying her a cent.

Crazy Weather

The old adage "If you don't like the weather, wait five minutes" is particularly apropos in Edmonton. Here are some incidents of our weird and wonderful weather, culled from the *Canadian Weather Trivia Calendar* and other sources:

Cold Snap

A cold spell in 1969 lasted 26 days and recorded temperatures as low as -40°C. The *Edmonton Journal* later issued certificates to residents reading, "I lived through Edmonton's record cold spell."

Giant Hailstones

Softball-sized hail rained down south of the city for 13 minutes on July 6, 1975 – some hailstones as heavy as 250 grams, one of the heaviest ever recorded in Canada. Wicked hailstorms in July 1953 killed as many as 30,000 ducks and other birds.

Air Quality

The air we breathe has rarely been as bad as on December 28, 1991 when mild 3°C temperatures caused smog-like conditions that trapped pollutants in the air and brought the air quality index to a dismal 10.

Alberta has been called a hotbed of UFO activity, an image encouraged by UFO researchers such as John Musgrave, an Edmonton man who in the 1960s and 1970s was Canada's most famous UFO researcher. He did academic work – for which he even received Canada Council funding – comparing UFO abduction stories to other historical tales of abduction (by witches, fairies, or other supernatural beings), enforcing his belief that UFO myths were cultural, not specifically alien, in origin.

Some of the earliest reports of what are believed to be paranormal phenomena – like UFO sightings, crop circles, and cattle mutilations – came from central and northern Alberta. More recently, the UFO 2000 conference was held in St. Paul in northern Alberta (a town that has its own UFO landing pad, an Alberta UFO Study Group, and a 1-888-SEE-UFOS sightings hotline). Edmonton itself is home to both the Alberta UFO Study Group and the Society of Earthbound Extraterrestrials (a group which gives members a lapel pin, a bumper sticker, and membership benefits like a map of the wormhole alien transit system). The natural home for annual *Star Trek* and Spock celebrations is, of course, Vulcan, Alberta.

It's a case for *The X-Files*: circular formations appear etched into grassy fields from here to Timbuktu, defying scientific explanation. Some speculate these so-called crop circles are caused by aliens or UFO landings; cooler heads insist the phenomena are deliberately caused by troublemaking humans. The latter proved to be the case in August 1999, when several large crop circles – a 20-metre orb surrounded by four six-metre circles to the north, south, east, and west – were discovered on the University of Alberta farm just southwest of campus. The tip-off that they were fake: the wheat stalks in the path of the circles were cut shorter than the rest of the field. (*Real* crop circles are said to be made up of patterns of bent, not broken, stalks.) Perhaps the prankster was just an entrepreneur at heart: in areas of England such as around Stonehenge, the occurrence of the spooky circles is so common they've become a revenue-generating tourist attraction.

Crime Wave

Cold weather caused a chilling crime wave in December 1995, when a rash of stolen cars plagued the city as motorists frequently left them running, unlocked, to warm up.

Early Snowfall

Snow ruined the indian summer of 1934 when 22.1 centimetres fell on September 23. The earliest ever recorded (since 1884) was in 1992, when the white stuff fell on August 21.

How Low Can You Go?

Lowest temperature ever was on January 19, 1886 when the mercury dropped to -49.4°C (a record that was nearly tied in the winter of 1993).

Are We Warm Yet?

The hottest summer ever recorded was in 1998, when the average mean temperature (May – August) was 19.3°C.

Ancient Burial Ground

In June 2000, a handful of First Nations members stood around a grassy patch in Edmonton's river valley burning sage and staking their claim in a century-long dispute about an old burial ground. Across the street from where the Epcor power plant sits today is the site where around 200 early Metis and European settlers are believed to be buried, near the old location of Fort Augustus (later moved and named Fort Edmonton). The graveyard is the old Hudson's Bay Company cemetery, used from 1800 to 1886. More than 30 skeletons have been uncovered over the years, usually by workmen or equipment digging in the area: five bodies were uncovered in 1943, four more in 1966, seven more by university students on a dig in 1967, evidence of two more in 1976, and so on. Despite the persuasive evidence that the burial site should be declared hallowed ground, Epcor has been pushing to tear down an existing plant and build a massive new one nearby. Native leaders buried a spear and erected crosses on the site, sacred symbols that are still keeping development at bay.

Ghost Stories

Versions of many of these spooky tales can be found in Barbara Smith's *Ghost Stories of Alberta* and *More Ghost Stories of Alberta*.

STAYING FOR DETENTION

The 86-year-old **Westmount Junior High School** (1125 131 St.) is said to be plagued by phantom footsteps and haunted hallways (and the gargoyles on the school's exterior do nothing to dispel its goth image). Two theories hold sway: one says that an early teacher, Felicia Graham, went missing after an outbreak of Spanish flu that saw the school closed for a month. Although her family offered a reward, she was never seen again and is said to walk the halls where she once taught. Another spirit-at-large could be a former student named Harold, who was accidentally locked in the school's tower one weekend and jumped to his death while trying to escape.

Klondike Kates

One of the icons of Edmonton's annual Klondike Days celebration, Klondike Kate, is actually a composite character. There was the first Kate, a pioneering Klondike woman from the gold rush days named Kate Ryan who bushwhacked her way to the Klondike gold fields and later settled in Vancouver with her golden fortune. She is buried in the Ocean View Burial Park and Mausoleum in Burnaby.

The second Kate was a Klondike showgirl, a young woman named Kathleen Eloisa Rockwell, who travelled to the Yukon with a musical theatre company and built a reputation with a "flame dance" she used to do ensconced in metres of red sequins and chiffon. Along with the Klondike Kate moniker, miners nicknamed her "the flame of the Yukon," and she travelled the world and made her fortune as a showgirl based on her fiery entertainment. In 1902, she fell in love with theatre magnate Alexander Pantages, who pledged his devotion but stole all her money and married another woman. This feisty Kate moved to Oregon, where she lived quietly until her death in 1957.

CLASS CLOWN

Another schoolhouse that rocks with paranormal happenings is the **McKay Avenue School** (*10425 99 Ave.*), now the Edmonton Public Schools Museum and Archives. Staff have reported chairs knocked over and pictures removed from walls, heat turned on and off, drawers opened and closed, doors locked and unlocked, and security system false alarms. Curious staff reportedly onco conductod a Ouija board investigation, and were told by a ghost named Peter that several spirits haunt the school. Peter himself is said to be a labourer who fell from the roof during construction of the school.

Bank Robbery Gone Bad

A clean getaway turned messy when three men who had just robbed a bank holed up in an apartment building in 1975. Reporting to the scene of a robbery at the Bank of Nova Scotia at 9512 163 Street, police were pointed to a nearby apartment building by witnesses on the scene. Two officers had cornered the men in the bathroom of an apartment unit when one of the criminals began firing, hitting officer Dick Bevan, breaking his arm and collapsing one lung. While caught in a tense nine-hour seige with police, one robber fired shots at a police car parked on the building's lawn, striking an officer in the chest. Constable Jerry Phelan survived with only bruises: the bullet hit a copy of the City Traffic Bylaw booket that was in his pocket. (It stopped at page 61 of the 80-page booklet.)

Gunman and robber Samuel Woods was captured and convicted, but within weeks escaped from the Fort Saskatchewan jail – causing temporary consternation for officer Bevan, who was thought to be a possible target for the escaped criminal.

Photo: Bruce Edwards/Edmonton Journal

You might say that Con Boland has had some trouble with women. Maybe its his rumoured predilection for kinky sex, but the prominent Edmonton photographer has been scorched, jabbed, and stabbed in the name of love. It all started back in the early 1990s, when Boland lived with a beautiful woman named Marilyn Tan (photo above). The relationship turned sour, and Boland later alleged that on a last-fling holiday to Palm Beach in June 1992 Tan waited until he was passed out after a vigourous S&M session and injected him with HIV. He later tested positive for the virus. In 1993, Boland answered his front door only to have sulphuric acid thrown at him by an unknown assailant, scarring his chest; he alleged that Tan was responsible for ordering the attack.

Marilyn Tan and three of her associates were later charged with a lengthy litany of offences (like aggravated assault, conspiracy to murder, uttering a death threat, administering a noxious substance with the intention of endangering a life, and conspiring to administer a noxious substance). Eventually they were acquitted of all charges, except for a death threat Tan had made against Boland's new girlfriend in 1992, for which she served 48 days in the Fort Saskatchewan Correctional Centre, where all those bars and chains no doubt only sharpened her dominatrix instincts.

Boland took another beating in 1997, when a woman named June Vivian stabbed him when she learned, after a night of intimacy, that he was HIV-positive. Boland required six stiches for a particularly nasty cut to his head, and also had cuts to his hands, back, and shoulders. Vivian was released on a six-month conditional sentence, although the judge, Percy Marshall, commented that he couldn't believe the woman didn't know about Boland's condition, since "virtually everyone in Alberta" had heard media reports about the notorious 1992 attack that Boland claims infected him with the virus.

KNOCK, KNOCK, KNOCKING ON THE PROJECTIONIST'S DOOR

The old floorboards of the **Princess Theatre** (10337 82 Ave.) sometimes resound with harmless but ghostly footsteps or knocks. Staff alone in the building late at night have reported footfalls on the third storey and knocking on the lobby walls and the projectionist's booth. Speculation is that the presence could be a holdover from the era when the Princess's upper floor was used as a rooming house.

WHOA, NELLIE

In the deep depths of the 86-year-old foundation of the **Macdonald Hotel** (10065 100 St.) lurks a ghost of the equine kind. When the ground was excavated in 1915, one mighty workhorse apparently died on the job and was buried in the rubble. After the grand hotel rose on the site, staff working in the utility area of the basement sometimes reported hearing the clopping of horses' hooves. Another theory proposes that an early laundry worker who died on the job is the real force at work.

For the last few years, the Edmonton Folk Music Festival program has consistently packed at least one surprise. The festival's house band, which frequently accompanies visiting musicians, has had a steady lineup for the last several years, with one unexpected lineup change. Drummer Bohdan Hluszko – who had played with the likes of Etta James, Jann Arden, and Sharon, Lois & Bram – "gave up his identity" in September 1997 and became a woman named Michelle Josef. The solid drumming is the same; the look is quite different. By way of explanation, the Folk Fest program states, "Occasionally, the Great Spirit grants an individual the opportunity to reincarnate without actually dying. Such is the case with Michelle Josef."

GHOST OF PREMIER PAST

Two buildings in the **Legislature** *(108 St. and 100 Ave.)* complex are host to haunted happenings that are attributed to Sir Frederick Haultain, the first premier of the Northwest Territories, prior to the naming and existence of the provinces of Alberta and Saskatchewan. Many thought that when those provinces joined Confederation in 1905 Haultain should have been made premier of one of them, but he wasn't. Perhaps it is a discontented Haultain who wanders the halls of the Legislature and the nearby Haultain Building, leaving footprint impressions in the carpet, conducting conversations in the offices, and prowling the hallways.

Keep It Clean

The opening of the **Down Under** gay bathhouse *(12224 Jasper Ave., 482-7960)* in 1998 brought back memories in Edmonton's gay community of a raid two decades ago that shut down a previous bathhouse and saw dozens of gay men arrested. For the first few months of 1981, Edmonton police investigated the Pisces Health Spa, finally raiding it on May 30 and charging its owners with running a common bawdy house. Police reported finding almost no health or exercise equipment on site, but plenty of sexual aids and 40 small cubicles, a "dark room," and a group "party room" that were apparently used for carnal pursuits.

Charged just for being found on the premises, only five men pleaded guilty and were fined $250, while 51 more stood for trial. (One of its owners, a physician and sometime university lecturer who kept a nearby medical practice, was called in the press the "Oscar Wilde of the 1980s.") The gay community charged that it was being unfairly harrassed, but the Pisces raid was seemingly part of a broader crackdown: it was the sixth bawdy house conviction that year in Edmonton.

Edmonton is not exactly the wild west, and the death of a police officer resonates powerfully in this largely peaceful community. Constable Ezio Faraone of the Edmonton Police Service was killed by two fleeing bank robbers on June 25, 1990. Apparently high on drugs, the pair fled the scene of the crime with Albert Foulston at the wheel and Jerry Crews hiding in the back seat. When Faraone stopped the car in an alley, Crews fired his shotgun, hitting Faraone in the heart and killing him. Crews and Foulston were convicted of first-degree murder and manslaughter, respectively. Faraone's needless death caused such an outpouring of grief in the community that more than $300,000 for a memorial was raised in a fundraising campaign. The brave officer's legacy is a small green space, **Ezio Faraone Park**, at the northwest entrance to the High Level Bridge, featuring a bronze statue by sculptor Danek Mozdzenski of the 33-year-old uniformed officer with a small child.

In 1998 another one of Edmonton's finest went down: a police dog named Caesar was killed in a bizarre schoolyard shooting. Reports of a distraught man firing a shotgun in the air as he crossed a popular school sporting field brought police to the scene. The suicidal man refused police requests to drop his gun and fired the shots that killed the canine before police returned fire, hitting him in the leg and torso. The Edmonton Police Service received such an outpouring of grief from dog lovers around the world that the volume of calls flooded their phone lines and the e-mails crashed its computer system.

HAVE GHOST, WILL TRAVEL

Its donors may have hoped that moving the so-called **Firkins House** from 7871 Saskatchewan Drive to Fort Edmonton Park would roust the spirit that had been known to sing, sit down to breakfast, and jump on the backs of the home's residents — but it didn't. The spectre, said to be a young boy who died while living there, followed the house across the city and caused some consternation for the Armed Forces crew who moved and restored it in Fort Edmonton. One worker had dirt and debris dumped on his head while alone in the house. A securely fastened four-pane window fell two storeys, but didn't break. Tools that were left in one spot were mysteriously found in another. A heavy iron radiator fell over for no apparent reason. Far from deterring visitors, the ghost stories seem to have made the house a popular park feature.

Political Danger

Not only has Alberta's Legislature borne witness to sniping and attacks of the verbal kind over the years, it has also been the scene for the crimes of at least two gunmen. A murder-suicide on October 27, 1977 was the apparent outcome of a love affair gone wrong. A man carrying a blue plastic suit bag containing a rifle entered the office of then-government services minister Horst Schmid at 8:30 a.m. Although Schmid wasn't in the office, one of his support staff, a young woman named Victoria Breitkruz, was already working. Breitkruz had previously dated the gun-toting man, one Guenther Hummel, but had left him the previous January. He fired a stray shot to announce his presence, took the young woman hostage, and within an hour had killed her then shot himself in the heart. Sadly, it appears the tragedy could have been prevented: security officers recalled that Hummel had been seen prowling around the Legislature twice in the weeks before the crime. And on the day before the fatal incident, he apparently told his employer at a local bakery that he planned to kill his former girlfriend.

More bullets flew in 1988, when, again in the early morning, Robert Crawford, armed with a rifle, eluded security. He entered the Legislature complex through the underground walkway system after firing some random shots on the Legislature grounds. One brave cabinet minister, who saw the gun-toting man climbing the stairs up from the pedway, later remarked, "I immediately went to my office probably faster than I ever have in my life." Crawford took the east elevator up to the second floor, and when its brass door opened, started shooting. Bullets whizzed by, one hitting a wooden moulding and deflecting into a security officer's thigh. Officers fired back, shooting and disabling the gunman. (You can still see the repaired bullet holes in a door frame, and dents in the elevator door and frame from police bullets.) It was later discovered that the Sylvan Lake man was apparently depressed because of a recent divorce and had left a suicide note on the Legislature grounds saying he wanted to shoot some police, listing his next of kin, and stating that he wanted to refuse any life-saving medical treatment. Crawford was institutionalized for psychological assessment after the incident.

HAUNTED MELODIES

The former janitor at **CKUA Radio** (4th floor, 10526 Jasper Ave.) just doesn't want to leave – he has reportedly been haunting the building since his death in the 1970s. The man, known as Sam to his colleagues, had a colourful past: rumoured to have been a notorious Toronto gangster in the 1940s, the bizarre story goes that he had made a threat on the life of former Alberta premier Ernest Manning and was lobotomized as a result. It is this quiet, docile Sam who sings in a clear tenor, occasionally appears as an apparition, and watches over some employees, even opening doors and so on to help them.

eureka moments

The world's eye has often turned to Edmonton when some medical or research breakthrough has caught the attention of the media. Here are just a few of the bizarre discoveries.

The Iceman Cometh

In 1984 the research team of University of Alberta physical and forensic anthropologist Owen Beattie announced that it had found the remains of two members of the ill-fated Franklin Expedition on Beechey Island in Canada's Arctic. The bodies of John Torrington and John Hartnell had been nearly perfectly preserved for 138 years in the ice and cold, and helped unlock some of the mysteries surrounding John Franklin's final, doomed expedition to find the Northwest Passage. The images of the eerily intact corpses were beamed around the world.

Insulin Shock

Photo: courtesy University of Alberta Archives

One largely unsung discovery is U of A biochemist John Collip's: he refined the technique of insulin extraction so that it could be used in treating patients with diabetes. Two of Collip's research collaborators, Banting and Macleod, later got the Nobel Prize for the discovery; Collip got the shaft. (In accepting, Banting "shared" his award with his colleague Best; Macleod "shared" his with Collip.) Collip had been invited to Toronto in the fall of 1921 to work on the insulin study team, and his contributions are said to have greatly advanced the insulin refining process. However, when the process was eventually patented it was in the name of the three other researchers, and the patent was given to the University of Toronto. Collip returned to the University of Alberta, and had a distinguished medical research career there and at McGill – but never received the glory he deserved for his work on the insulin discovery.

THEY'RE FIRED

Two old fire stations since converted into ambulance stations still bear traces of their former inhabitants. At the old Number Five station in the east end, footsteps are heard, vehicle doors are opened and slammed in the bays, and once all the station phones rang although all lines were open. The spirit is said to be a firefighter who is reported to have died either while sleeping or in the course of fighting a fire. Across town at the old station Number Four in the west end, another former firefighter raises and lowers the garage doors, opens and closes doors in the station, occasionally speaks, and helps keep the night watch. Again, a firefighter who reportedly died in the former fire hall is the culprit; in a unique twist, one rumour has him dying while sitting on the toilet – a crappy way to die.

Super Serpent

Photo: Lotus Studio

DEFENDING SACRED GROUND

At the **College Plaza** apartment tower *(8210 111 St.)*, the spirit of an ancient Native chief once confronted a University of Alberta professor. The apparition, dressed as an Indian brave in full regalia, told the prof to scram from the site, where he said Native elders were buried.

Researcher Michael Caldwell discovered the evolutionary "missing link": a metre-long serpent with small hind legs that links today's slithery beasts to massive sea creatures that existed in the dinosaur age. The U of A researcher co-authored a paper in the April 1997 issue of the prestigious journal *Nature* that shed new light on a 97-million-year-old fossil that had been sitting in a Jerusalem museum for 20 years, previously thought to be a reptile. Caldwell's discovery garnered much attention from scientists and theologians alike, who had previously believed that snakes slithered – not walked – the earth, inspiring terror and tempting fair maidens.

Patriotic Fever

We're all used to seeing the red maple leaf flying high on flagpoles across the country, but few realize the design comes from a former Edmontonian. George Stanley left Edmonton after his graduation from the U of A in 1929 to attend Oxford University as a Rhodes Scholar. Later, the historian returned to Canada and found an academic position in New Brunswick, where he lived most of the rest of his life, achieving the rank of that province's lieutenant governor. In the 1960s, when a parliamentary committee struggled to find a design for the proposed new national flag, it consulted Stanley, one of the country's most renowned historians. He provided a quick sketch of a stylized maple leaf and two vertical bars of red that became the basis for the flag that was first flown in 1965 and still flies today.

Wintertime, and the living is *hard* – that sums up eight months of the year in Edmonton. Make life a little easier on yourself with this insider guide to the city's must-see hangouts, must-have products, must-eat goodies, and must-get services.

Strike It Rich

Flip over some of those souvenir matchbooks you've idly picked up on your travels to a Vegas casino or the Cannes Film Festival – chances are a few of them will read Cougar Match Corp. of Nisku (just south of Edmonton), the only match manufacturer in Canada. The Wolski family runs one of only a handful of plants in the world making paper matchbooks, and has supplied them to luxury hotels like the Sahara and to producers of films like *The Wedding Singer* (a quarter of the company's business is in the U.S.) at the rate of about 100 million books of matches a year.

Alley Kat Brewing Co.

Neil Herbst started this award-winning micro-brewery in 1995, and has won a handful of gold and silver medals at the World Brewing Championships in Chicago for varieties like Aprikat, Alley Kat Amber, Full Moon Ale, Scona Gold, Olde Deuteronomy, Redneck, and the Oktoberfest-style lager Ein Prosit. Tours of the brewery are available on Thursdays and Fridays from 2-4 p.m. A staffer's concoction of Alley Kat Amber-infused barbecue sauce (available on the company website) won first prize in a *City Palate* recipe contest.
9929 60 Ave., 436-8922

For years, a shack near the University of Alberta campus called the Tuck Shop served the city's favourite cinnamon buns. After the Tuck Shop was torn down in 1970 the beloved buns were resurrected on campus. Most recently, they've been made at the CAB (Central Academic Building) cafeteria, where they disappear faster than a student's tuition money. Make your own, according to this secret recipe, courtesy of *New Trail* magazine:

TUCK SHOP CINNAMON BUNS

Use an electric mixer, as the dough is soft and requires a lot of beating.

2 pkg. instant yeast
½ cup warm water
2 tbsp. sugar
2 cups boiling water
3 tbsp. margarine
2 tsp. salt
3 tbsp. sugar
5 ¼ cups flour (total)
3 eggs

Cinnamon Topping
⅓ cup melted margarine
1 cup sugar
1 ½ tsp. cinnamon

Soften yeast in warm water with sugar dissolved in it. Let sit about 10 minutes. In a large bowl, melt margarine in the boiling water and add salt and sugar. Let the mixture cool a bit, then add two cups of the flour and beat hard until very smooth and creamy (about five minutes). Add the yeast mixture, along with the eggs and the rest of the flour. (You may add a little more flour if the mixture is too soft to handle, but the less flour you use the better the buns will be.) Beat until dough is very smooth and soft. Cover and let rise in a warm place until doubled in bulk (about one hour).

Put the melted margarine in a flat pan and mix the cinnamon and sugar together. After the dough has risen, turn it onto a floured work surface and let sit for 5-10 minutes to firm up. Cut the dough into pieces the size of an orange, and dip each one first into the melted butter, then into the sugar-cinnamon mixture. Stretch it to a 4-5 inch-long rope, then tie in a knot. Place the knots (allow about three inches for each one) in a 9x12x2" pan, and let rise for about 45 minutes. Bake at 375° for 30 minutes. Makes 18 buns.

CHEF TUTTLE'S PITA BITS

Yes, Virginia, there is a real Chef Tuttle, and he is a NAIT-trained chef. While working as a personal chef in 1995, he made some tasty baked snacking treats from seasoned, toasted bits of pita bread. His client liked them so much he convinced Tuttle to go into business, and the delicious flavoured morsels — they come in hickory barbecue, cinnamon and sugar, onion and chive, lightly salted, and original — are manufactured in Edmonton and can now be found at Safeway, IGA, Save-On Foods, and Co-op stores. Even though they're made with real butter, they're dramatically lower in fat than other snack food items like chips, and taste great right out of the bag or with a dip.

6756 99 St., 438-7190

Smooth and Juicy

You'll be skipping your Wheaties at home every morning once you've sampled the creamy smoothies, flavour-packed juices, and invigorating shots of nutrients served up by local juice bars.

Booster Juice

These are springing up around town faster than wheatgrass shoots. Your choice of dozens of combos of fruit and flavoured smoothies (including mocha, peanut butter and banana, and "power" mixtures) made with fresh homemade non-fat yogurt, and each one comes with one free "booster" shot of nutrients blended to boost your protein, energy, brain, or immune system levels.
10 Edmonton-area locations

Juice Fare

Have a fruit smoothie, a Rejuvenator (a meal replacement drink), or a Muscle Builder (a high-calorie, high-protein, vitamin-enriched shake). They can make most smoothies non-dairy on request, and every drink comes with one free nutrient shot.
10636 82 Ave., 439-0363

Gotta Hava Java

Where *else* would you expect to find the best and strongest cup o' joe but on a university campus? For a loonie, **Java Jive** makes the finest coffees (fancy and straight) in town at three U of A locations *(SUB, 438-4883; HUB Mall, 433-5573 and 433-7617)*. Luckily, you can still access this treasure without the parking hassles or tuition prices. The **Java Jive Coffee Factory** *(9929 77 Ave., 432-9148)* sells this black gold (including fair trade and certified organic beans), roasted on-site, at very reasonable by-the-pound prices alongside coffee paraphernalia of every description. Not open on Sundays (when you probably need it the most).

For friends getting together for a coffee klatsch, we like the long, narrow room at **Block 1912** *(10361 82 Ave., 433-6575)*, where the eclectic mix of couches, tables, and chairs is slightly reminiscent of *Friends* and the management is family-run. Light entrées (running to lasagna, casseroles, and quiches) are made on-site, in summer there's a popular Italian ice cream counter at the front, and a good selection of baked goods and biscotti always hits the spot. Always great, current reading material, too.

Other spots that inspire loyalty among those who love the bean are the two **Sugar Bowl** cafés *(10922 88 Ave., 433-8369; 10724 124 St., 451-1038)*. The south-side location has folksy-rootsy music on Saturday nights, and both make good, mellow hangouts. **Remedy** *(8631 109 St., 433-3096)* is an urban coffeehouse with a twist: you can also have an alcoholic bevvy and play pool. They specialize in those newfangled health drinks with various natural immune-boosting and healing properties. As long as they taste this good, we don't care if they're good for us.

It's Easy Being Green

Edmonton has been increasingly eco-friendly since 1989, when it became the first city in North America to recycle milk cartons. In 1999, it won the Best Municipal Program Award from the Alberta Recycling Council for its composting and recycling program. Today, its blue bag program (the offspring of a successful blue box program) is the envy of cities around the world: users dump all their recyclable garbage into one bag, and the contents are sorted at a materials recovery facility at the **Edmonton Waste Management Centre** in the city's southeast (the old Clover Bar landfill site). The city banks about $1.5 million a year from the sale of recycled materials.

With the recently built **Edmonton Compost Facility** – at the size of four football fields, it's North America's largest – our city is becoming one of the first in the country to recycle more than 50 percent of its waste. The $100 million compost facility, opened in March 2000 and owned and operated by TransAlta, mechanically separates compostable and non-compostable items from residential garbage collected around the city. The self-generated heat in the compost piles can reach 70°C as the starch, sugar, and cellulose in cardboard, paper, textiles, and food waste breaks down over the course of about a month into a rich, Grade-B industrial compost.

Other unique environmental facilities include **Eco Stations** *(11430 143 St., 5150 99 St.)*, which safely recycle hazardous household waste from paint to old refrigerators. If you're the type who thinks poking around in heaps of stinking garbage is a real good time, the city will arrange tours of its recycling facilities. *496-5403*

Make Beautiful Music

If only Jimi Hendrix had known about **Nicoll Guitar Co.** *(9913 82 Ave., 433-3545)*. They'll not only repair or refurbish used guitars, they create custom instruments and offer workshops on guitar construction.

Thinking of moving to the other side of the tracks or the street? According to Edmonton Police Service data, here are the top scorers for neighbourhood crime in 2000, with the number of incidents over the year.

Residential break and entry
Alberta Avenue (149)
Boyle Street (149)
Inglewood (120)
McCauley (100)
Central McDougall (87)

Commercial break and entry
Downtown (169)
Oliver (76)
Strathcona Industrial Park (50)
McCauley (44)
Central McDougall (41)

Theft
Downtown (1,209)
Oliver (589)
Spruce Avenue (521)
Central McDougall (373)
McCauley (353)

Vehicle Theft
Downtown (184)
Oliver (125)
Boyle Street (120)
Alberta Avenue (120)
Spruce Avenue (110)

Medical Firsts

The Faculty of Medicine at the University of Alberta has produced an amazing number of medical achievements over the years, beginning with James Collip's contributions to developing insulin as a treatment for diabetes in 1923.

1956
The first open-heart surgery in Western Canada is performed here.

1961
The first kidney dialysis in Western Canada performed in Edmonton.

1967
Western Canada's first kidney transplant at U of A Hospitals.

1985
Canada's first heart transplant occurs in Edmonton.

1989
Edmonton is the site of Western Canada's earliest liver transplant.

1989
Canada's first islet cell transplant operation performed in Edmonton as a treatment for diabetes.

1990
Clinical trials begin on the world's first anti-viral treatment for Hepatitis B, pioneered by an Edmonton researcher.

video connoisseur

If you're not in a blockbuster mood, these videophile haunts will provide something to suit your fancy:

Alternative Video Spot

The Staff Picks and Fearless sections yield some surprises, but there's a solid selection of both Hollywood and indie flicks, and even a section for local independent filmmakers. *10050 82 Ave., 439-2233*

Pride Video

A gay and lesbian friendly store with typical and alternative offerings. *2nd floor, 10121 124 St., 452-7743*

Sneak Preview Video

This south-side neighbourhood spot has sections grouped by director, star, genre or theme, and even decade. Check out the Movies for the Adventurous section (cult and just plain weird flicks) and a changing palate of sections like "Movies About Food" or "Movies With Dazzling Style." Huge selection of classics; helpful staff. *4047 106 St., 437-3182*

re-inventing the wheel

Inventing Edmontonians seem to move far away before having that critical lightbulb moment. Here's a sampling of the weird and wonderful stuff invented by the geniuses that have inhabited our city:

Answering Machine

An early prototype of the modern answering machine was invented in Edmonton by Roman Gonsett in 1912. In 1940, Gonsett's son Faust invented the two-way radio after leaving Alberta and moving to California.

Artificial Turf

Monsanto employee James Bromley already held 29 U.S. patents when the creators of Houston's Astrodome approached him to come up with a substitute for natural grass. The Edmonton-educated engineer came up with the product that revolutionized the sports world in 1966: Astroturf.

The Bomb

While working on the Manhattan Project, U of A graduate Clarence Johnson helped build a barrier through which gaseous uranium could be directed to obtain fissionable material – an important step in the successful creation of the atom bomb.

Crash Position Indicator

This device that guides rescuers to the scene of an aircraft crash was patented by former Edmontonian Harry Stevenson while he worked for the Canadian Navy's Flight Research Laboratory.

Dental Fillings

U of A metallurgical engineering professor William Youdelis invented a harder, lighter, and longer-lasting dental amalgam at the urging of his brother, U of A-educated dentist Ralph Youdelis, in the 1960s. It is sold worldwide under the name Dispersalloy.

Best of the City

Those annual readers' polls in local publications have got to be good for something. Here are a few unusual city "bests":

Best Public Bathroom
City Hall
Hotel Macdonald
15th floor, Canada Place (includes a shower and gold-plated fixtures)

Best Elevator
Canada Place
First Edmonton Place
Commerce Place

Best Dojo
Temple Kung Fu
Neil Dunnigan School of Karate
Arashi-Do Karate Schools

Best Place to Score Dope
Gazebo Park
Whyte Avenue
School

Best Place to Have Public Sex
Legislature grounds
River Valley
Hawrelak Park

Biggest Eyesore
Logo flower beds on Whitemud Drive
Delta Hotel paint job
Epcor's Rossdale Plant

Electron Microscope

Former U of A grad student Albert Prebus collaborated on the creation of North America's first true transmission electron microscope while studying at the University of Toronto in the late 1930s.

Fastbagger

Former mechanic Patrick Larkin makes yard work easier with his plastic device that holds standard outdoor garbage bags up and open so grass, plant clippings, and leaves can be quickly bagged and disposed.

Horseshoe Tire

Elgin Court May came up with the idea for a tire covered in a horseshoe-patterned tread (hey, it works for horses) as an alternative to winter chains, and produced it in Edmonton in 1917.

Oil Sands

The process used today to extract oil from the sticky, dark oil sands isn't much different than the procedure invented by Karl Clark in the old Power Plant (now a restaurant and bar) on the university campus in the 1940s.

Photocopier

U of A graduate Carl Miller was working at the Minnesota Mining and Manufacturing Company in the 1940s when he took cellophane wrap from a box of candy, covered it with a heat-sensitive salt, and shined infrared light on it to produce the world's first thermographic copy — the technology that led to 3M's revolutionary Thermo-Fax copying machine.

Quarks

U of A graduate Richard Taylor received the Nobel Prize in 1990 for his work on a Stanford University research team that discovered the first physical evidence for the particles known as quarks.

get inked

Lots of Edmontonians make the drive to the venerable Smilin' Buddha Tattoo in Calgary, but there are plenty of fine local establishments where you can get inked. Naturally, make sure to check their Health Board certification and sterilization standards before exposing your fleshy bits.

Bear's Skin Art

An award-winning artist and custom and freehand designs; located in the funky 124th Street area.
10522 124 St., 482-3876

Ink Machine Custom Tattoo

The folks at Ink Machine pride themselves on avoiding spontaneity at all costs. Their artwork is all custom designed and prepared ahead of time. The award-winning team also do designs on themselves.
9523 Jasper Ave., 423-0267

Sister's

For women only, this body art studio offers henna and traditional tattooing, piercing, and permanent makeup tattooing along with a soothing cup of tea and calming aromatherapy.
4108 36 St., 452-0635

Zipp's Tattooing and Museum

If you're researching a custom design, get inspiration from the displays of a huge variety of tattoo art.
10150A 82 Ave., 439-0519

Fine Wine

Every oenophile has their favourite spot, and particularly in a province where the liquor industry is privatized, the choices are legion. Here are a few purveyors of the rotting grape that have solid creds:

Cristall's Wine Market
This popular destination store in the Kingsway area holds many product tastings and has highly knowledgeable staff. They're very accommodating with choosing and delivering cases for large special events, too.
11459 Kingsway Ave., 455-8888

picture-perfect spots

Vinomania

Many restaurants consult with this downtown shop to put their wine lists together, so you know they've got the knowledge. Specializing in hard-to-find and undervalued (i.e., undiscovered and hence underpriced) bottles, there's something here for every taste and budget. The same owners also operate **Wine & Spirits Warehouse Cost Plus** (11452 Jasper Ave., 488-7973). 10180 101 St., 428-VINO

The Wine Cellar

It bills itself as "Canada's foremost independent wine merchant," and the selection lives up to the hype. They have Alberta's largest variety of Bordeaux and Burgundy, and premium Californian and Italian wines. 12421 102 Ave., 488-9463

These are the places where you're most likely to see an elaborately attired wedding party alternately sipping champagne and arguing on a sunny summer afternoon. Many locations (including city-owned Muttart and Fort Edmonton) charge for photography privileges, so check ahead.

Lee Pavilion

The Citadel Theatre's indoor oasis is a two-storey atrium filled with exotic plants and a towering waterfall. (Warning: the humidity is hell on make-up.)

99 St. and 102 Ave., 425-1820

Legislature Grounds

Big enough for several groups to share, the prettily landscaped grounds (including a fountain/wading pool), along with the grand staircase and other features of the Beaux Arts building, scream "photo op."
108 St. and 99 Ave., 427-7362

Muttart Conservatory

These four glass pyramids filled with exotic flowers and plants are a delightful year-round backdrop; in summer the grounds outside are pretty with the striking structures in the background.
9626 96A St., 496-8735

Rutherford House

This quaint brick house with its elegant pillars and restored historic interior (complete with staff in period costume) is a charming setting. With an attached restaurant/tearoom, it can even host entire functions.
11153 Saskatchewan Dr., 427-3995

gourmet grocers

If you've noticed a preponderance of upscale food and grocery stores locally, you're not alone: Statistics Canada data from 1998 shows that Edmontonians spend more than any other households in the country on food – a whopping $6,305 a year. How do you like them (organic, designer, imported) apples?

The Big Fresh

What used to be an old Earl's restaurant is now a mecca for everything earth-friendly, from organic produce and packaged goods to prepared meatless entrees, natural cosmetics, and a huge selection of bulk foods and grains (12120 Jasper Ave., 433-7374). If it bears more than a slight resemblance to **Terra Natural Food Market** (10313 82 Ave., 433-6807), that's because it was started by former Terra employees. With growing concern over pesticide-laden and genetically modified food, there's room enough in these markets for everyone.

Debaji's

The upscale grocery market in Edmonton was pioneered by the Debaji family, whose ill-fated market foray into West Edmonton Mall in the 1980s was before its time. They resurrected the ultra-fresh, high-quality **Debaji's Fresh Market** concept in the 1990s in the Parkallen area and the rest is history – this Wetaskiwin family now runs a few successful outlets in Calgary, too. From flowers to dessert, this is dinner-party one-stop shopping and a great place to pick up unusual (giant, juicy apple pears) and organic produce, meats, and deli items.
7115 109 St., 496-9559

From the Good Earth

This humble fruit and veg stall in the Highlands features good, fresh stuff several cuts above supermarket quality, usually in season and within price range. For instance, a big, juicy whole pineapple might go for as little as two bucks, and a big sack of juicing oranges for a fiver.
11809 66 St., 479-8671

Fit to be Tea'd

They say tea is the new coffee ... or something like that. It's definitely a trend that's hit Edmonton in force, with a handful of new tea houses in the last year. At spots like **Tranquili Tea** (102-10235 124 St., 482-4150) and the **Russian Tea Room** (10312 Jasper Ave., 426-0000), part of the tea house atmosphere is the tea-leaf readings that are offered by appointment. Spots like **Nellie's Tea Shoppe** (12606 118 Ave., 452-9429), **Rutherford House** (11153 Saskatchewan Dr., 427-3995), and the **Macdonald Hotel** (10065 100 St., 429-6424) serve traditional high tea, complete with finger sandwiches and tiered trays of tiny goodies. The Mac's tea is offered from May to August and at other times of the year by special request; call a day in advance to reserve and pre-order at any of these locations.

Acquired Tastes Tea Company

A few blocks away, another cozy tea shop has a unique wedding or party favour program: go in and sample and select a custom tea blend, which the shop will then package in individual labelled canisters suitable for gifting. Then, when your guests run out, then can go back to Acquired Tastes and re-order your custom blend – sort of like a reverse bridal registry.

12516 102 Ave., 414-6041

Steeps: the Urban Teahouse

Brothers Brendan and Paul Waye call themselves "the two tea guys," and more than live up to that moniker. With a smell and atmosphere that's less heady than a coffeehouse (you can't even get a coffee here), this High Street spot serves and sells over 100 varieties of herbal, black, white, and green loose tea authentically steeped in elegant little press-style pots. The boys are the only Canadian manufacturer to make and bottle their own chai tea concentrate, made right in Edmonton and available from the in-store cooler and various local outlets. It's a subtle, spicy blend that's less sweet and cloying than the major U.S. commercial varieties because it's based on an authentic Indian recipe. Side note: the spacious Steeps bathroom has been voted visitors' favourite in the city by two local radio station polls.

12411 Stony Plain Rd., 488-1505

Sunterra Colonial Market

The old Colonial market is now a full-service grocery store with many upscale extras like online grocery ordering and delivery, a recipe club, prepared meals to go, and membership perks and discounts. The founding Price family (they also run the popular Sunterra deli and café downtown) got its start in wholesale agriculture, so they know their stuff.

5728 111 St., 434-2610

Urban Fare

The Vancouver Yaletown experience comes to Edmonton with this concept born from the Overwaitea/Save-on-Foods empire. The Crestwood location made local headlines with news of the authentic French bread (flown over from Paris daily) available for a mere hundred bucks. There's also prosciutto from Rome and olives from Athens for the discerning gourmet, and a butcher shop, bakery, seafood counter, flower shop, coffee bar, and a counter for light bites and take-out meals. It's all done up in sleek chrome and stainless steel, and among the aisles of toothpaste and pasta you'll find retro-cool products like milk in old-fashioned glass bottles. There's also a ubiquitous membership card for discounts and rewards.

9680 142 St., 482-0021

We All Scream

Photo: Sharon Wade

Given Edmonton's weather, you might not expect it to be an ice-cream loving town. In fact, on July 24, 1988 the biggest ice cream sundae in the world was built here to celebrate the 60th anniversary of Palm Dairies – a record that still holds in the *Guinness Book of Records*. The gigantic treat used 20,110 kilograms of ice cream, 4,360 kilograms of topping, 90 kilograms of whipped cream, 50 kilograms of peanuts, and 50 kilograms of cherries. It was built using a forklift, hoes, and rakes in the fountain in the middle of the lower level of Edmonton Centre, where an adjacent store's sign got splashed with rivers of butterscotch topping. Once its seven-metre diameter had been verified, spectators got to dig in and enjoy.

Another local ice-cream legend is **Pinocchio Italian Ice Cream**, a second-generation family business started by his parents nearly 20 years ago and now run by Tom Ursino. They supply the creamy frozen stuff to more than 100 local hotels and restaurants as well as local retail outlets like Urban Fare, IGA stores, and the Italian

Centre Shop. Pinocchio's no longer has its own parlour, but you can still get a cone at the **Perk Avenue** coffee shop (9640 142 St., 453-6172).
100, 11737 108 Ave., for locations call 455-1905.

Out, Damn Spot

If these fine dry cleaners can't get it out, it's there for good.

The Cleanery
Specializing in leather and suede goods.
11210 109 Ave., 426-0510

Gellibrand's Excellence in Dry Cleaning
Great service, and that little jelly bean snack hits the spot.
17030 90 Ave., 481-9538

Valtone Cleaners
They do a great job with cleaning and preserving wedding dresses.
Whitemud Crossing, 4211 106 St., 436-5672

CUTS FOR KIDS
Looking to shear the locks of the young 'uns? In a St. Albert strip mall is **Bambeenos Fun Cuts for Kids**, a salon designed to appeal to the little person. They boast a play centre and tractor-chairs, but most ingenious are the televisions and video machines at every station, so your little cutie can watch their favourite cartoon while getting that new 'do.
11 Bellerose Drive, 460-0880

The pampered pooch will feel right at home in Edmonton, where a variety of decidedly luxurious services for pets thrive.

Pick up a yummy snack for the well-behaved pooch while shopping for your own goodies at Urban Fare *(9680 142 St., 482-0021)*, which carries products by **Paw Prints Gourmet Pet Bakery** including pet muffins and bagels, breath mints, and treats with gourmet flavours like cranberry turkey, sun-dried tomato pizza, and spinach quiche. Products have no salt, refined sugar, fillers, preservative, or fat. **Wags and Wishes** *(7338 82 Ave., 466-4777)* goes a step further with not only 70 varieties of treats and biscuits, but birthday cakes suitable for doggies and kitties for $5 and up – veterinarian-certified to be healthy.

The **Paw Spa** *(10447 124 St., 414-0431)* provides traditional pet grooming services along with a doggy day care – we're not talking kennels and cages, here, we're talking comfy couches and chairs for lounging. Dogs even get a walk for the $10/day fee. **Calico Hills Kitty Lodge** *(418-6369)* provides a similar service for cats, with a kitty gym, indoor play area, and a cozy fireplace. For $8-$10/day they'll pamper and play with your feline.

If it's holistic care your pet craves, send them for a therapy session with cat therapist Natalia Krawetz at Wakaba *(453-2340)* or dog therapist Irene Darius at Higgins, Darius and Associates *(434-2034)*. Put your pet back in line with a session with chiropractor Dan Martin *(612-10216 124 St., 482-6644)*, who has treated famous humans (skaters Kurt Browning and Kristy Sargeant, singer Bobby Curtola) and plenty of animals (more than 1,000 racehorses and countless dogs and cats). Martin is certified by the American Veterinary Chiropractic Association, and is one of only a few Canadians performing the specialty.

DOG DAYS OF THE WAR

When vets (that's veterans, not veterinarians) returned from overseas and piled onto trains headed back to Edmonton after the Second World War, one of them contained an extra passenger: a small dog. The canine had bonded with Edmonton soldier Jim Trueman when he was stationed in Holland, and it became the informal mascot of his unit, the Loyal Edmonton Regiment. After the war ended, the sentimental soldier smuggled the puppy back to Canada inside his coat. It popped out long enough to be immortalized in a photograph taken by Albert Blythe when the soldier debarked on the platform in Edmonton.

Photo: Provincial Archives of Alberta (BL987/7)

digital revolutionaries

You may not think of Edmonton as Silicon Valley North, but the city has spawned its share of digital wizards.

Bioware Corp.

Two medical doctors with a jones for computers got their start by programming some new and better medical software in med school. That led them back to their teenage passion, video games, and soon Ray Muzyka and Greg Zeschuk were spending more time using joysticks than tongue depressors. Their first successful game was *Shattered Steel*, quickly followed by the acclaimed *Baldur's Gate* (named best role-playing game at the Electronic Entertainment Expo in Atlanta, the largest video game conference in the world) and *MDK2*. It has also struck a deal with Lucas Arts Entertainment Co. to create the first *Star Wars* role-playing video game, expected to be released in 2002. Today Bioware employs dozens of young programmers at its funky Whyte Avenue offices.
302-10508 82 Ave., 430-0164

Docspace

Two brothers who grew up on an Alberta hog and grain farm went on to found the first Internet company offering a high-level Web file delivery and storage system. The company's IPO garnered $535 million in the heady days of 2000, but times weren't always so good. Evan and Shane Chrapko (the "h" is silent – go ahead, laugh, but they're millionaires) confess to living on next to nothing and eating Spam while developing their innovative system from the roots of management and software companies they previously owned. The company is based in Toronto.

Car Washes

Maybe it's the weather, but Edmontonians seem inordinately obsessed with keeping their cars clean. We're not talking do-it-yourself here, but 100 percent soft cloth, hand-washed, and detailed luxury.

Bubbles Car Wash and Detail Centres
11828 104 Ave., 448-9274

10538 82 Ave., 433-1540

16907 Stony Plain Rd., 484-4949

10212 108 St., 423-5206

13804 127 St., 456-7474

Cupid's Car Wash & Detail Centre
7303 103 St., 439-5664

Minit Car Wash
11614 Jasper Ave., 482-7669

10070 178 St., 484-2220

Deep Blue and Chinook

In 1996, when the computer dubbed Deep Blue met world chess champion Gary Kasparov, the machine won one game, but lost the match. But Deep Blue won a six-game rematch in 1997, beating Kasparov 3.5 games to 2.5. Former Edmontonian Murray Campbell is a one-time Alberta junior chess champion who was one of the original grad students at Carnegie-Mellon who developed the Deep Blue prototype, and was part of the team behind programming the man-eating Deep Blue.

Another Edmontonian, U of A computing science professor Jonathan Schaeffer, is the human face behind Chinook, the computer recognized by the *Guinness Book of World Records* as the world man-machine champion of checkers. Schaeffer is the author of *One Jump Ahead*, a book about the development of Chinook. You can play against the wily computer online at *www.cs.ualberta.ca/~chinook/*.

Personal Chef

If you're spending a fortune eating out, reduce your cash outlay but not the quality of your meals by employing a personal chef from **Tastes Like More** *(15 Olympia Ct., St. Albert, 910-3156)*. This service uses your own home kitchen to prepare multiple-taste meals that can be stored in the refrigerator or freezer; preparation instructions included. Complete service of 10 meals for two (including entrées and side dishes) starts at less than $300 – compare that to restaurant prices, consider the convenience, and it's a steal. Makes a great gift for a new mom or a senior, too.

WHY DIRTY THE KITCHEN?

Gail Hall's **Gourmet Goodies** has earned a reputation as one of the tastiest and most popular catering outfits in town. Now they have a retail take-out store *(10665 109 St., 438-1234)* where you can pick up hors d'oeuvres, full dinners-to-go, and gourmet food products. A smart Gourmet Goodies innovation is the Friday night TV dinners: order on Thursday and pick up a three-course meal for just $10.95 on your way home from work Friday. They'll also cater all manner of special events, in your home or elsewhere. The **Runaway Spoon Bistro and Catering Co.** *(12417 Stony Plain Rd., 488-6181)* has the right idea: they'll rent you the whole bistro for a private party for 15-45 people and let you choose from a set of menus or whip one up to your specifications. They'll also cater any event with a minimum of four people.

to market, to market

Callingwood Farmers' Market

This quiet west-end community turns an ordinary strip-mall courtyard into a bustling market on Wednesdays (noon to 6 p.m.) and Sundays (10 a.m. to 3 p.m.) in the summer. That way, you have access to dozens of stalls of produce, bedding plants, furniture, and crafts, and the 75 shops and services of the Marketplace at Callingwood (including a Running Room store and the Bagel Bin bakery and café).
69 Ave. and 178 St.

Capilano Mall Market

Held every Saturday year-round from 9:30 a.m. to 5:30 p.m.
5004 98 Ave., 465-0987

City Market on 97th

A century ago the Rice Street Market (where the Milner Library is now) was the only game in town. Today, the downtown market tradition has been revitalized on 97th Street with fresh meats and produce, flowers and preserves, and arts and crafts available every Saturday.
10153 97 St., 424-9001

Old Strathcona Farmers' Market

Open year-round in the old bus barns, this market hosts produce, meat, baked goods, and prepared foods (preserves, snacks, and condiments) along with arts and crafts. Saturdays from 8 a.m. to 3 p.m.; free parking across the street.
10310 83 Ave.

Cook Up a Storm

If you're a stickler for the best and most authentic ingredients, try these specialty shops:

Acme Meat Market

With 80 years of experience, the meat here is high quality and cut right. They carry beef, lamb, chicken, and pork in any shape or form you'd care to consider.
9561 76 Ave., 433-1812

Billingsgate Fish Co.

The annual June LobsterFest is a local favourite, but year-round you'll find the best local fresh and frozen fish, shellfish, and seafood go-withs like seasoning mixes and sushi-making supplies.
7331 104 St., 433-0091

St. Albert Farmers' Market

The largest outdoor farmers' market in Western Canada, this one shuts down traffic in front of St. Albert Place every Saturday between July and September with a huge selection of food, crafts, and entertainment. The city also runs smaller indoor markets at various locations year-round. Runs from 10 a.m. to 3 p.m.; free parking. *St. Anne St. and St. Thomas St., 458-2833*

Italian Centre Shop

The heart and soul of this Little Italy institution is the deli counter that covers one long, entire wall. If your mouth is watering as you make your selections, have the counter staff craft you a sandwich with your choice of meat and cheese. More varieties of antipasto, canned tomatoes, and pasta than you've ever seen under one roof. *10878 95 St., 424-4869*

Omonia Foods

Greek foods like fat kalamata olives and creamy feta cheese are the specialties of this grocery. *10605 102 St., 426-6210*

Strathcona Chinatown Mall

A bakery, restaurants, a huge Chinese grocery, and clothing, kitchenware, and Asian import shops *(118-7915 104 St., 437-7419)*. Similar variety can be found downtown at the **Lucky 97** complex *(10725 99 St., 424-8100)* or on the streets of Chinatown.

get baked

Why spend $100 on an authentic French baguette from Urban Fare when you can have European-quality artisan bread, made right here in the city, for about $98 less? Here are some of the hot spots for sweet and savoury baked treats.

Bagel Bin Bakery & Bistro

Some of the best bagels in the city and great cakes, including a unique European cheesecake with nuts and raisins (by the slice or whole). A fairly new addition is a lunch and coffee counter and small eating area. *226-6655 178 St., 481-572*

Bon Ton Bakery

The Edelmann family's bagels have a rabid following. This newly renovated institution also features a whole host of specialty breads – including an acclaimed Omega 3 flax-seed based bread – and yummy Hungarian pastries. *8720 149 St., 489-7717*

French Meadow
Artisan Bakery Café

The Whyte Avenue location shares quarters with **Paddy's International Cheese Market** – an unbeatable combination. *11212 Jasper Ave., 414-6089; 10736 82 Ave., 413-8045*

Italian Bakery
Co. Ltd.

Get those crispy, crusty Italian restaurant-style buns and breads here. *10646 97 St., 424-4830; 4118 118 Ave., 474-2248*

La Favorite
Pastry Shop

Perfect pastries, elegant petit fours, Belgian chocolates, and decadent cakes, including wedding cakes. *11401 95 St., 477-2084; 12431 102 Ave., 482-7024; 70-19 Bellerose Dr., St. Albert, 459-4583*

Tree Stone Bakery

These breads are chewy and have complex flavours, the result of natural leavening and long rising times. *8612 99 St., 433-5924*

SPECIAL-NEEDS BREAD
Kinnikinnick

Gluten-free baked goods and packaged foods, including baking mixes, cereals, and pasta. *10306 112 St., 424-2900*

THE NUT MAN COMETH

Started in Calgary in 1984, the Nut Man Company has been dispensing snack foods, novelty items, and smiles ever since to bored office workers across the prairies. If you can't wait another few weeks for your regular nutty man to cross the company threshold, and you just *have* to have your fix of corn nuts or chocolate mints or a mechanical singing fish right away, then head to the **Nut Man Outlet** *(5113 99 St., 439-7757)*, which sells bags of all the company's best-selling sweet and savoury goodies.

COMPANY'S COMING

The best cookbooks always seem to be the ones produced by loving hands, like those you buy from service clubs or at church bake sales, stuffed with well-worn, well-tasted family favourites. That's the feel that a **Company's Coming** cookbook achieves, thanks to the homespun touch of the company's matriarch, former Vermilion caterer Jean Paré. The company's tag line says it all: "Everyday recipes tested by millions." Company's Coming is now a mini-empire, publishing not only Canada's best-selling cookbook series but a bi-monthly magazine, *Cooking at Home*, out of its Edmonton headquarters, which also houses its Recipe Factory test kitchen.
2311 96 St., 450-6223

Bee-Bell Health Bakery

Don't let the name throw you off – alongside the healthy and organic breads they have a tasty selection of full-sugar, full-fat cookies and cakes.
10416 80 Ave., 439-3247

Buns and Roses Organic Wholegrain Bakery

Varieties of bread include yeast-free, bran, flax, rye, and a dozen more. They can accommodate most special dietary or religious needs, and also make simple soup and sandwich lunches and special coffees in-house.
6519 111 St., 438-0098

mom, i'm bored

Here are a few off-the-beaten-path things to spring on the kiddies when they've worn out the PlayStation and your patience.

Seismic Sundays

The **Edmonton Art Gallery** provides children's activities (free for EAG members, or included with regular admission prices) every Sunday that are fun, creative, and educational, as they're inspired by current exhibits. There's also a children's gallery with everyday activities.
2 Sir Winston Churchill Squ., 422-6223

Climbing the Walls

The **Vertically Inclined Rock Gym** offers introductory courses, gear rentals, and group programs for kids. You could teach your kids worse things than cooperation, teamwork, and trust.
8523 Argyll Rd., 496-9390

Beady-Eyed

Beadworks and other local bead shops offer classes for beaders of any level. A bonus: instills thrifty values in kids as they make their own funky, inexpensive adornments.
10324 82 Ave., 433-9559

Birthday Bashes

The City of Edmonton makes local facilities available for children's birthday parties. How about a pioneer baking party or a summer picnic in the park at the **John Walter Museum** or **Fort Edmonton Park** *(496-8778)*? A Zoo Clue mystery or a sleepover party at the **Valley Zoo**, or a Bug-Mania birthday at the **John Janzen Nature Centre** *(496-2925)*? They'll also arrange a Pirates' Plunder or Mermaid Magic party at the **Kinsmen Sports Centre** *(496-7309)*. Various options are also available for the river valley parks *(496-2987)*, or **Muttart Conservatory** *(496-8736)*.

Go Shopping

When all else fails, buy them something to keep them busy (and quiet). Instead of the usual pilgrimage to the big-box toy store, try the **Science Shop** *(Southgate Centre, 435-0519)* for telescopes, microscopes, and puzzles for kids; or **Kites & Other Delights** *(West Edmonton Mall, 444-1256)* for all things floatable and flyable, and tons of craft and hobby kits.

You Sexy Thing

Suffice to say that whatever turns you on, there's probably a local fanciers' club for it. Here are just a few:

THE LIFESTYLE
Those who are in it know what it means — it's jargon for couples who swing, baby, swing. Most hold regular social nights that are organized via e-mail for confidentiality to, you know, weed out the freaks. Check out these Edmonton clubs.

Fantasy Nites
www.fantasy-nites.com

The Secret Garden
www.compusmart.ab.ca/thesecretgarden/

Intimate Times
www.intimate-times.com

NUDISTS
If you love to get naked just for the heck of it, you better surround yourself with like-minded individuals.

Helios Edmonton
Box 8, RR 2, Tofield, 662-2886

fitness secrets

Beyond the bright lights of the big fitness chains are these less well-known local spots to huff and heft:

Centre Club

A great downtown location is the draw for this executive gym with squash and racquetball, an indoor track, gym, and fitness classes.
10120 103 Ave., 425-3333

Macdonald Health Club

Located in the venerable hotel, this gym and spa (including pool, whirlpool, sauna, and steam room) is open to hotel guests and members.
10065 100 St., 429-6423

MacEwan Centre for Sport and Wellness

The college's student fitness facility offers day-passes and memberships to the public for its pool, racquet courts, gym, and steam room. It also offers fitness classes.
10700 104 Ave., 497-5300

Stadium Fitness Centre

Hidden within Commonwealth Stadium, this club has weight equipment, a gym, and indoor racquetball and outdoor tennis courts.
11000 Stadium Rd., 496-6999

University of Alberta Fitness and Lifestyle Centre

As well as providing subsidized use to university students, staff, and faculty, this well-equipped facility offers community memberships.
Van Vliet Centre, University of Alberta, 492-2231

Bare Naked Boys Club of Edmonton
47-10024 82 Ave., 471-6993 or bnbc@interbaun.com

FUR FANS
If you like hairy, or are hairy, this one is for you: a club for hair men and their admirers meets at Buddy's Pub *(11725B Jasper Ave., 488-6636)* the first and third Saturdays of the month.

The B.E.A.R.S. of Edmonton
47-10024 82 Ave., or www.freenet.edmonton.ab.ca/~bears

IN THE PRIVACY OF YOUR OWN HOME
Intimate Attitudes
This Medicine Hat-based company will send an Edmonton-area consultant to your home with a selection of erotic novelties, books, games, videos, and lingerie for your group's perusal. The tone is fun and relaxed, with the utmost discretion in private purchasing.
1-888-886-4099

the look for less

Are you a high-maintenance guy or gal with a low-maintenance budget? Go glamourous without going broke with these beauty bargains:

The Spa Clubs

This full-service discount salon and day spa offers discounts on its already-reasonable prices to those who buy an annual one-year membership. For instance, member price on a shampoo, cut, and style is under $30; a manicure is just $14; around $50 for a leg and bikini wax. Packages (including bridal spa packages) and gift certificates are available at both locations. *11214 Jasper Ave., 423-CLUB; 10642 82 Ave., 437-SPA2*

Marvel College

For the chintziest among us, this hairstyling and esthetic school offers services by its students at greatly discounted prices. Sure, it takes a little longer, but students are carefully supervised and check with instructors every step of the way. Unbeatable prices include $8.50 for a ladies shampoo, cut, and style; $8.50 for a manicure or $17 for a pedicure; and around $30 for a full leg and bikini wax. Professional estheticians and stylists are also available for an approximately 50 percent premium – still lower than most salon and spa prices. *10018 106 St., 424-4171 ext. 126 (hair) or 122 (esthetics)*

Bah, Humbug

By the time the end of December rolls around, winter in Edmonton is one-third over and that's cause enough to celebrate. Here are some of the annual seasonal festivities that go on around town:

Bright Nights
This winter festival in Hawrelak Park includes a drive-through seasonal light show and activities like sleigh and hay rides, entertainment, and more. Admission to the light display is per-carload, with proceeds going to charity.

Candy Cane Lane
Neighbours on 148 Street (between 92 and 100 Avenues) turned a local display into an annual civic event with their elaborate lights and decorations. Starting in mid-December, you can cruise through at a snail's pace or better yet walk through on foot and drop off a donation for the Food Bank.

Redneck's Haircut Emporium

It might not cut the mustard with the fashionable crowd, but you'll have a good time at Redneck's. The kitschy log cabin decor, combined with a big-screen TV and pool table, make haircut anxiety a thing of the past – and the cheap price (around 10 bucks) doesn't hurt either.
4115 106 St., 431-0118; 10807 82 Ave., 413-8855

And Hair We Are

Another weapon in the war against the mullet cut is this men's only spot that consistently wins local raves and reader polls.
2nd floor, 10219 109 St., 439-4056

University of Alberta Dentistry Student Clinic

If your chompers are less than perfect and pearly white, you might consult U of A dental students at a discount price. Dentistry and dental hygiene students working in a supervised environment complete procedures ranging from cleanings and fillings to root canals and braces – at half the fee schedule recommended by the Alberta Dental Association. You'll require an initial screening consultation, and appointments take longer (from two to three hours), but if you don't have dental insurance this place is a godsend. Closed between mid-July and mid-August.
Dentistry/Pharmacy Centre, 492-4436

...When Less is More

For the ultimate spa experience, you can't beat **Eveline Charles Salons and Spas**, a world-class, award-winning company started by the woman herself right here in Edmonton (formerly known as Bianco Nero, which is now a separately owned company). The West Edmonton Mall location *(424-5666)* is a cool, calming oasis of white marble and gentle, loving care. Schedule plenty of time for your esthetic services so you can relax in the lounge sipping chilled juice or water, take a leisurely steam, and indulge in the sample products in the change rooms.

index

index

index

index

index

index

index

index

index

CHARLENE ROOKE lived in the Edmonton area for 21 years before making tentative forays to Toronto (to attend the journalism program at Ryerson Polytechnic University) and Calgary (to edit *Avenue* magazine). A graduate of the University of Alberta, she began collecting obscure, trivial, and profane Edmonton anecdotes while an editor at the University of Alberta alumni magazine in the 1990s. Her writing has appeared in *Realm*, *Financial Post*, and *Calgary* magazines and she is active in the Alberta Magazine Publishers Association and the Western Magazine Awards. Her favorite Edmonton haunts are the Yardbird Suite (jazz) and the Sidetrack Cafe (music and nachos).